PRAISE FOR *HERE & NOW: GIRLS WRITE NOW 2024 ANTHOLOGY*

"The Girls Write Now anthology is full of urgent, beautiful, and original writing that delighted me, challenged me, broke my heart. I'm so happy we get to hear these voices."

—**KAYLA MIN ANDREWS**, editor of mother Katherine Min's posthumous novel, *The Fetishist*

"As a longtime mentor with Girls Write Now, I saw firsthand how this organization inspires and empowers young people to harness the power of their own stories. The impact of that goes well beyond the words on the page. By crafting their own narratives, mentees are given the support to dream big, create the change they want to see, and even find emotional healing. It is truly a gift for the next generation to have access to this uplifting community, especially in today's complicated world."

—**GRACE BASTIDAS**, editor-in-chief of *Parents*

"More now than ever, it is crucial that we create space for our young women to find the language they'll need to assert themselves in a world that seeks to oppress them. In the Girls Write Now anthology, we watch the voices of our next generation take shape before our eyes, and unfurling from its pages, we find hope for a better future."

—**TAYLOR BYAS**, author of *I Done Clicked My Heels Three Times*

"Girls Write Now elevates underrepresented voices with stories that need to be told."

—**AYESHA CURRY**, Girls Write Now honoree, CEO of Sweet July, and cofounder of Eat. Learn. Play.

"I hope you will experience every remarkable piece, each one written from a particular point of view no one else has, by writers from myriad backgrounds and perspectives."

—**ABI DARÉ**, Girls Write Now honoree, philanthropist, entrepreneur, and author of *And So I Roar*

"This isn't a book, it's a world! Each of these incredible young writers gives us her voice, her life, and the bond that she's formed with her Girls Write Now mentor. Plunge in and feel awestruck, and joyful."

—**SUSAN CHOI**, author of *Trust Exercise*

"These are the voices of humility, resilience, and determination. *Here & Now* is not just a compilation of words from today's generation, it is a personal look into the hearts and souls of our future."

—**ANNA GOMEZ**, CFO of Mischief and author of *My Goodbye Girl* and the From Kona with Love series

"The Girls Write Now anthology features diverse voices of today's emerging leaders who brilliantly guide you through uncharted territories with stories that resonate with the human experience."

—**CHARNAIE GORDON**, author of *Lift Every Voice and Change* and *Etta Extraordinaire*

"Sometimes just beginning a sentence with 'I' takes courage. The stories that emerge from Girls Write Now are a thrilling testament to that courage, and to the creativity, insight, and pride it can inspire."

—**LISA GRUNWALD**, author of *The Evolution of Annabel Craig*

"At this critical moment in time, when windows of universal truths are too easily shuttered, Girls Write Now draws back the curtains. The creative brilliance of this diverse group of young writers will dazzle you and make you realize we are more alike within our shared humanity than not."

—**ELLEN HOPKINS**, author of *Crank*

"As a mentor myself, I am so proud to be involved with the Girls Write Now organization. The work this foundation does is so important, and that's evident in the vibrant voices of the young women sprawled across these pages."

—**CANDICE JALILI**, author of *Finding Famous: A Mashad Family Novel* and *Just Send the Text: An Expert's Guide to Letting Go of the Stress and Anxiety of Modern Dating*

"Having once been a poverty-stricken girl who dreamt of becoming an author, I know the contribution of Girls Write Now is palpable. It empowers young women to transform their dreams into reality and rewrite their stories of limitation into ones of limitless opportunity."

—**KARENA KILCOYNE**, author of *Rise Above the Story*

"This anthology—with its kaleidoscope of genre, themes, and ideas—gives us a glimpse into what is possible when young girls are given the space, guidance, and creative license to express themselves on their own terms. A vital collection from an incredible organization."

—**GABRIELLE KORN**, author of *Yours for the Taking*

"There is always possibility, mystery, and hope in young women. Finding voice to that, especially with the written word, can be really, really hard. Girls Write Now supports, nourishes, and provides a bridge to telling the stories we so desperately need to hear. And we thank you!"

—**MAJA KRISTIN**, Girls Write Now honoree, philanthropist, entrepreneur, and author of *Instructions Not Included*

"A vibrant community built to amplify the stories of young women and gender-expansive youth, Girls Write Now is doing essential work. The writing in this collection is fired by the power that comes with finding our voices. I am moved by these writers' passion and inspired by their singular words."

—**R. O. KWON**, author of *Exhibit*

"The Girls Write Now anthology offers a chorus of voices—young and perceptive and impassioned voices—that might not have been heard otherwise. To encourage and provide a platform to these writers is an essential step toward a more empathetic future."

—**KELSEY NORRIS**, author of *House Gone Quiet*

"Girls Write Now is a beacon of empowerment, fostering a culture of expression and growth among young women. Their anthology, *Here & Now,* is a testament to the power and potential of these voices. These stories, crafted with raw emotion and authenticity, present a promising future shaped by the strength and creativity of today's youth."

—**NADYA OKAMOTO**, author of *Period Power: A Manifesto for the Menstrual Movement*

"What a marvel this book is, a bulletin from the next generation, full of brilliance and heart. These stories handily reassure us that today's girls are ready to take on the world, to speak powerfully and eloquently of the things that matter most, to them and to all of us."

—**ANN PACKER**, author of *The Children's Crusade*

"Encouraging the next generation of girls to find, use, and amplify their voices will change the world. Girls Write Now powerfully inspires our girls to do just that through supporting writers and creative thinkers to make themselves heard."

—**KATE T. PARKER**, author of *Force of Nature* and *Strong Is the New Pretty*

"Are we willing to embrace the bittersweet beauty of our collective humanity by listening to the voices of our younger selves? *Here & Now: Girls Write Now 2024 Anthology* poignantly captures the sentiment of some of our most observant and silenced. Girls Write Now has gifted us an anthology that will compel you to listen and take action by inspiring you to remember what is truly at stake."

—**JAMES RHEE**, entrepreneur and author of the bestseller *red helicopter,* TED speaker, and Howard University Johnson Chair of Entrepreneurship

"Girls Write Now is a vital tool for amplifying the next generation of storytellers, empowering them to lift their voices and share their truth. We need these stories now more than ever."

—**EMMA SCOTT**, author of *Full Tilt*

"If we're going to build a brighter future, we need all the voices, stories, and beautiful noise these girls have to share."

—**NINA SIMON**, author of *Mother-Daughter Murder Night*

"I can think of nothing more vital to our society right now than the wisdom and clarity of young women and gender-expansive youth. Girls Write Now provides this next generation of powerful thinkers with a platform that nurtures, strengthens, and amplifies their voices, and we are all better for it."

—**KATE SPENCER**, author of *In a New York Minute*

"These are the voices I want to hear. These are the stories I want to learn from. Girls Write Now shows us what's possible when we give young people a microphone, a megaphone, a seat at the table—a pen."

—**MEGAN STIELSTRA**, author of *The Wrong Way to Save Your Life*

"Now, more than ever, the world needs the voices of strong girls who speak their truth in stories and poems. The Girls Write Now anthology is full of passion and discovery, dreams and struggles, the power of lived experience transformed on the page."

—**DIANA WHITNEY**, author of *You Don't Have to Be Everything: Poems for Girls Becoming Themselves*

"Confidence, opportunity, and support. These are the words that come to mind when thinking of Girls Write Now and all that the organization encompasses. By pushing back on the systemic barriers of gender, race, and economic status, Girls Write Now gives girls from underrepresented backgrounds the confidence to make their voices heard and the opportunity to become the leaders of the future, while providing support throughout their journey."

—**JON YAGED**, CEO of Macmillan Publishers and Girls Write Now honoree

"Sometimes you come across a piece of writing that grabs you, holds you close, yet transports you. Writing like that is rare, but it fills these pages. This Girls Write Now anthology thrums with electric work, in many formats, from new voices mentored by seasoned pros. Reading it will have you tuning in to a powerful frequency—and tuning out the noise of the breakroom, bus, or bookstore. Or, honestly, whichever place that starts with a 'b' you choose. Just keep the flow."

—**LARISSA ZAGERIS**, coauthor of *My Lady's Choosing*

GIRLS WRITE NOW

HERE & NOW

2024 ANTHOLOGY

GIRLS WRITE NOW

HERE & NOW

2024 ANTHOLOGY

FOREWORD BY
DONNA HILL

INTRODUCTION BY
FORSYTH HARMON

girls write now

Published 2024

Printed in the United States

Print ISBN: 978-0-9962772-9-7

E-ISBN: 978-1-948340-62-5

Library of Congress Control Number: 2024903266
Copyright © 2024 by Girls Write Now, Inc.

Cover design by Dominique Jones

For information, write to:
Girls Write Now, 247 West 37th Street, Suite 1000
New York, NY 10018

info@girlswritenow.org
girlswritenow.org

GIRLS WRITE NOW

HERE & NOW

2024 ANTHOLOGY

Dedicated to Girls Write Now Mentors

over 25 Years of Transformative Storytelling

To write is to give a definite shape to our pain, and confusion and hope and joy. It doesn't just leave a record, it names what needs naming. It gives us the vocabulary to understand what we are going through and to understand everyone around us.

—Excerpted from the speech "Goodness, Beauty, and Truth: The Value of Art in Times of Crisis," given by R. F. Kuang, author of *Yellowface* and Girls Write Now honoree

HERE & NOW: GIRLS WRITE NOW 2024 ANTHOLOGY

Suspecting I might need a little extra inspiration to finish a short play I was writing about an asteroid disaster, my Girls Write Now mentor suggested we visit the Hayden Planetarium at New York City's American Museum of Natural History. We settled into our chairs and looked up in anticipation, ready to be transported into the abyss. Soon we were watching stars and patterned celestial rings dance across that mysterious place where past and future coexist. It was magical.

As I thought about the stars, the planets, the cosmic dust, the accretion of galactic stuff that tells the story of our universe, I realized that I, too, hoard "stuff": notes, tickets, lists, and a whole lot of dreams. Others keep relics, furniture, photographs, or paintings, but it's all in the service of telling *our* stories, navigating *our* personal universes. We feel the urge to collect things to help us understand, to keep track, to learn. After we've studied the details, when we know our pasts and can imagine our futures and the place where the two might meet, we are equipped to tell our tales.

Entering the world of storytelling is a daring act. We are at our most vulnerable when we say our thoughts out loud. It's then, just as it is when we look to the stars, that we can't help but feel our smallness. Maybe that's what makes us brave. We realize that we mirror the universe—its loss and light, its power and destruction—and know that by putting memories and ideas on paper we are opening portals into worlds that offer different perspectives and possibilities. To have the capacity to write like that—on the page or for the screen or through any medium—is a gift. And allowing readers to enter your mind as you travel through caves of wonder, thought, and imagination is an act of generosity.

Working on *Here & Now: Girls Write Now 2024 Anthology* has given me and so many others the opportunity to explore ourselves and see how far our minds can wander when given the space and time. And what stories the contributors tell! Their works are constructive, unapologetic, and beautiful; they fully embody thought, mind, and spirit—forming a vivid picture of our world today: the past and the future, the here and the now.

We on the Anthology Committee are glad that this time capsule has found you, wherever you are. Your here and now is undoubtedly a different place than the rest of us reside in. But we all live under the same moon and stars, and so we reach out to you in peace and kindness.

EMILY TOLIVER is a Girls Write Now mentee working with her mentor, Suzie Bolotin, as an editor on the Anthology Editorial Committee. Emily is a graduate of New York City's Repertory Company High School for Theatre Arts and a rising senior at The New School, where she is majoring in literary studies and journalism, exploring the possibilities of storytelling. Her work has been published in *The Brooklyn Reader, The Last Girls Club,* and *DarkWinter Literary Magazine.*

ANTHOLOGY EDITORIAL COMMITTEE

EDITOR

Molly MacDermot

COMMITTEE CO-CHAIRS

Annaya Baynes
Rosie Black
Meg Cassidy
Mariah Dwyer
Amy Fusselman
Jenissa Graham
Leigh Haber
Becca James
Vahni Kurra
Soyolmaa Lkhagvadorj
Nadine Matthews
Carol Paik
Lisbett Rodriguez
Anne Sanderson
Marisa Siegel
Kiki T.
Maryellen Tighe
Sophia Torres

COMMITTEE EDITORS

Nan Bauer-Maglin
Audrey Bergen
Susan Bolotin
Anne Caceres-Gonzalez
Andrea Cepeda
Martina Clark
Erin D. Coffey
Nicole Comly
Dara Daré
Katie Della Mora
Tess Forte
Gabriela Galvin
Catherine Greenman
Daphney Guillaume
Lily He
Nicole Goldberg Henry
Fiona Hernandez
Donna Hill
Kayah Hodge
Waeza Jagirdar
Lauren Kiel
Colleen Markley

Amaya Michaelides
Leslie Pantaleon
Elle Gonzalez Rose
Patricia Rossi
Mara Santilli
Ashna Shah
Victoria Siebor
Madeline Stone
Emily Toliver
Madeline Wallace
Rebecca Lowry Warchut
Liza Wyles

PROMOTIONS CHAIR

Livia Nelson

EDITORIAL STAFF

Azia Armstead, Community Coordinator
Annaya Baynes, Fellow
Sally Familia, Community Coordinator
Margery Hannah, Community Manager
Jessica Jagtiani, Community Manager
Vahni Kurra, Senior Community & Marketing Coordinator
Molly MacDermot, Director of Special Initiatives
Emily Méndez, Editor-in-Residence
Elmer Meza, Salesforce & Systems Manager
Lisbett Rodriguez, Programs & Systems Senior Coordinator
Erica Silberman, Director of Engagement & Partnerships

CONTENTS

Stories that depict sensitive topics are necessary for many reasons. Facing the most difficult parts of the human experience can both help others feel less alone and inspire readers to work toward a better future. However, we recognize that certain topics may be distressing when they catch readers off guard. That is why we have included a Content Warning for some of the stories.

FOREWORD

DONNA HILL

Books and reading have been my companions for as far back as I can remember. As a young girl, during my free time, when I was not in school or at a Girl Scouts meeting, I was in the Macon Street library. I devoured Agatha Christie mysteries, imagined myself raining havoc on the hapless mortals from my perch on Mount Olympus, or pined after the dark and brooding heroes in *Wuthering Heights* and *Jane Eyre*. Those were my reference points. My North Star. Growing up as a Black girl in Bedford-Stuyvesant, Brooklyn, there were no books with characters that looked like me or lived the life that I understood. As a young reader, I simply believed "that's just the way it is." I never fathomed that I could do what I loved—write. I had no mentor, no models. I had no Girls Write Now. But as the literary icon Toni Morrison once noted, if the book is not out there, write the story you want to read.

These young, gifted women of Girls Write Now have in their grasp the support and nurturing that writers long for, that I wish I'd had in my early years. They are putting to paper the stories that are not out there—*their* stories. They are taking up Morrison's charge. The mentoring community of Girls Write Now is preparing each of these young women to not only express themselves through writing, but to uncover who they are, and offering a pathway to all they can become. A Girls Write Now mentor can change lives.

I am honored and humbled to have served as a mentor for more than five years, to give back to blossoming writers so much of what I've learned, to watch my mentee go from shy and reserved, to serving as an emcee for a Girls Write Now event, to graduating from college. All of these young women are success stories, and on the pages of this year's anthology they bare their souls, share with the world all that they are, and offer a vision of their future selves. That takes courage. That takes love. That takes the magic of Girls Write Now.

DONNA HILL is a Girls Write Now mentor, Anthology Editorial Committee member, and the author of *Confessions in B-Flat* and *I Am Ayah: The Way Home.*

INTRODUCTION

FORSYTH HARMON

When I was a seven-year-old girl, I spent a lot of time at the local thrift store on our small town's main street. My grandmother worked there, and I'd accompany her on her after-school shifts. Sometimes I'd sit with her at the donations window, tearing open black plastic bags of one woman's discards, wool slacks and silk blouses spilling out, or digging through cardboard boxes labeled *attic* in black marker, hoping to be surprised by something wonderful. Or I'd wander the store, restacking mismatched porcelain plates, trying on a pair of too-big high heels that hadn't been there the week before.

One late-winter afternoon, lemon light gilding the store through the front picture window, I spotted something new hanging from the costume jewelry rack. A star-shaped gold-plated charm glittered at the end of a long gold chain. I took the star in my palm. On its face, engraved in capital serif letters, were the words *TURN YOUR SCARS.* I flipped it over. Its opposite face read *INTO STARS.*

Turn your scars into stars.

I contemplated the scab on my recently skinned knee, the small crater on my mother's cheek where there'd once been a mole, the white line along my father's jaw where he'd taken shrapnel in Vietnam. I imagined each of these scars becoming little gold stars we'd send up into the dark night sky. My grandmother was sweet enough to buy me this trinket, and I wore it around my neck for many years. As a teenager, and a writer, I'd finger this star at my collarbone, considering the aphorism's more metaphorical dimension.

As a Girls Write Now mentor lucky enough to have worked with Dom Dawes, my mentee, and today reviewing the contents of this gorgeous new 2024 anthology, I'm awestruck by the courageous and beautiful ways in which Girls Write Now writers have lived through the pandemic and the complex years that have since followed, finding their strength and their voices to produce the glittering works of poetry and prose that follow. From a love letter to a long-gone home, to a meditation on the Japanese art of kintsugi, to soulful reflections on love, joy, and grief, these young writers and *Here & Now* anthology contributors have each sent up a star, offering light, direction, and hope for the glittering cosmos of the future.

2024 brings us the age of Aquarius. This is the age of community, innovation, revolution, and collective liberation. This is the age of light. Here we are. Now's the time. Look up.

FORSYTH HARMON is a Girls Write Now mentor. She's the author of the illustrated novel *Justine,* as well as the illustrator of national bestseller *Girlhood* by Melissa Febos and *The Art of the Affair* by Catherine Lacey. She received both a B.A. and an MFA from Columbia University and lives in New York.

GIRLS WRITE NOW

HERE & NOW

2024 ANTHOLOGY

FOLAKE AINA

Folake is a Bronx-based African educator and creative. She has a dual degree in urban planning and globalization and is dedicated to finding resources to uplift her communities.

MENTEE'S ANECDOTE:

Girls Write Now has empowered me to use my voice. Working with Shenny has allowed me to block out the judgment I fear and to allow positive energy to flow throughout my writing process. While creating this piece for the anthology, I was able to get great advice from my Girls Write Now staff lead, Vahni Kurra. Through my writing, I want to help myself and others cope with the feeling of anxiety and not being enough, because we are all intrinsically valuable as human beings.

SHENNY SHANTAY

Shenny Shantay, a college freshman who is passionate about storytelling, aims to pursue her passion in writing and shed light on underrepresented communities so they are seen.

PEER MENTEE'S ANECDOTE:

Joining the Girls Write Now community has been a wonderful time. The support and encouragement from fellow writers have been invaluable, inspiring me to explore new genres and styles in my writing.

BIRTHDAY ANXIETY

FOLAKE AINA

I turned twenty-five on February 6, and I felt like I didn't have much to show for it, but I realized I was letting my anxiety get the best of me.

I am to be loved, a day in celebration
from the time bakers lay each letter on frosting
As loved as a name is used before the person enters the world
Another year of living, of wonder, to think of what to contribute
Expectations on clouds and scene above, from those who were not aware
Conscious around strangers, family feels like danger, when you have nothing to show
But I realize My gift is life, to share the fate of existing
Taking steps of firsts, in this new age

ASMA AL-MASYABI

Asma Al-Masyabi is always writing. Poetry, personal essays, and stories stain her fingers dark with ink. She tries to find her reflection in these musings.

MENTEE'S ANECDOTE:

Nyilah Thomas is the kind of writer whose work you can't read just once. I could write a long list of the things I obsess about in her writing—the bold voice, the perfect amount of humor, the way she separates her stanzas—but I don't have the word count for that. I love learning more about her through her beautiful poetry and prose in our weekly sessions, and all our time spent together geeking over our favorite poetry. Nyilah is the one who truly introduced me to spoken-word poetry, and my YouTube algorithm thanks her profusely for it.

NYILAH THOMAS

Nyilah Thomas puts pen to paper to obsess about love, loss, religion, and her daily experiences in poetry, prose, and personal essays.

PEER MENTEE'S ANECDOTE:

Asma Al-Masyabi is one of the greats. Reading Asma's pieces always invokes so many emotions, images, and ideas, leaving me stunned like a deer peering into headlights. Her work hits home, and her feedback is a delight. I love Saturdays at 3 p.m., because that's when I get to catch up with Asma about our lives and, even more recently, share our mutual love for spoken-word poetry and even a playlist for performances. I hope to one day see Asma perform, because her voice journeys you into the poem. Remember her name, folks; she's that good!

I'M AFRAID YOU'LL END UP SEEING ME THE WAY I SEE MYSELF

ASMA AL-MASYABI

Here are the things I don't want anyone else to know. Here is the person I don't want anyone else to see.

When I was younger I dreamed of a hermit's life for myself. Cottage in the woods, a shelf of books, a lone stranger knocking on my door and I do not answer. They are lost and I make like a ghost. Like water vapor. I am young and I am always making a ghost of myself. I trace the outline I might take up if I could not be seen.

My heart seized at the thought of asking a store employee a question. I was in the way of a man browsing books in the library and could not wring myself any smaller. My mother asked if I wanted to attend a writing club and I loved writing but could not—*could not*—be in a room full of people's eyes tracing my being, each unique soul turned in sharp thought toward my own. I shook my head around a silent wish and cried, later, fists pale-tight around all I wasn't.

They have kind eyes and soft smiles. At the end of class, we push the desks back together, a chore turned ritual, and I thank them for their responses to a poem. We all walk the same way and start chatting (I beg my heart to slow down, to be less strange, to live in the cold air and the words around me). When they invite me to coffee, I give thanks to everything I can think of on the walk to Starbucks. I thank the pavement and the clouds and my thick-soled boots. I thank the creaking of my ribs that has grown quiet after so long.

I like to say I have learned to do hard things. I've learned to speak up, to barge into unfamiliar territory and declare that there are things that I want and then to pursue them. I've embraced failure. I've learned to be alone. Sometimes the hard thing is sending an email, or ordering fries. Sometimes it is sitting by a person and being a person, laughter and conversation freeing all the weight you learned only from yourself, watching it drift to and fro. There are hard things, and there are *hard* things. Sometimes I have to learn to breathe.

Later, I ask a small question and she gives a big answer and while she talks I wish I could reach out with my words and tell her that I can never understand, but I understand, and I am listening. Instead, I just listen and while we are walking we get lost and the weather is cold, the sun blotted by clouds, the wind blowing right through us. I am the only one of us who knows the way, but I don't bother to ask where we are going. We trudge through half-melted snow, too cold to talk.

I've learned that fear is not diminishing. It lives in the same shape as the air. The same shape as you. You move, and it moves with you, a delayed shadow. Like an afterimage. The burning of a light that is no longer light darkened in your vision.

Even after I lose us, lose the perfect words, after we shiver under bone-white sky, she still smiles. She learns I am not so good at directions, that I exit buildings out of opposite doors, thoughtless. Learns I am practiced at listening but still try to give words as well as silence. Learns I am afraid of endings but never let that stop me from attempting to grow beginnings.

I failed once, to put a word to everything. When I saw a word and thought it was mine, I took it home and felt the air of how it might explain my fears in one long string of letters. I cried when I realized it didn't belong to me. I learned, instead, that I was an unexplained, strange thing. That there was nothing I could hold on to when my body compressed itself as it realized that to exist meant to be perceived.

What is lost when heavy things rise, like an anchor strung onto a light blue balloon? Up, up, up, so easily, it feels like falling. Like the wind could laugh and blow it all away.

When outside, my eyes move toward the clouds, almost on instinct. They draw me in, their defined edges, the bits of them that fade into the space around them. You would never know from looking that they are heavy bastards. That they can weigh billions of pounds, all water vapor, particles, and air. The only reason they remain hovering above is because they are slightly less dense than the air beneath them. There is nothing weightless in their towering construction.

Not too long ago my fears held themselves in the cavern of my mouth and the emptiness that filled my chest. After being afraid so long it feels like nothing at all. Nothing, nothing, nothing. A bubble of air expanding in my lungs, blocking the way to my throat. I smile easily, but my eyes are transparent. I close them when I am alone.

AYAH AL-MASYABI

Ayah Al-Masyabi is a writer, artist, and aspiring journalist who spends her time watching soccer news, thinking about new projects, and laughing at her favorite sitcoms.

MENTEE'S ANECDOTE:

Working with Anne is the highlight of every week we meet. I always look forward to talking to her. Whether it be about books or how our weeks are, it is always a joy! My favorite part of this year was the days we revealed the "exquisite corpses" we'd collectively assembled. I was so nervous before, but it was like magic—how our words worked so perfectly together, making beautiful pieces. I especially loved being able to read Anne's work, which is so thoughtful and poetic. I am learning so much about writing and art from a great friend!

ANNE HELLMAN

Anne Hellman is a Brooklyn-based writer and the founder of The Grandmother Project. Other than writing fiction, Anne published *Design Brooklyn* with Abrams in 2013.

MENTOR'S ANECDOTE:

This year, Ayah and I ventured further into the universe of fiction-making. Ayah never stops exploring and doesn't shy away from innovative ideas, those new "rooms" in the stories she writes. I am certain Ayah's new novel will illuminate her unique mind. We delved into "exquisite corpse" pieces, redacting each line until we unveiled them all, and were happy to find we create psychically together. A card Ayah gave to me reads "There's still time . . . ," and I think of all the stories we want to write, how they do take time. That's just the beauty of it. Thank you, Ayah.

BROKEN

AYAH AL-MASYABI

A short story about the connection between a girl and her necklace.

She'd worn the necklace ever since she'd gotten it, at age eleven. It was a small, gold (or so she thought) oval on a long gold chain. When she first put it around her neck, the oval reached the bottom of her stomach. Years later, when she turned sixteen, it would finally fall above her belly button, just where she liked.

Because she was a shy girl with few friends, nobody noticed that she always wore it until two years after she put it on, when she was thirteen. "Why do you wear that all the time?" they started to ask her every day at lunch. At first she was hesitant, a multitude of thoughts running through her mind, thoughts like *Why should I tell them?* and *What if they thought I was crazy?* As her friends stared at her, waiting for some magical or mystical answer, she would hold on to the oval, but not too hard or its silky texture would cause it to slip through her fingers. She'd flip her dark curly hair out of her face, let go of the necklace, and fold her arms as she waited for the awkward silence to end. Eventually, someone would feel so uncomfortable that they'd change the subject.

This continued for a little over three weeks, and then they gave up on being able to hear her strange story. The truth was, she didn't wear the necklace because it made her pretty, although that was a plus, or because it reminded her of someone. She wore it because when she'd received it, she'd been hopeless and had felt alone. Nothing changed after she got the necklace; she still felt the same. But it reminded her that people still loved her, even when she was broken.

RAISA ANIQA

Raisa Aniqa is a senior at Stuyvesant High School. She will be attending Sarah Lawrence College. This is her first year at Girls Write Now.

MENTEE'S ANECDOTE:

The best part about Julia being my mentor is that we're both total geeks with a huge love for superhero comics. Our personalities just clicked, for which I am immensely grateful. Having that connection with her from the start made me feel so much more comfortable sharing my writing and working on it with someone else. I will forever be grateful to her for helping me not just work on my technical issues with writing but also be more honest and confident in what I write.

JULIA MERCADO

Julia Mercado is a Girls Write Now mentee alum, a Queens-based writer, and a podcast host. As a recruiter, she has hired creatives for more than thirty magazines, including *Marie Claire* and *Cosmopolitan*.

MENTOR'S ANECDOTE:

When I met Raisa, I wasn't sure if I could help her with her writing because it was already very strong, but as we bonded over our love of Marvel and writing, it became easier to connect to Raisa and her words. Together, we're working to get her out of the mindset that she is a "bad writer." All a writer needs is a little direction. Raisa's a great writer and she only grows as we continue to work out the kinks in her writing. I'm always so proud of what comes out after every session we have together.

WHO WE COME FROM

RAISA ANIQA

As a first-generation American, I've always carried with me an intense fascination with my past. This is the story of my most notorious ancestor, and my unease at the rest, who have been forgotten.

During mealtimes as a child, along with the handfuls of rice she would put into my mouth, my mother would spoon-feed me her family's history, all of which could be traced back to one man.

Monir's ship steered off course in the midst of a cyclone. He was one of few survivors, with the number of people onboard and alive dwindling as time passed. By God's grace, the ship docked at the Sandwip Ship Ghat.

He sailed the Meghna River into the Bay of Bengal, though from where we do not know. Perhaps from Assam, or Paschimbanga, with the original body being either the Brahmaputra or the Ganga. But there's also reason to believe he could've been from Odisha or Bihar, or Kashmir or Punjab. (Why is there reason to believe such? Because we must trust the words we've circulated for so long. If we do not give weight to our own theories, no matter how distant from the realm of reality they may be, then who will? It simply would not do to disrespect our elders and say *No, that doesn't seem quite right.*)

Monir was tall and fair-skinned, and had hazel eyes. This is how we know he was not what people would now consider Bangladeshi. Additionally, his tongue was unlike ours—even among ethnic Bengalis, the linguistic quirks of dialects make them nearly mutually intelligible—for it was more elegant, more kind. His voice carried such rich smoothness that he made even the Sandwipya dialect he would come to speak sound kind when it otherwise sounds brutal.

His differences, his superiority, made him a man worthy of veneration. Even when he eventually fell from otherworldly heights to the levels of commoners due to years of association and, thus, familiarization. He became a man of the island, but in the small community of Harispur, Sandwip, where he had staked his claim and built a house for himself, his wife, and their eventual children, he was still seen as more.

In taking a native bride, Monir created a new line, one with ties to both the world at large and its spirit of adventure, and a small island of fishermen, shipworkers, and farmers in the Bay of Bengal.

For over a century, his descendants stayed on the island, a token of their gratitude to him and all he did. But they still weaved together fictions of his heroic journey across treacherous waters, as though he were Odysseus.

For over a century, they stayed. But they've clearly since left.

With time, once-familiar lands can become not just foreign, but foreigners. The opposite is also true, a cyclical pattern of migration where identities are transformed by location and locations are transformed by identity. As generations pass, roots are continuously pulled out of the ground and replanted elsewhere. When we leave, we leave behind families, memories, and names. We leave behind entire histories, though we desperately try to take as much of them with us as we can hold in our small pockets and limited luggage.

We leave behind burial grounds, if there were ever any at all. Too many of us were haphazardly put into the soil, with no accompanying grave markers to identify us by.

There is a pond in front of our ancestral home of seven generations, one removed from my own. It is where we would get our drinking water, where our children would swim and play, where we would fish, where we would garden. This pond defines our family identity just as much as the four mud buildings with tin roofs on our complex—as in, still, even decades after we've all scattered.

Monur'go Bari. That's what they call us, our family. That house in Harispur, with the pond? With the dirt road and the tiny creek? That's Monu's house.

We're Monu for Monir, my great-great-great-great-great-grandfather. The man who came from everywhere and nowhere in the early nineteenth century, who married an island girl descended from Arakanese pirates and, in settling down with her, created a local dynasty.

On the other side of the pond is a makeshift cemetery, the resting place of generations of women in my family, including Monir's wife.

When we leave home, we leave an imprint elsewhere. We forget those who have stayed, who were there in the first place, almost as though we never knew them at all.

We remember the name of a man no one alive remembers, but we forget those who have nurtured our heritage. We forget the person to whom we owe it all; Monir couldn't have created our family without the culture—*her* culture—he adopted and made his own.

"What about his wife?" I asked my mother the day she revealed to me the name of our myth of an ancestor.

"What about her?"

"What was her name?"

"Oh, that does not matter. She was only his wife."

"And the woman who created our family. The one who birthed us. Is she not important?"

JAMILAH ARAF

Jamilah Araf (she/her) is currently a high school junior at the Baccalaureate School for Global Education.

MENTEE'S ANECDOTE:

This year, I have been more overwhelmed by school and extracurricular requirements than ever before. Through it all, Kate has been nothing but supportive. In fact, our meetings have become a great and necessary escape. This year, we started doing collaborative prompts, which have led to hilarious stories, such as our short stories about Barbie and Ken. I am so lucky to have been matched with such a great mentor and to have her throughout my Girls Write Now journey.

KATE RILEY

Kate Riley (she/her) is the institutional giving manager at the Brooklyn Conservatory of Music.

MENTOR'S ANECDOTE:

I'm so glad we're on this adventure together: three years running! Jamilah continues to inspire and impress me; her writing conveys a depth of emotion, economy of phrasing, and clarity of viewpoint. Her fearlessness to try new genres and activities—launching a new school club, exploring photojournalism, and rocking high school debate—is a powerful reminder to be interested *and* interesting. Our one-to-ones are a balm and a kick in the pants. It's a treasure to scaffold on the connection and skills we've developed in the last two years and to see her confidence and mastery grow.

EL OCÉANO, MI AMOR

JAMILAH ARAF

Content Warning: Drowning, PTSD

A woman living in a beach town is recovering from trauma caused by a boating accident. Despite her initial fears, she eventually falls in love with the ocean again.

Her window framed the scene like a postcard. The wooden boardwalk held tourists, college kids on spring break, and old couples taking walks. Though they were far away, snippets of their conversations could still be heard from her room. Behind them, the shore, with sand as soft as powder and waves even softer. A clear line in the ocean about ten feet out separated turquoise from sapphire. Separating safety from danger. No one dared to cross this line. Parents yelled at their children not to swim too far out while couples took selfies with the gorgeous blues in the background. If you listened really closely, you could hear gasps from those witnessing its beauty for the first time all the way from her room. But she wasn't trying to listen for those reactions or the chatter. All of her senses were further out into the distance, beyond the boardwalk and the shore. She could only hear the sound of large waves breaking against the surface, only see the sapphire blue sizzling from the summer sun, only smell salt and blood. It was this scent that left her stuck in her bed all hours of the day. Why did she keep moving to beach towns? Why didn't she just move to a concrete jungle or a small farm? Why couldn't she just look away?

During the day, she was possessed by the ocean out in front of her. At night, she was possessed by the ocean in her memory. Much like the one she lived by, the ocean she had ventured into was a beast. She could still remember their ship, one of the best, being flipped like a pancake. She could still see the wood come apart like sand. She remembers her crewmates, their heads sinking in one by one. It's really a miracle she survived, if you call this survival.

After months of pleasant weather, she awoke one morning to a murky gray sky instead of the usual blue. The rain was coming down hard, and the winds were howling. This explained the lack of crowds on the shore and the boardwalks. She watched droplets fly in through her open window. The carpeted floor began to hold a puddle, forcing her to leave her safe spot.

Now she was closer to the ocean than she ever had been. It took only a few feet for this obsession to turn into a pull. As if her feet had a mind of their own, they slid into some old flip-flops and started running. She had to get there before the sun wiggled out from behind the clouds and the crowds came flocking back.

She came to a complete stop on the sand. A wave stretched out toward her as if it wanted to grab her by the foot and drag her in. But it had just missed the tips of her flip-flops, leaving it up to her to make the move.

Even after being chained to her bed by nightmares of her crewmates' screams, she didn't hesitate to run in. The feeling was not mutual, however, as she sensed that the ocean was trying to push her out. But she fought back. She jumped over the waves it sent and stood up every time they knocked her down. She kept going.

By this point, she was far beyond the safe zone, though she didn't seem to notice. She didn't know when she was going to turn back or *if* she was going to turn back. It sounded ridiculous, but there was nothing for her on land. Nothing like this.

Now the ocean was annoyed. It had hoped to push her out, then hoped she would leave on her own. Its patience had run out. It sent a wave the size of a skyscraper, one she could not escape in time. Before she could react, it ate her. She was left doing cartwheels in the ocean but was too far out to be pushed to shore. Once she slowed down, she didn't rush to grab air. She opened her eyes, taking in the gorgeous colors around her. She felt like a fly in a piece of stained glass. Even without the beating sun, the ocean still sparkled. Entranced by the sight, she forgot to go up. The ocean seized the opportunity, sending in another big wave. She didn't go spinning, but the shock had caused her to let go of her breath. A rush of salt water entered her mouth, the cold shooting through her insides. It wasn't painful, it was refreshing. More refreshing than a glass of cool water on a sunny day. She drank it all in and smiled. As if it were her inaugural sip, she decided from there on that she wanted to swim and drown in these waves.

Her window had framed her love like a photograph.

SHAYLA ASTUDILLO

Shayla Astudillo (they/them) is an Ecuadorian American poet who is studying English. They spend their time reading, writing new poems, and doing skincare!

MENTEE'S ANECDOTE:

Danielle has been there through all the ups and downs. She somehow always knows what to say to me, especially when I don't have the words. I have counted on her for the past four years to tell me the truth, support me, and be someone I can call upon. Her advice and ideas come from the heart and she's always had my best interest at heart. I am so grateful to have her as a mentor, and I can't wait to continue seeing her journey.

DANIELLE MAZZEO

Danielle Mazzeo is from New York City, where she spends her time with books, her cats, and being a grant writer.

MENTOR'S ANECDOTE:

Shayla and I have been working together through Girls Write Now for four years, and it has been such a pleasure and honor to watch Shayla grow as a writer, thinker, and young adult. They are incredibly generous in their work, willing to share so much of themselves while also caring deeply for their readers. In an era of their life that has seen so many changes, Shayla continues to show resilience, strength, and an eagerness to learn. I can't wait to see what's next for them!

OUR WORLD AND MY WORLD AS OF TODAY COLLECTION.

SHAYLA ASTUDILLO

The world and I have been communicating lately. This collection of poems shows how our conversation went.

THE "REPEATED CHANGE" SONNET

The world has become a dark place darling,
With no flowers growing from volcanoes
No stability . . . red ink sweeps railing
You hope. but no such thing with the *veneno.*
The trees are no longer viridescent
Their eyes cannot open, the smoke too strong
Then, we the adult as adolescent
It's about time we realize our wrong
The black weapon is pointing at their heads
Should we stay quiet, or scream with no air
No longer bright and young nice newlyweds
Scream, scream, we have been taken by the pair.
Breathe, Breathe, hold your hands together darling.
Prosper, together, without their snarling.

A COMPILATION OF ME TRYING TO BE YOURS

I've told you all
about my writing, my words, and how much they mean to me.
It's been a wonderful thing really.
I think it's time I look beyond myself.

Why do I write? What do my words do for you?
Well, a part of me hopes they comfort the part of your soul that you have left to
rotten.

Another part of me hopes that I tell a
true story.
A story of a repeated past.
Do you understand,
the past has become a cycle and aren't **I** just lucky to be here right now.
Ah, back to me. Apologies, it's a habit.
The flowers bloom,
the leaves fall,
the grievances rise,
the people die.
Repetitive, isn't it?
Let me say it again.
The flowers bloom,
the leaves fall,
the grievances rise,
the people die.
I want this to be bigger than me.
I want all the words I've been talking about for all this time to be bigger than me.
Let it be bigger because I don't know if I can take my presence being nothing in this world.

Take my pain, take my wrath, and take my joy.

Take it.
Turn it into something no one's seen before.
I know I'm just talking of myself again, old habits die hard.
Let's, just, act,
like we care.

ENTONCES

Esto es para usted.
Un idioma donde no me viene las palabras.
Pienso, pienso y todo que sale son los recuerdos de usted.
Mis palabras no salen con felicidad, ni salen con tristeza.
Vienen sin confianza y sin amor.
Yo no conozco el piso que yo piso, o el aire que respiro.
Sin embargo, si recuerdo el dolor.
Creo que sientes lo mismo.
Sigue, sigue, dolor que no es completamente mío.
Recuerdo cuando el dolor se hizo mio, y te lo regreso.
Es tuyo.

I'LL SEE YOU AROUND

My voice has become shaken. Hasn't been used in quite a long time.
It is shaking when it speaks, trust me.
That will not stop it from seeing you again.
They are excited to speak to you.
With all its good and bad listening.
It will come back with the voice of reason.
        my voice.
Welcome Back.

ELIO AVILES

Elio (they/he) is a fifteen-year-old writer with an interest in space, photography, and art. They enjoy writing fantasy and horror, and wish to share their work!

MENTEE'S ANECDOTE:

I was pretty nervous about working with somebody I'd never met, but that fear quickly went away upon our first meeting. My peer Paige is a wonderful person. She is very cool, creative, and active. On top of all that, she does theater and sports; Paige is also, of course, a wonderful writer—from her descriptions to the built-up tension as well as her scripts, Paige's writing is impressive! Paige is a very welcoming person, and I have enjoyed our meetings together. I am incredibly grateful to have a peer like them!

PAIGE BLAIR

Paige is a high school sophomore with numerous poetry and scriptwriting accolades who enjoys listening to podcasts and thinking about fictional characters in her free time.

PEER MENTEE'S ANECDOTE:

Working with Elio this past year has been such a great experience! It's so fun to talk to them about writing, and they inspire me to be a better writer with their drive and skill. It's awesome to be connected to another aspiring author my age, and I can't wait to see where their writing takes them!

ASLAN

ELIO AVILES

With tons of celestial references, this poem is about a lonely child struggling with their beauty, self-worth, and relationships.

I was a child of the moon
Cursed by wretched beauty only the evil
Could find.
A child blessed by the gods
And loved by all those with desire.
Beautiful was I to all those who knew
What a treat I was truly
Created to be.
A child born to malign and pain and blood.
Far too cold was I just as the
Moon
Who held beauty much sweeter—distilled and true. The moon whose
Beauty had left me behind with the rubble and the dirt as I
Scrambled to pick up anything of value to
Increase my true worth.
This beauty I was
Given.
This beauty I held was not
Beautiful at all.
I was an angel untrue.
Like Icarus chasing the sun, I
Chased after the moon—after the one who
Left me behind.
My wings were uneven—bloody and torn.
The moon had no wings
But a halo hung

Around her head.
A beautiful thing such reminding us all of
Her pure worth.
My beauty.
My beauty is blood. My beauty is
Gone.
Gone all to her who
In all her glow
Had forgotten me and my dirt.
I was a child burned by the sun and
Forgotten by the moon.
Born from violence and evil and
Malign and
Grief.

LYDIA BACH

Lydia Bach is a high school student in New York City. She enjoys reading, writing, and singing.

MENTEE'S ANECDOTE:

Being a mentee at Girls Write Now has been, more than anything, a way of finding community. My friends and the various adults in my life are always surprised to find out how much I love to write. Since becoming a part of Girls Write Now, I have found other teenagers who enjoy writing as much as I do, and who want to pursue writing more seriously. It has been a really great experience for me, from the monthly studios to just hearing what other people my age have to say about writing. I'm excited to keep participating!

AZIA ARMSTEAD

Azia Armstead is a poet from Richmond, Virginia. She is currently a community coordinator at Girls Write Now, where she also teaches poetry.

MENTOR'S ANECDOTE:

As a reader, I want to inhabit the moment Lydia has given us a glimpse into. She utilizes a keen brevity in this succinct poem in which the speaker is an observer of an intimate moment between their grandmother and her close friend at the end of their life. Bearing witness to this tenderness evokes a stillness, engendering an unknowing within the speaker about life and its meaning. I'm called to this poem again and again.

THE DYING FRIEND

LYDIA BACH

This piece is simple, yet I hope it can still be striking to whomever reads it. I have been thinking about writing this poem for a very long time.

My grandmother reads Yeats
to her dying friend.
I am not sure what life means anymore.

TILDA BARTLETT

Tilda (she/her) is a junior from New York City. She enjoys doing anything creative, such as writing, drawing, painting, sewing, or filmmaking. She also plays soccer and runs.

MENTEE'S ANECDOTE:

Devon has been an amazing mentor to me and helped me come so far as a writer. She's been very reliable, even though sometimes I am not, and is very understanding. This year, compared to all my other years in Girls Write Now, we've worked on so many pieces together and I really just enjoy meeting with her every week.

DEVON FORWARD

Devon Forward is a news writer covering all things celebrity, entertainment, and pop culture for *Parade* who spends her free time exploring creative writing.

MENTOR'S ANECDOTE:

Throughout our time working together during the mentorship program, Tilda and I have explored a variety of creative writing projects and styles. She continually impresses me with her unique voice and talent for naturally creating a vivid world with her words that invite the reader in, while I barely had a grasp on essay writing at her age. I hope I have been helpful in her writing journey, but I've learned just as much myself, with Tilda's creativity inspiring me to challenge myself in my own writing ventures.

IT WON'T LAST FOREVER

TILDA BARTLETT

I wrote this piece as I was thinking about the pressures of fading beauty and the standards society holds for women.

Sometimes I wonder what life would be like if I could look in the mirror one day thirty years in the future and not tug my face taut as I watch my mother do now. Sometimes I wonder what it would be like if I could express my emotions without worrying about leaving a mark.

It might seem naïve or self-involved to be worried about these things now, and even though I try to, I cannot escape the fear of disintegrating beauty. Women are surrounded by their peers, always telling them to enjoy it while it lasts, or, one of my favorites, "I remember when I still looked like that." It's difficult to hear those who reminisce and look forward to my future. Especially when they imply that the future may not be something I should dream of, but rather something I should be wary of.

I know some people say that aging is a blessing, which I don't disagree with. It's simply hard to find the truth in that statement when I fear I'm in possession of something I know I won't have forever.

Women are treated like we have some sort of an expiration date, like we're some milk that becomes rotten the longer we exist. It becomes hard to embrace getting older when everyone and everything around me is telling me that these years will be the best of your life. How do you enjoy something when you know it won't last forever?

ARISLENY BENITEZ-LINAREZ

Arisleny is a current high school junior and a nature fan. For some reason or another, some type of nature always shows up in her writing.

MENTEE'S ANECDOTE:

Samantha has been a really inspiring and encouraging mentor. She has always supported me and always had a positive attitude. I really appreciate her as not only a mentor and a role model, but also a friend. I will never forget the times we got boba, when we not only wrote, but also bonded, and of course I can't forget playing Connect Four with her.

SAMANTHA ISALES HERNANDEZ

Samantha Isales is a former mentee and current mentor at Girls Write Now who enjoys blending activism and world issues in her writing.

MENTOR'S ANECDOTE:

Writing with Arisleny is lots of fun. She always finds fun and creative ways to write about literally anything. She is someone who truly empowers others to find their voices as writers, which has encouraged me as a mentor to push myself even more. I really admire the thoughtfulness that she puts into her writing, and I am always looking forward to reading anything she works on. Her ability to make the most boring of topics into descriptive and intriguing pieces has been fun to watch and learn from. I am excited for what's to come!

WHEN A GARDEN CRIES, A PERFECT GARDEN IS STAINED

ARISLENY BENITEZ-LINAREZ

We were sitting on the phone together, trying to figure out what we could write about that felt close to both of our hearts. We decided to use nature to write about mental health.

PART 1

A perfect flower
Covered in blood

I once believed if I held that perfect flower.
Any one small thing.
It would light up my garden, allowing for more to grow.
But a little flower,
I have no more.
It felt as though every single leaf, tree, and animal I've touched
has become stained with the idea that nothing's right.
Slowly it seeps into my garden.
Covering everything I love with anguish and anxiety.
No flowers can grow in the soil so dry.
Though you would've believed the tears from the waterfall would have moistened it.
Transition from a believable almost perfect-like state.
To one where it feels like the literal ground has been pulled from under you.
The constant loss of friends makes you feel despair and it seems as though nothing is right.

Try and try as you might, everything only seems to get worse.
Never had the garden looked so gloomy.
And never had the girl been depressed by the garden.
You see, the girl often lets many people into her garden so that they too can be happy.
But people aren't always nice and they litter and ruin the poor garden.
The girl, always believing in other people first, had no idea how to banish them from the garden, and so they remained.
Trashing the girl's loveliest possessions with anger and hatred.
The girl could only marvel at the mess they'd made.
And as the poor garden was dying before now all that was left by the travelers was nothing more than sadness, depression, and self-hatred.
See, hatred is contagious.
Once someone tells you they hate you it's hard not to tell yourself that.
In front of a waterfall, the girl's reflection looks back at her as tears begin to fall on skin that she once used to love.
Even her skin crawls thinking of the vile words said.
She needs to learn to defend herself.
A boundary as tall as the waterfall will be put in place.
Maybe that'll keep the unruly settlers from trampling her garden ever again.
For now the girl sits in her garden.
Looking at the remains of things she'd once loved.
The twirling leaves, showing the dances she once used to love.

She looked out into her garden.
Seeing how broken her own flowers and ground were.
She must do something
She gets up
And prays for water
None comes
She sits there
Praying for water
And the soil remains dry
She asks "why has the world forsaken me?"
At that time
The waterfall becomes so loud the girl couldn't ignore it anymore
She went up to it

"If you want a vibrant garden,
You have to keep it vibrant.
Love yourself enough,
To keep it safe for you."

PART 2

In came the intruder
The one that stole the flowers that I so delicately planted
I stood up all night practicing my techniques
So that the tulips and the roses
The sunflowers and the violets all lasted
Under the moon's light, they very shortly lived
Listen to me now, this was not the first time the intruder got its way
A few days ago, it came and poured the water I worked all night to collect
Killing the tulips and the roses, the sunflowers and the violets

See, it took lots of crying to collect that amount of tear-water
After watching gardens be exterminated around the world
And particularly in the Middle East
I could not sleep
I stood up all week collecting my tears
I watched gardeners yell and demand for the exterminator to stop
No one listened
The long hours of crying filled my jar
They say that if you pray under the moon, collect your tears, and pour them over your garden, then maybe a miracle will go far
I am angry
and sad
and mad
and truly distraught
The note on the jar read "water-tears do not touch"
And again the intruder went and poured it all
If there is one thing I'd tell this intruder it is that while I love sharing my tulips and violets and roses and sunflowers,
Their actions have now killed my garden and the tear-water has dried up

The pain of a dead garden will live deep in my heart

MADELINE BERBERIAN-HUTCHINSON

Madeline is a junior at Stuyvesant High School and lives in Brooklyn, New York. She is a writer, poet, sister, and daughter.

MENTEE'S ANECDOTE:

Jackie and I have met in coffee shops, sharing our writing and prompting each other. These settings, dynamic in ambiance and imbued in rich nurturance, parallel the value gained by our mentoring collaboration. Jackie has generously offered me a strong sense of being seen and heard. She values my work and has attended every one of my accomplishments. Jackie is brilliant, as a person, writer, and mentor. Her support has helped me evolve, breaking the barriers I created within myself. Jackie is the person I constantly aspire to be.

JACKIE HOMAN

Jackie Homan leads content and campaign development for a mental health nonprofit. She enjoys creative writing, rock climbing, and visiting museums.

MENTOR'S ANECDOTE:

It is a true honor to work with Madeline for a second year. Throughout our time together, I've witnessed Madeline's writing sharpen and evolve, while she maintains such a clear voice that is unquestionably her own. Madeline has also stepped out of her comfort zone to try new forms—I had the privilege of watching her perform spoken word at the New York City Youth Poet Laureate Commencement. Madeline is exceptionally talented, creative, and self-aware, and I am confident her work will make a profound impact in this world.

VOGELS/GIRLS

MADELINE BERBERIAN-HUTCHINSON

An ode to southern Germany and my cousin, Marlene.

I. (2018)

Knee-deep in the shallow end of the riverbed, we sat crouched in the bordering brush.
(I did not yet know that the ticks were biting at my strappy sandaled heels,
the venom festering inside us) and our calves began to shake from the cold rush of the river
and the hours of waiting on relatives who did not remember our names. In the water, darkness
clung to our thighs as our panoptical sun ran alongside her cousin
in between the leaves, saluting a creased god.
The breeze drew her wisps of fine hair against my eyelashes.
Our language is shaded in between heavy blinks, so our eyelids begin to sing.
She taught me, in broken English, how to even our tiny palms (render them
an unfamiliar flatness, no German or girl had ever known) so the fireflies
would land in the softest part of our grasp—which was every part of me.

Our mothers called us to the dinner table with the leaves and the stained tablecloth.
We grabbed our last shiny rocks by the fistful, and I folded
my checkered Sunday dress, cut from the tablecloth, upward
to keep the rocks safely in my grasp and wondered if this is what it's like

to be a mother. Specks of purple nail polish floating down the stream, our bliss dripped
onto the gravel path as we tripped on our toes up the hill.

The grain of our grandfather's unpolished wooden bench sliced
against the underbelly of my thighs and her face
split in two, her *teeth* proudly bearing the *scene* where
I tattooed my name on her wrist
with chalk, hers near my shoulder.

In an abbreviated breath, she told me *I had our family*
until you and this sentiment had left me with a complicated guilt
until I bit back my (grand)mother tongue: I later learned
that she truncated her double "S" and meant to say she hated our family,
for in German the difference between having and hating is found in a single beat.

II. (2023)

The photos our fathers took of us had their blurry fingertips on the frame, and the river ran black, a dark, unforgiving sludge. The pool (where her little brother almost drowned) was filled with concrete, and her blue-eyed horse had died, buried near the patch of edelweiss where we screamed, for the first time, curses in English.

Me not knowing the word for nostalgia, her not knowing the word
for oil spill, we tried to explain what had elapsed, tried to explain
why the hair on our legs and the lilac grass in the field were so closely shaven.

But the word for exhalation had not yet sprouted in either of our disjointed lexicons.
I now know diasporic and dysphoric still sound the same on my tongue: neither
the land nor the body will ever be mine.

JACQUELINE BERNABE

Jacqueline Bernabe is a busy college student interested in medicine, writing, and traveling who enjoys discovering new artists, films, and spending time with friends and family.

MENTEE'S ANECDOTE:

Although Shrien and I have been in collaboration for only a few months, it feels like I have known her much longer. From the first day we met, she has made me feel seen and has pushed me to explore and write about the things I truly wanted to express. I always look forward to our meetings, especially the ones that occur at the café we frequent on the Upper West Side, where we laugh, relate, write, and bond with each other. I am excited to continue writing with her and hope to take her to get some pupusas soon!

SHRIEN ALSHABASY

Shrien Alshabasy (S.M. Figgs) is a first-generation Egyptian American writing an urban fantasy set in her home of New York City.

MENTOR'S ANECDOTE:

When Jacqueline and I met to discuss her anthology piece for this year, we made a list of different ideas and topics that she felt were important to her. The previous piece we worked on dealt heavily with her father's passing, an experience I could understand, as someone who lost her mother at a young age. After she wrote out her list of topics, I could sense Jacqueline gravitating hesitantly to the idea of writing about grief and her body. I encouraged her to head toward the thing that intrigued her, and this beautiful piece is the product.

MY TEARS HAVE TRAVELED

JACQUELINE BERNABE

Content Warning: Fatphobia, Death of Parent, Blood

A reflection of my tears throughout my life.

Mami, could I possibly start using tampons now?

I was expecting my mother to groan and perhaps even give me a lecture when I asked her this question. She simply laughed as if I was asking the most outrageous and ridiculous question—the ones where you're so stunned that all you can do is cackle—and that's what she did while I stood, red in the face, eyebrows furrowed, and could feel my eyes ready to release the subsequent tears of shame.

At that moment, I wish she had yelled instead.

I couldn't hold it in, so I rushed to the bathroom. This shabby bathroom, too small for a family of six, had been converted into my sanctuary over the years. It was here where I cried the first time I got my period because I had bled through and didn't realize it. I was used to sitting on the cold tiles, clutching my stomach from the nausea that my first couple of periods would bring. This bathroom had its own peculiar way of being there for me when I felt the shame that came with my intolerable development. Now was no exception, with the tune of my mother's laugh still ringing in my ears. Looking back, I don't think it was the laugh, itself, that bothered me. It was more the fact that the laugh was a reminder of this endless cycle of embarrassment when it came to my body and the transformation I was going through. There were many things I couldn't control when it came to my body, yet when I did gain even a bit of strength to stand up, that strength disintegrated. It was replaced with the humiliation that I still hadn't gotten used to.

The only thing that could cement me was sitting alone in the bathroom with a dread that I kept to myself, too scared to ever let her out.

By the time I was fourteen, my period had continued to be something that I saw every so often—like a family member that annoys you and you surprisingly see only on Christmas. My period was severely irregular, which, unbeknownst to me, was due to polycystic ovary syndrome. At the time, I didn't know what that was, so I never chose to look it up or inform myself about it, choosing instead to sulk and be a moody preteen. I wanted to stop the race, but my body was winning against my mind. I felt fourteen years old.

But the day I finally got my menstrual again, I felt like I became a "woman" again.

It wasn't the sound of the packed buses filled with locals going to work or the familiar lady who walked up and down the streets yelling out "Pan francés!" that woke me up. It was the blood running down my thighs. My period had returned unannounced. I was looking forward to this day, as it was the day my family and I had planned to go to the beach. A day that was supposed to be spent splashing in the waters, writing messages in the sand, smelling the charcoal fumes that emit from the grill—a smell I used to relish—and getting my summer vacation in El Salvador started. It was supposed to be a family beach day, and nothing compared to spending summer with family.

It was also the day that my dad died.

I cried earlier that day because I knew I wasn't going to enjoy the day, but now I was crying because I didn't know if my family or I would ever enjoy the rest of our lives. My cramps felt sharper and sharper, as if the anguish in my mind had also manifested and crawled around my body. I was still a child, yet, on the same day, my desire to be naïve flew away. Perhaps it was even naïve to think that I could desire this in the first place. I was no longer a child. I was a young woman. If the physical embodiment of blood leaving my body—a belief that my family, and even me for a while, shared—didn't show it, then it was seen in the way I had to explain and retell the story of the day my dad died. I controlled my breathing, and I trained myself to fly into an alternate universe I had created in my head so I wouldn't have to think about the fact that he wouldn't appear in any new family photos.

All I could tell myself was that time will heal, *time will heal*, which meant that from then on, I kept thinking about the future. I kept thinking about how one day I was going to look back and all that grief I experienced was going to disappear and . . .

I'm now nineteen and, although I don't cry when I talk about my dad anymore, I still picture my fourteen-year-old self in tears on the beach the day he died. I wish I could tell her that it will be okay.

LUCA BERNSTEIN

Luca Bernstein is a senior in high school who has always loved writing and exploring the world. She looks forward to what her future holds and how writing will be a part of it!

MENTEE'S ANECDOTE:

The second I met Sara, I immediately felt a connection, even over Zoom. I would spend the whole week looking forward to the hour we met over Zoom. She would share writing she found and we would respond to prompts relating to what we'd just read. This is how we spent most of our pair sessions, excluding the times she would help me apply to internships and submit my writing for competitions. I was repeatedly blown away by Sara's work and always appreciated the insight and help she gave me in our pair sessions. She is like the older sister I always wished I had, but also so much more than that. Even when I felt like I couldn't write anything, Sara always managed to get something out of me; even throughout some really hard times in my life, she was there supporting and encouraging me more than anyone. When things felt crazy and out of control, I always knew I had that hour with Sara where I could put everything aside and just focus on writing.

SARA FELSENSTEIN

Sara Felsenstein is a brand and content strategy director in New York City who believes everyday adventures make the best stories.

MENTOR'S ANECDOTE:

From my first Zoom meeting with Luca three years ago, I was blown away by her intelligence, creativity, and talent. Fast-forward to 2024, we're now meeting in East Village coffee shops, and I'm amazed by how much Luca has grown as a writer and a person; she is so confident in her own voice. At nearly every meeting, she writes something that inspires me, or shares a view on life that makes me think more deeply about my own. Our mentoring relationship has grown so much over the years. I'll miss Luca next year, but I can't wait to see where her talents take her next!

EATING (GOD) DISORDER

LUCA BERNSTEIN

Content Warning: Religious Trauma

This poem is about my experience growing up being forced to be kosher.

CRAB—maryland/ our annual family holidays which we used
to have when we were still a family/ still invited/ crab/ one of
my favorite things in the world which I love more than
anything/ instead of eating I had to watch the eating/ by my
cousins/ who would try and sneak me bites/ of crab under the
table.

Deut. 14:10 ***"And whatsoever hath not fins and scales ye shall not eat;
it is unclean unto you."***

BACON—carlos/ happy family/ happy Sunday breakfasts/
unfamiliar happy Sunday family breakfasts/ almost as foreign
as the bacon to me/ ate a pack not knowing you're not
supposed to eat the entire pack/ high levels of cholesterol
didn't bother me.

Lev. 11:4 ***"Nevertheless these shall ye not eat of them that only chew
the cud, or of them that only part the hoof."***

OYSTERS—oyster happy hour/ an hour in which I knew
Mom and I would be happy/ pro oyster eaters don't require the
red sauce/ but my mom was just trying to improve her health/
at six years old/ I would gulp them down/ a dollar each/
although they meant much more to me.

Deut. 14:10 ***"And whatsoever hath not fins and scales ye shall not eat; it is unclean unto you."***

MARSHMALLOWS—filled the cups of my friends' hot chocolates/ at my birthday party/ a bowl filled with mini-marshmallows/ rested on the table/ mini-marshmallows that weren't meant for mini me/ so instead/ snuck to me by Mom in the bathroom at my own birthday party.

Deut. 14:8 ***"Because he parteth the hoof but cheweth not the cud, he is unclean unto you; of their flesh ye shall not eat, and their carcasses ye shall not touch."***

SAN PANINO CHICKEN SANDWICH—the unofficial after-school lunch of my elementary school/ my honesty would make my nanny a liar/ in trouble/ San Pa Knee ohh, how do I pronounce it?/ smelt on me by Stepmom/ smelt on me the way someone smells a recovering alcoholic who hasn't recovered from alcohol/ all for a San Pa Knee ohh chicken sandwich/ which I didn't know I had to sneak/ which resulted in me learning about responsibility.

Lev. 7:26 ***"Moreover you shall eat no blood whatsoever, whether of fowl or of animal, in any of your dwellings. Whoever eats any blood, that person shall be cut off from his people."***

She smelled something "not kosher" on me
And told my father, Luca smells like a chicken sandwich.

The Forbidden fruits of God/ the forbidden fruits he forbade from me/ forbidding me/
prohibiting me/ from living out my childhood dreams/ instead of sneaking sweets/ I would sneak foods I knew/ I shouldn't/ couldn't eat/ the rules which god put on me/ cause god said/ God/ said and spoke/ unlike me/ whose voice was too afraid to say anything of reality/ so instead I spoke through food/ Bacon's Rebellion/ Bacon was my rebellion/ against/
the rules which god tried to put on me.

KAYLA BOWMAN

Having studied professional and creative writing at Spelman College, Kayla Bowman writes on issues of intimacy, interior life, and intrapersonal/interpersonal relationships.

MENTEE'S ANECDOTE:

Tatyana's mentorship is a gift, holding space for all tiers of life. We discuss friendships gone awry, family traditions, and first dates. Whether I am inspired or unmotivated, she pushes me forward. Tatyana meets me where I am while supporting my growth toward the writer I aim to become. With a "How is your soul?" I'm reminded of the safe space we've created and I'm allowed to show up as my truest self. With her help, I've challenged my inner critic by writing imperfectly, resulting in a graceful commitment to the writerly life I couldn't accomplish before meeting my mentor.

TATYANA WHITE-JENKINS

Tatyana White-Jenkins is a Virginia-based writer with a passion for poetry and creative nonfiction.

MENTOR'S ANECDOTE:

After first meeting with Kayla, I knew this mentorship was written in the stars. She is like the little sister I never had. I love that our conversations cover topics such as "embracing the cringe" in our writing, the highs and lows of being only children, and our love of Beyoncé.

It's a privilege to walk alongside Kayla in her writing journey and provide her with the tools and advice I've collected over the years. Working with her serves as a reminder of best practices in my own writing. Her vibrant words, knack for deep storytelling, and enthusiasm inspire me.

WELLSPRING

KAYLA BOWMAN

May our first source of acceptance be from within—an abundance of unconditional love awaits us there. Connecting with it renders peace unattainable in external pursuits.

In the opening of Spring, when fragrance from a hundred rising roses
infuses the air, a hundred honeybees race toward the scent in the crisp cold,
before the morning sun can touch the dewy ground.

Their wings can be heard from afar
as a single tulip among the roses waits to feel the soft fuzz
of a bee's legs landing on its petals.
The 101st flower watches the roses and bees dance to an innate song.
And waits.
And waits.

Daylight returns and sheathes the tulip without it having danced along.
She watches as nature's couple exchange a nectar so golden it blends in with the rising sun,
and wishes to taste an admiration so sweet.

Her petals, dressed in cream like a summer bride
and soft as feathers,
become a new color, with burnt
red leaking through their centers and spreading up
toward the feather's curves.

Rough as matrimonial lace, they stick out among the velvety, rich-red petals.
Maybe this will win her nectar.

Petals of mesh contort and divorce 'til they span out
and form a poor resemblance to the roses,
beautifully fanned like the decorated wings of a peacock.
They push away from the center 'til it crumbles around the edges,
and the stem begins splintering down its core.
Just enough to feel the soft fuzz
of a bee's legs land on the impostor velvet petals.

A wobbly dance ensues and
mutes the wind swirling in the background.
The tulip's tender body follows the tiny lead of the honeybee
as the two create euphoric splendor,
peace as quiet as morning awakening the day,
a nectar as golden as the sun rising behind them.

Once the soft fuzz is gone,
and the tulip is alone with her nectar,
she observes the treasure as one does the stars of an open night sky.
But the shiny appearance she remembers is missing,
and the buttery texture which she imagined to melt at the touch
has a coldness that suffocates the skin and numbs the limbs.
Is this what barehanded shape-shifting earns you?
Biting away bloody pieces of yourself
until a palatable thing remains.
She tastes it, hoping for a sweet kiss to receive her adoration,
but its sourness leaves bite marks on the edges of her tongue,
and a queasiness brewing in her stomach.
Eyes wincing in anger and disgust,
she spews the nectar and sees it spread out on the ground before her—
Her prize.

The sun makes its scope over the other half of the world
as the tulip analyzes her lacy petals under the moon's light,

growing more discolored around their pointy ends by the hour
and more brittle to the touch.
She turns her face up toward the light, but her splintering stem can't carry the weight,
so it hangs toward the ground instead.

The swirling wind sweeps one disintegrating
petal away with it,
revealing a single cream-colored bud in its place—
still green around the root,
but soft as cotton to the touch—
hardly seen if not for the withering of the surrounding petals.

With the absent weight,
a deep inhale runs from the bud and up through the drying stem,
reconnecting it with an estranged self,
familiar and comforting,
a quiet and faithful presence.

At the exhale,
another rose leaf releases its grasp,
and petals once spread out and contorted
now curl inward,
intertwining and weaving.

As crimson adorns the hills and troughs of the field,
a milk-and-honey cream grows from the roots of a stem once broken.
While the moon and sun switch places,
the tulip remeets herself—
greeting the land as the rising sun does,
climbing over the high grounds first, then reaching down into the valleys.
The birds pay tribute to her arrival,
their whistles blending with the incoming flight of a hundred honeybees—
so well she barely notices their dance with the roses begin,
focused instead on uprooting the final mesh petal
with an inhale that runs through a stem now upstanding.

At the exhale, she releases a nectar of her own—
sweet as honeydew,
warm like one hand held in another.
A stream running forever,
with a fragrance infusing the air
and intertwining with that of a hundred rising roses.

SUMMER BOXER

Summer Boxer is a sophomore in high school at The Madeira School and is a current first-year mentee at Girls Write Now.

MENTEE'S ANECDOTE:

Girls Write Now has helped me become a better writer and reader! I have loved all of the opportunities and special memories it has given me. My mentor, Hanna, is an incredible guide and truly an inspiration. My best memory with Hanna is when we met for the first time at a coffee shop in New York City to catch up and talk. I am so grateful I get to learn from her and have her feedback!

HANNA R. NEIER

Hanna Neier is a Brooklyn-based freelance writer whose work has appeared in *The Jerusalem Post*, *POPSUGAR*, *Lilith*, *Motherly*, *Kveller*, and other publications.

MENTOR'S ANECDOTE:

Getting to know Summer has been amazing! Her enthusiasm and eagerness to write are inspiring. She shows up at every meeting with a bright smile, insightful questions, and a willingness to grow as a writer. At just fifteen, she's already a talented wordsmith with tons of imagination, and I know her drive and writing will take her far in life. The highlight of my time with Summer so far? Getting to meet her in person on her recent trip to New York City. I feel so fortunate to have been matched with Summer and look forward to watching her grow!

WAVE HELLO

SUMMER BOXER

This poem is about the beauty of the ocean. Sometimes, in life, it can be hard to notice the little things.

Waves have minds of their own
Their movement flows throughout the ocean
Viewing who to love or hate along the soft beach
Wiping people from their feet
Decisions are up to them
Fortunately they were always kind to me as a kid
Letting me get to know them
Playing games of tag
They let me win
They say hello
They have seen all of me
Three years old and unable to swim
The waves keeping me out of diving in deep
Seven-year-old me in a purple two-piece bikini
Knowing how to swim and hating the yellow sun
Keeping me cool from the heat and calming the sunburn
Eleven years old and scared of my own body
Keeping me hidden
Twelve years old with eyes full of tears
Missing faces at the dinner table
Waves spraying me with cold water
Keeping me grounded and mindful of the sunny day
Now fifteen years old with a pink smile ear to ear
I can tell the waves are happy
They are saying hello to me
The waves hug the rocks

My leg pushes the cold water away but only droplets respond
I thank them for their love
But they don't reply
They only wave back
A little girl comes beside me
Couldn't be more than three years old
Her mother watching and staying close
But waves have minds of their own
Luckily they like her
And are waiting to see her grow up
Summer, my mom calls from behind
I say goodbye to the waves, tell them I'll be back soon
I wanted to stay
But the waves have others to greet

KAIA BOYER

Kaia Boyer is an author from San Francisco, California, with words in *The Daily Drunk* mag and elsewhere. She is currently revising her second novel.

MENTEE'S ANECDOTE:

Working with Daniella has been such a blast and so beneficial to my work. Specifically, I remember when working on my college essays, I was absolutely at a loss for what to write for a specific prompt and brought it to our biweekly meeting session for ideas and workshopping. After we talked for merely thirty minutes about it, Daniella had helped me come up with a whole list of suggestions I could write off of. That essay ended up being one of my favorites I have ever written, and I certainly would not be the writer I am today without her.

DANIELLA FAURA

Daniella Faura is a financial markets analyst living in Brooklyn. When she's not wrapped up in numbers, you can find her writing short stories and essays.

MENTOR'S ANECDOTE:

When first meeting Kaia, I could feel their spark through Zoom and almost 3,000 miles away. As fellow Californians, we connected over our hobbyist knowledge of astrology and the struggle that is writing a personal statement without giving yourself the ick. Their energy and voice always lift off the page whenever I read their work, and it always leaves me feeling inspired. I deeply admire Kaia's confidence, drive, and commitment to their goals. Their future is so bright, and I am grateful I can be a small part of it.

"LISTEN"

KAIA BOYER

Sometimes you know better, sometimes you confront the part of you that knows better, sometimes you refuse to listen anyway.

maybe i should just go for it.

okay, listen.
there's something *different* about them.
and i know that's cliché and naïve of me
you can lecture me about it until the
currents have changed their ways
and the tides have stopped pulling
at my gut, telling me that you've gotta
run, run, run, you know these white flags
and they're stained with blood,
but—but.
i want to say i feel stranded with no way out,
but there's been boats passing and
they scrape the sand before taking right on off.
so help me?

okay fine, then. listen.
you know, god, you've really done it now—you know,
you've only ever wanted someone to tear your heart out
and marvel at it as if that's adoration.
you want the pain
you want the agony.
that's what this is, isn't it?
knowing they don't want you,
knowing their thoughts are preoccupied by

red lips and—god, you really don't know,
it makes you sick to think about and you still don't—
you know, i'll leave it here, you know
you want the feeling of sinking until you don't
know what's the water and what's the land,
what's salt, what's sand?, what's pure.

but it shouldn't hurt too bad, i think.
stay here for a second, just listen, hear me out—
if every bone breaks at once at least
i wouldn't have to focus on one spot.
if my lungs fill with water instead of air i think
i'll pause to have some to drink.
right?

no, look—
you're blinded by streaks of sunlight
until the seasons change and
you can see, stranded in the cold snow,
for how long they've left you behind.
do you think you'd be talking to me
if you didn't recognize the hurt in your chest,
the rotting pomegranate pit in your heart?
you know better!
i'm begging you to know better.
i'm digging my knees into the gritty sand,
letting the waves wash up on my dress,
stain it with the tears that you know are going to come.

no, i'm begging *you* to understand,
i have never felt this way before.
i know it well, i've never felt its grip yet
the marks it leaves are sharp, but familiar.
it's borderline peculiar—tried, but true.
there's a twinge in my chest that thrums and sings,
soaring to the peak of a snow-capped mountain
whenever i peer at them, stealing glances,
cause yes, you and i both know i can only steal,

and thieve and rob and uptake,
because yes, they're not mine.

they're not.

yeah, they're not.

so, y'know,

maybe i wait it out.
i'm good at waiting, you know?
and i think they like me, just a little bit.
i think that's better than nothing.
i think that's better than wallowing around
in the cold waiting for good things to catch up to me.

okay.

"on a journey to fix yourself" and you
run yourself straight out of sight of the lighthouse.
i'll be here when you're ready for salvation
and not looking for a stained helping hand.

all right.
i'll just go grab theirs.
intertwine our fingers until i bring them down with me too.

. . .

good, now you get it

PALMARES BUSTAMANTE

Palmares is a high school student and costumer at Fiorello H. LaGuardia High School of Music and Performing Arts in New York City who is passionate about diversity in the arts.

MENTEE'S ANECDOTE:

Kydee is not only a mentor guiding me on my journey, but is also incredibly inspiring to me in her own journey. I look up to her professionally, and personally, as she is such a kind and intelligent mentor. When we first met, we clicked instantly, and I knew that we would become great friends. She has taught me so many things, not only in my hope to change the world, but also in the person that I want to be. I am so fortunate to have met someone who matches my energy every step of the way.

KYDEE WILLIAMS

Kydee is a manager of Diversity, Equity, and Inclusion with the Walt Disney Company, based in New York City, who is passionate about traveling.

MENTOR'S ANECDOTE:

When Palmares and I met, we immediately had a lot in common, from our shared hobbies to our goals. We were very excited to work together throughout the year. We have made a lot of progress on her nonprofit and I cannot wait to see all of the plans go into motion. Whether it was building her website, starting a LinkedIn page, or going over an essay, we have always found ourselves laughing, learning, and having fun.

TALE OF A MOUNTAIN BIRD

PALMARES BUSTAMANTE

The voice of a bird bound to a mountain that is inspired by the experience of an individual being an advocate for their beliefs.

I have always been known as an unmovable mountain,
A stubborn object, a hardheaded girl.
Always called so by the kind who relies on gold, glass, and pearls.
I was always the one to be feared, the one too tied into the ground.
Because in my blood, and in my veins, to it I am bound.

I am happy to be part of a mountain, a force, a string.
I am excited to drink from the flowing rivers overrun with salmon in spring.
I am gleeful to pick the ripe fruit in the summer, and lay in the beams of sun.
But I, unlike you, am willing to stay there, even when the warmth is done.

When the winter plunges forward and the land is barren, I am who remains.
I am there to plant the tulip buds in the dead of the cold and rain.
I hold on to the grass and the falling leaves, even when the nights get long.
So lo and behold when I stick around, and am blessed with March's song.

I found my mountain when I realized you were quick to lose your own.
Too frightened to think you would have to be there all alone.

Too scared to face the simple fact that you and I both know.
You love to see the summer days, but are terrified of snow.

You will always live on the roaming planes flush with golden wheat.
You will always have a belly full, and desire for more to eat.
You will always be the one to roam in circles with your land-loving herd.
But I'll let you in on a secret—you will forever wish you could fly like a mountain bird.

I think that it confuses you how being tethered could set me free.
It is because I can go anywhere and build a mountain with my feet.
I can roam through the skies, travel the clouds, then land back on the earth.
Because my mountain knows that wherever I go, it is in service to her.

So I have always been labeled as the girl to be one with her creed.
But I, one day, can say I died with my mountain,
Where can you be buried?

CHRISTIANE CALIXTE

Christiane Calixte is a journalist and writer from Brooklyn. She has been a participant in Girls Write Now for three years.

MENTEE'S ANECDOTE:

I absolutely love working with Luria; she's consistently challenged ideas that I've presented, prompting me to hone them further. She urges me to be confident in my writing throughout the development of my craft. Whether it's for feedback on finding my voice and style in writing or even for hair-care tips, I know I can count on Luria for anything. Together, we've focused on the intricate specificities of my habits in writing, and I've improved in a way that shall be of great use throughout all endeavors. I am grateful for the incredible writer, mentor, and friend that Luria is.

LURIA FREEMAN

Luria Freeman is a Brooklyn-based correspondent, producer, and writer. She's originally from Chicago, Illinois, and graduated from the University of Missouri's School of Journalism.

MENTOR'S ANECDOTE:

Christiane has a wonderful imagination. When she first told me the plot for "Woman vs. LEGO," I was immediately excited to see where she would take the story. I've been consistently impressed with her work ethic, especially while she's also juggling schoolwork and other responsibilities. She takes feedback well, and she's truly committed to pushing herself to be a better writer. Christiane has so many dreams for her craft, and I know she has the talent and tenacity to achieve all of them.

WOMAN VS. LEGO (EXCERPT)

CHRISTIANE CALIXTE

One woman's terrible day is about to get worse. This piece is an excerpt of "Woman vs. LEGO," the entirety of which is posted on Christiane Calixte's Girls Write Now author page.

She pondered how she ever could have found herself in a situation like this in the first place. During the evening, after the agency abruptly fired her from her all-too-irritating position as a costumed character for children's birthday parties, she was subjected to further humiliation as she pleaded with her landlord with hopes that the deadline for her rental payment could once again be pushed back. The two-bedroom flat, decorated with blue-black speckles of pungent mold and scented with the effusion of deceased rodents, was the only option in terms of a place to live that she and her two sons had, even if they happened to have cockroaches as fellow roommates.

This fact, however, was scarcely enough to convince the landlord, who had long been quite accommodating, to extend the saddened mother further grace. After months of delaying her fate, Leslie had run out of excuses. And her landlord knew that she'd run out of excuses.

So, this time, in spite of the cold tears that flooded from her eyes, in spite of the long strings of mucus trailing from her nostrils, and in spite of the pain she felt as she pressed her phone against her ear and felt the pressure of fake earrings poking into her skin, Leslie was utterly helpless.

That she would find herself in such a predicament alone was an injustice. Here was she, a tired, underappreciated mother, working three—now two—jobs for the sake of her family's stability. If only her petulant ex-husband, in the midst of his sudden midlife crisis, would bring himself to attend even slightly to the well-being of the children or at the very least contribute a cent to their caretaking, only then would she have the hope of a somewhat less erratic life. His nonchalance toward the state of his very own sons was nothing other than despicable.

And where were those whom Leslie considered to be her friends during this time, her darkest hour? Surely the dismayed Leslie should have some level of support to lean on. Yet it seemed as if all those close to her had been whisked away by various, perhaps contrived, preoccupations since the moment she opened up to them about the hardships she was going through. For instance, her old sorority sisters were flooding her Instagram feed while they adorned themselves with designer jewelry and makeup in preparation for a lavish destination wedding in Dubai. They promised Leslie, who lacked both the time and the funds to attend, that they'd send pictures of the event, as if photos of them having fun without her would provide her any morsel of comfort.

When the call with her landlord ended, Leslie understood that she had no more time to throw herself a pity party. With the moon now shining in the starry night sky, her boys would be, beyond a doubt, ever more ravenous. Wiping the crust of dry tears and blowing her nose, she began to slog to the kitchen, slowly dragging one foot in front of the other over and over again.

And she ruminated.

Of course, she wanted to focus on leading her household. But like a dissonant cacophony, a screeching variety of cares and worries called for her to listen. She thought about her humiliation. She was a grown, forty-two-year-old woman reduced to the likes of a babbling, incoherent baby. She wiped a pot with her rough, callused hands.

She thought about the rent payment. In the likely scenario that she should be evicted, could she send her children to their grandmother's house? How would they feel about such a difficult transition? Would it even be ethical to burden her own mother with this?

She gathered the vegetables to wash. She fumbled as they almost fell out of her hands.

She thought about her loneliness. With those closest to her abandoning her, could she ever trust anyone again?

She picked up the cutting board and knife. As she moved to start cooking, her hands trembled. She questioned why she couldn't maintain her composure, berating herself with negative thoughts. She was a prisoner to her own anxieties, and was unable to find the key.

She dropped everything and began to pace around the kitchen. The cacophony grew louder and more dissonant. Her mind raced with thoughts about her strife, one worry replacing the other and so on. Her heart seemed to beat its way out of her chest. Everything was in her head, but the awful din of her concerns was so loud. She longed for the mental agony to stop. She longed for something to take her mind off *everything.*

The mental noise stubbornly intensified.

And then her hope for it to stop was realized in an unfortunate way.

Leslie jumped and screamed. In excruciating pain, she lifted her foot in abject horror. Turning the sole of her foot upward, she examined the injustice she had been subjected to. She heard the soft clank of a small object falling to the ground.

Leslie had stepped on a LEGO.

CARISSA CEASOR

Carissa Ceasor is a student of rhetoric and writing and Black studies at the University of Texas and a member of the speech team, and participates in Girls Write Now's Lead 360 learning journey.

MENTEE'S ANECDOTE:

Walking around the Museum of Modern Art with Kate was one of my favorite experiences from my summer in New York City. She lives in Brooklyn and I live in Austin, so most of our mentorship has been online. But last summer I was able to visit a gallery where her art was displayed, and I tried pho with her for the very first time. It was a great way to learn that we click the same way in person as we do online.

KATE PARVENSKI

Kate Parvenski is a Brooklyn-based multimedia producer documenting artist stories through video, photography, and writing.

MENTOR'S ANECDOTE:

Working with Carissa has been a true delight. I am continually in awe of her creativity, unique vision, and infectious enthusiasm. Even though we're time zones apart, I've been lucky to witness Carissa add brilliance to anything she tackles: from crafting novels and workshopping poems to illustrating characters or experimenting with her new camera. Her thoughtful contributions and insights shine brightly in any room she enters. Meeting Carissa in person was a genuine highlight of my summer and I loved being able to chat art and life with her over a meal. I'm so grateful for our creative connection!

PALPITATION

CARISSA CEASOR

I wanted to write a poem about the anxiety of racial trauma—of not being able to recognize when danger is and isn't there.

Rabbit, run, duck and cover
Fluttering of heartstrings for fears now far'way.
When they paint you, it is big-eyed,
Tooth blunt like a lead pipe, rabid.

Rabbit, push brush and hide now,
By design, you are lithe, stretched long,
You were built to reach for forward,
Fuck the fight, you are flight *and* fancy.

What 'bout cortisol can kill you that
You didn't already have coming?
What twitching fever-mare have you
Not already become? and when

They paint you, you are bloodstained.
Whose blood?

ANDREA CEPEDA

Andrea (she/her) is an English major at the University of North Texas. In her spare time, she enjoys reading, rewatching her favorite shows, and romanticizing her life. Andrea is a member of the 2024 Anthology Editorial Committee.

MENTEE'S ANECDOTE:

Colleen is an amazing mentor! We spend about fifteen minutes each meeting just catching up and debriefing about life. She has given me great advice about my writing, but also has provided me with support and encouragement in my life endeavors. It's been a pleasure to hear her words of wisdom, anecdotes, and understanding in shared life experiences. Our monthly meetings have truly grown into something that I look forward to, and I couldn't ask for a better mentor.

COLLEEN MARKLEY

Colleen Markley is a writer, speaker, and fan of the Oxford comma. Links to her published essays and short fiction can be found at Colleen Markley.com. Colleen is a member of the 2024 Anthology Editorial Committee.

MENTOR'S ANECDOTE:

How delighted I was to be paired with Andrea! She has a fabulous perspective in everything she writes, combining kindness and compassion for life's difficulties. Don't let that fool you. She's also got fantastic fire inside that pours onto the page, reminding you she sees everything, and she's taking notes. Andrea wields words to call out injustice, disrespect, and opportunities for our fellow humanity to step up to be their very best—just like she models for all of us, both on and off the page. I can't wait to see what Andrea does next.

RETRACTION, AT AGE NINETEEN

ANDREA CEPEDA

A reflection on the factors that caused introversion and overthinking tendencies.

She used to be so carefree. So happy. She used to say that she wasn't shy, in fact, quite the opposite.

She used to be able to claim that she could walk up to anyone and make conversation with them, no problem. With no fear of being rejected. No fear of being perceived as weird. She used to believe she could make all the friends in the world.

When she reflects on her childhood, she remembers nothing but happy memories, because those were the only things that mattered. She remembers when her parents were still together, and all six of them lived in a house, with a big backyard, or so she always thought it was. Her best memories were those of going outside with her brother and sister, with her cousins, and running through the sprinklers, even if they weren't fully clothed. When her brother and cousins, who were older than her and her sister, would lure them onto the seesaw, only to keep them stranded up there, screaming and pleading to be let down.

When she reflects on those gentle memories, she remembers fall. When the leaves would tumble from the trees and leave them bare. Her dad would have those big brown paper sacks from Ace Hardware, and they would spend weekend mornings raking the leaves, creating massive piles, and jumping on them.

When she reflects on the best years of her childhood, those entering middle school, and even those approaching the beginning of her teenage years, she misses the girl that she used to be. Even then, she was never really popular, but that didn't matter. Because she surrounded herself with people that actually enjoyed her company. She surrounded herself with people who had the same interests and passions.

But she grew up, and she realized that people wouldn't always care about her. That no matter how hard she tried, she couldn't please everyone. That some way or another, someone was going to find something they didn't like about her. Because the thing about the real world is that once someone makes up their mind about you, labels you with an opinion that they believe to be true, they're most likely never going to change it.

So she retreated into herself. She lost her confidence. She stopped being so verbal about her passions with just anyone. She became selective. She became an overthinker, a people pleaser. And she's been trying to find herself, to reintroduce herself to the girl she used to be. The one she still believes she can become. The one who's going to be loud, whether everyone likes it or not.

AMANDA CHEN

Amanda Chen will be attending Northeastern University in Fall 2024. She plans on studying data science and economics.

MENTEE'S ANECDOTE:

When I first met Stephanie, I thought she was really funny. When we worked together and started writing, she gave me great advice. Stephanie has a way with words that helps concisely gather my thoughts in a much more sophisticated way. We both bonded over social issues surrounding gender, which allowed us to work effectively. I am extremely grateful as a mentee to have such a wonderful and passionate mentor that can guide me through the Girls Write Now program.

STEPHANIE GOLDEN

Stephanie Golden is a Brooklyn book author, ghostwriter, journalist, and book doctor. Her book *The Women Outside: Meanings and Myths of Homelessness* won two awards.

MENTOR'S ANECDOTE:

I could tell when I met Amanda last fall that she has a powerful mind and is willing to tackle tough topics. And we share an interest in bringing awareness to social issues. So it was a great pleasure to work with her to clarify her ideas and refine their expression for her essay about sexual harassment. Watching her discover how to explore her own feelings and reactions and use them to illuminate how this experience continues to plague women and girls exemplifies why I love being a mentor.

TRAIN RIDE TO DANGER STATION

AMANDA CHEN

An uncomfortable experience among girls and women is sexual harassment, something that I encountered on the train, which left me furious.

I prefer to take the express N train because it will get me home faster. Occasionally, I take the F train with my friend when she forgets to get off at her stop. However, she gets off in Manhattan, while I have nineteen stops before I get home in Brooklyn. When I get off school, the trains are packed with other students and individuals I assume just got off work. However, two months ago on a Thursday, I noticed a man wearing a ski mask and sunglasses as I followed my usual routine when taking the F train home. I ignored him because I'm used to seeing strange individuals on the train. Most of the time if I ignored it, it wouldn't bother me. He had gone from train car to train car, and I noticed him again when he sat across from me. I was mostly alone on the train with a few people farther down. As I looked up from my phone, I noticed his hands down his pants with a slight movement that seemed creepy. He noticed my gaze and stared at me throughout the train ride. When I got up to get off, not because it was my station, but because I was scared, he got up and moved toward the door. Lucky for me, the doors closed in his face. The only person who noticed this was an older woman, the only other woman in the car, who got off at the same stop. On the train, she had been watching both of us and now she told me that she noticed him fidgeting with his pants and watched him. She got on the next train, but I waited until the next train came to minimize the chances of running into him again.

For the next few months, I changed the way I traveled. I no longer take the F train anywhere around 4 p.m., to avoid such an incident again. I am much more alert to my surroundings, especially when changing trains. Sometimes I am afraid someone is following me home, so I walk a couple of blocks away from my apartment to make sure that I have lost them. This happens more in the summer, but occasionally over the school year. I always check my surroundings or walk with a friend.

As the oldest of three siblings and a daughter of immigrant parents, I didn't have anyone to consult about this issue, so I started consulting with my friends. One friend noted that if he was wearing a ski mask and glasses, it wasn't the first time that he had done this, and so I question: How many other girls has this happened to besides me? Out of the six friends that I asked, four had been harassed this way, and the other two were uncomfortable talking about it, unsure how to respond. Another friend told me that as she waited on the platform, a man approached her, saying, "You're cute," and when she stepped away from him, he inched closer to her. Another woman stepped up and asked if she was all right and if the man was bothering her. She scolded him for bothering my friend and told him to leave. A third friend shared that on Halloween, she and her friends were at the subway station and were continuously catcalled and followed by a man. They asked him repeatedly to stop, but he didn't. They ended up walking fast into a crowded area outside the subway, where he stopped following them. "That's usually what happens. I'm sure you can relate—like you can't confront them," she said.

This happens to a lot of teenage girls. I've noticed that around the age of fifteen, we started to change how we said goodbye. When I was ten, I said, "Goodbye, see you tomorrow." But now we mostly say, "Bye, get home safe," or, "Bye, text me when you get home." We have to deal with tough situations like these because we can't say no to them.

At the time of this shift, I had just returned from two years of online learning during COVID-19 and mentally still felt like an eighth-grader. As I grew up physically, I had to catch up mentally in the sense of having to adapt to how men perceived me. Although I'm not sure if my peers also felt mentally stuck in eighth grade, for me being so unprepared made it more shocking.

Months later, I haven't encountered the man on the F train again. But the anger never went away. It made me realize that this was just the beginning of many uncomfortable incidents I would have to face.

Sometimes I think about this experience and a rush of emotions overwhelms me. I'm furious because of my vulnerability—I have no power to make the person stop. I can only hope that sharing these experiences will bring more light to the issue, because this isn't just happening to one person, it's a universal experience among girls and women.

MICHELLE CHEN

Michelle Chen is a Master of Arts in Teaching English (MAT) student at Stony Brook University, where they enjoy presenting at conferences and receiving grants to fund their creative writing.

MENTEE'S ANECDOTE:

Jena is a versatile and passionate writer and academic with wonderful prompts, advice, and twinning dyed hair (purple, ash blond) with me, and I was very excited to learn about them and share many stories (spoken, written). Our adventures include browsing sci-fi fantasy and cookbooks and sitting outdoors at Books Are Magic, and watching Losar at the Rubin Museum of Art with dances and butter sculptures, before getting a spicy lamb burger and silken tofu at Xi'an Famous Foods! Without Jena, I would have been less organized. With them, I now have more confidence to present at conferences and observe in schools.

JENA BARCHAS-LICHTENSTEIN

Jena Barchas-Lichtenstein is a linguistic anthropologist at Knology with a Ph.D. from UCLA, as well as associate editor of Public Anthropologies at *American Anthropologist*.

MENTOR'S ANECDOTE:

Michelle is an experienced, brilliant, and courageous creative writer just starting graduate school—lucky me, to get to learn from and with them! We went to the same high school (about fifteen years apart) and we both love speculative literary fiction. Right now I'm reading *Folklorn*, a book they recommended, and it's blowing my mind.

It's been so much fun to share ideas and get to know each other. We write over video call using the Pomodoro Technique. When our schedules make it possible to meet in person, we check out bookstores and museums and food around the city.

THE PARTRIDGE PAPERS OF LI QING ZHAO (EXCERPT)

MICHELLE CHEN

An ekphrasis poem illustrating the life and experiences of Li Qing Zhao, eleventh-century poetess and collector in an era rife with power struggles, court intrigue, and an evocative and fantastical natural world.

EKPHRASIS FOR LI QING ZHAO

The waters sweep   gondoliers' fingers—
  only   her now.
        Spring's skipped out:
  a hazy mist
        looms
cloud falling too close to earth.
  Air thickened with   apples deformed
stone paths   away
        on the shore.
A thousand years before Newton charted
  apple loosened by God's tremors
  apple hewed close to her
split along a divot.
        Ten   twenty meters deep she thinks
        she approaches the pond's center
As she lifts   the oar
  pokes
        it into her ribs   wincing laying it across
        the boat gunwales   she feels free to enter her own mind

like a tortoise
withdraws   from intuited (false / real?)   danger
into earthenware shell.
She sees
floating home for otters   crystal lotuses padded
by thin green plates   drifting like the porcelain detritus
of family feasts   placemats for the drowned.

She wants   to squash them
as she passes,
those red and white blooms   mainly white
like bone through   each petal's center.   Red's only   an
afterthought
staining so little   it's like glances of   mold on rice
caught
before any real harm.   Flies dart
orange stem
where yellow grains   hundreds of times   smaller than
the end of her cold fingertip
spread onto
sprightly black ends of   bumblebees
who alight upon   serving ladies' elbows with fanfare
set off   series of beizi sleeve flutters   shadowy shouts   dizzying
swats.

Water lifts   sky holds   but each   lotus center
floats
still   at her feet   the central magma   a forbidden planet
a shard
of honeycomb   that aforementioned bees
dropped
from their newly startled   streaked bodies.   Lotus pads darker
than a pine forest's understory   hide cranes
lifting   from roughshod
shores.
They soar
north   following summer   toward Nanjing's libraries
return   with convulsive blisters of snow

newly wed.
her room at the residency
screens patterned with webbed elm fold up quick
cots plumped with the rarest feathershorn lacquered rounded
backs
of elm chairs long-legged bed-frames nightstands
for the same stretch
of night per day all she wishes
is a green glass horse that swirls loyally
beneath her hull,
coming up for air once per shi a trembling gnat bolting with
life, that runs with her ink on calligraphy sheets to remove
the wet dripping tracts a blinking and shaven dwarf
dressed in deep blue hanfu for dolls bending down robe
pooling into mud lifting the rubber doorstop
on her imagination.

That is to say
in solar terms
the time of Lesser Fullness passing into Grain in Ear she lingers
why she'd begun her love of poetry.
After Mingcheng's shivering
death from malaria
Zhang Ruzhou's ruthless
pillaging of her books
what remains is
water that passes below her knees an alternate universe
her body holding the space. Here the balance of oak float
under her control dangling cranes
frozen in the sky they
leave
movable signs all over the province. Their nests
unfold into sticks fall from trees reabsorb into the earth
drift of her words pulling backwards like prey in a trap.
Animals hunt are hunted—
humans flicker fail like rotting apples under
merchants' straw sandals shirk time loyalty—

but her collection will reach beyond
any forgettable element of nature
in this instant on papers shorn from willow pulp
the keenest axes mind sprawling heavy as zitan in her ink
strokes,
zitan a wood
worthy as
gold as dense being the only wood that
sinks
in
water.
And in that particular take on
life living seeing the lotus pads
black smudges around her, looking
in a way was not
looking
she'd been fixed coal-red glow of the
horizon
with the village's lantern-lit passageways on her right, and though
the sun is high leaves nothing to escape it, in her heart
it has long fallen
out of
sight.
The blacks shatter smudge all
around her little wrists
ash-green tunic, splash into rivulets her novice yet determined
rowing,
all the way into the center of existence. there
comes
to be a crane, still living, saliva crumbling down its beak her hand
around
its neck, enough to dig beneath contour feathers find down splitting
off from stress, the only black section lithe,
cirrus -like
body
painterly
splashes on its southernmost wing pits, she
holds branch out of her face on a foraging trip cherries

toadstools
at Purple Mountain.
The pinks flame on each lotus pad eating down each point, on these
sharp
petals
cut from gods' quartz. So her waist dress the only white wisp for
acres, frogs burbling humorously and dragonflies
launching
what she imagines bites itinerant wing-clips on her
own clay
hand,
shaped by Nüwa blasted through stone oven she runs it softly
through the dark stains of the lake the ones that are not there but all
she can see in the tremulous faces of the lotus flowers. Just you wait,
midday's going to draw more color out, as too
much sunlight destroys
the edges of our sight.

ANNE CHRISTELLE CHERY

Anne is a lover of all things film and media and is exploring her interests in writing, starting with poetry. This is her first poem!

MENTEE'S ANECDOTE:

Working with Jenny has been encouraging. When I set my goals she roots for me to complete them, and when I bring in concerns about life or writing she assures me in both. My main creative goals this year have been to work more on my poetry writing and my interest in film. We have started and completed a couple of those projects.

JENNIFER STEPHENS

Jenny Stephens is a literary agent who enjoys jogging outside, eating food, and yoga. Originally from Maine, she now lives in New York City with her family and their cat.

MENTOR'S ANECDOTE:

Anne's writing is incredible and I feel so grateful to be working and learning together this year. When we met this fall, I was immediately struck by her creativity, sense of humor, honesty, and openness. She has an amazing eye for detail when describing things or experiences, and it's been so fun to see her infuse her poetry or other writing with those vivid descriptions. I can't wait to see what she writes and creates next.

CHECK

ANNE CHRISTELLE CHERY

This poem is a reflection of my struggle with anxiety.

I swing my legs over my bed
I have to get ready for the day.
I set out my bowl,
it's dirty
I clean it
Instant oatmeal isn't instant enough
I look in the fridge I think I'll just have yogurt today
I wash my bowl again
I contemplate but it'll just take too long to make,
1:20 on the microwave feels like an eternity
when you're already late.
Instead
I eat a bowl of worry,
the edges of the *w*'s and the pointy ends of the *y*'s are sharp,
they are hard to chew and they upset my stomach.
The *o*'s with their round shape should be easier to go down
but they get stuck in my throat,
unwilling to move.
The *r*'s rebel
the curvy parts lodge in my throat and they threaten to climb back up.
Before I leave the house, I'll pack my umbrella, in case it rains.
I have to wash up
I tried to wash yesterday away but it stained my skin I can only try to hide it.
I do my hair,
and I can't help it but I put my worry on my face.

I put some light worry on my eyelids, and I carefully paint the worry on my lips,
I tie it all up by brushing some worry on the apples of my cheeks.
I get dressed in my worry and I wear worry on my feet.
Before I head out the door I check my list for my worry. Have I got my worry, check. Have I got my worry for the train, check. Have I got my worry for the store.
Surely, I need my worry before I head out the door.
Where's my worry for school . . . When I get to school I'm ill-prepared. It was a sunny day.
How do I better prepare for this . . .
I know I'll worry some more.

JULIA CHOI

Julia Choi is a high school student who enjoys writing poetry. She is part of her school's golf team and enjoys listening to music.

MENTEE'S ANECDOTE:

Working with Robin has truly been amazing. She has helped me grow not only as a writer but also as an individual through her feedback on my work and life advice. I am able to be comfortable around her, for example, being vulnerable and sharing my thoughts with her. When we discuss the poem we read together, she always inspires me with new ideas and encourages me to not give up on my writing.

ROBIN MESSING

Robin Messing is a prize-winning poet, fiction writer, and occasional essayist.

MENTOR'S ANECDOTE:

One of the highlights of my week is meeting with Julia Choi. We share the events and feelings of our week. We read poems together. What could be more wonderful? I am always enlightened and surprised by Julia's responses to and interpretations of the works we read. It is a thrill to see her writing evolve, to be present for her enthusiasm, curiosity, wonder, and her caring spirit. What a privilege. What a joy.

SAYING GOODBYE TO MY GRANDMOTHER

JULIA CHOI

This was the moment when my mom received a call from my uncle saying that my grandmother was sick.

For a moment, she stopped breathing.
Her hands gripped her apron,
her body sank into the couch.
My mother's tired eyes stared directly at mine
and, with a small gesture of her hands,
she pointed her index finger upstairs.

I remained hidden at the top of the stairs
awaiting the sounds of laughter,
the addition of small, sly comments about me and my sister,
and the complaints about the little things
that were going wrong in our household,
but the house was silent.

Small mumbles and quiet sobs
walked up to where I was.
I stared out the window as shades
of orange and yellow engulfed the sky.

The window reflected an image of my mother,
her eyes, painted in anguish and pain,
I finally understood death's approach.

Sitting still at the top of the stairs,
I learned how to say goodbye
from a distance.

FAIZA CHOWDHURY

Faiza (she/her) is a college student passionate about advancing the narratives and resilience of South Asian and immigrant women through medical practice and storytelling.

MENTEE'S ANECDOTE:

Shabel has been instrumental in nurturing my passion and building my confidence in writing, especially with my novel in progress. She is an incredible resource and provides thoughtful, personalized feedback and resources to help me confront my fears of capturing history and navigating historical research. Each monthly meeting with Shabel not only leaves me creatively inspired, but also marks the resolution of any lingering writer's block. The warmth and unwavering faith she expresses in my writing are truly uplifting, making the journey all the more rewarding. I am so grateful for Shabel.

SHABEL CASTRO

Shabel is a proud mentor with Girls Write Now. She is an attorney and seeks to create stories centering on migration, Black womanhood, and family.

MENTOR'S ANECDOTE:

Working with Faiza has been a gift. She creates stories that center voices that are not always represented. I am impressed by how she employs beautiful, poetic language to capture honest and difficult events. It has been exciting to see her commitment to craft and passion for writing, which translates on the page. I am truly honored to have a glimpse into the first workings of her amazing historical fiction novel. Faiza's writing has inspired me to be braver in my work. I look forward to getting my book signed by Faiza when she inevitably gets published!

A BLOODLINE'S END

FAIZA CHOWDHURY

A motherland and a mother yearn for the children they've lost.

In the ten years it has cradled my bones, the white cloth that wraps me has soiled. I lie in the depths of my homeland beneath the earth that I no longer know. Beneath the soil that my sons and daughter played on, and tucked from the air that once kissed their youthful cheeks, I sleep in the company of my ancestors. I am the last to join them; before long, this burial ground will be yielded to make way for the town's newfound prosperity.

The children I bore have found a humble abode in lands my eyes never dreamed of. This motherland of theirs could never support the summit of their dreams, and this I understand. A mother always wants the best for her children. I am lonely, but shouldn't complain when our family home is the loneliest. I hear it wailing not far from where I lie; it laments the loss of its soul. For it was born from the blood, sweat, and tears of our humble roots. The money we saved moving between mud-walled huts, cleaning houses, spreading the divine knowledge of Arabic, and teaching algebra was put toward this home. This beautiful bungalow* was our apotheosis, nourished by our happiness and strength.

Over the wire, my children have turned this bungalow into a rental and now vapid people come and go. Their rooms stripped bare, and no trace of them left behind. The kitchen has rusted, and its floor is dusted with the aged longing for another family meal circle, where aromatic spices wafted through the air and plates were exchanged amid the animated conversations echoing across the walls.

* Bungalow: An architectural style originating in the Bengal region. Although now referring to small, cottage-like houses in the Western context, prior to the twentieth century, bungalows were associated with status and were of grander size. This definition is still applicable in South Asia.

Now the blood has run dry. Before my memory dissipated in the mortal world, my sons and daughter would call from abroad, talking ill, demanding their patrimonial shares.

Did they not arrive as bonded foreigners in that land? A land that was not kind to them in the beginning, whose people were not so kind, either. Did they not only have each other, a warm gleam of hope and recollection amid the harsh blue-collar work and English abuse? Their bloods interconnected, their mouths suckling on the same nipple. Like lateral roots seeking nutrients far from the mother tree, they have ventured far from their sole anchor in that foreign land. Or had they always been the roots of the banyan tree, which even aboveground appears entangled and twisted—scarcely whole, sufficed, and parasitically nourished until opportunities beckoned overseas?

No one has since stepped foot in this land, the motherland, not even in my passing. The mosque where the ancestors before me, myself, and my children learned the holy words of the Qur'an is not as it was. The sacred echoes of the minaret's call to prayer, which could be heard kilometers away and kept me sane in my slumber, have faded. I wonder if my children keep the reminder of God on the tip of their tongues.

In this soil, this bloodline has witnessed the rise and fall of great empires: the Gupta, Bengal Sultanate, and Mughals. It has survived British oppression, famines, a partition that nearly tore it apart, and a liberation war to preserve its identity. Like the lost art of Dhaka muslin, I sense this lineage succumbing at the hands of the West. The echoes of my mother tongue ring faintly from the lips of my grandchildren. This bloodline has had a long run, but with me lies its demise.

LILURA CHRISTOPHER

Rogerline "Lilura" Christopher (they/he) is a part-time college student majoring in social work. In his free time, they're trying to pump out endless art.

MENTEE'S ANECDOTE:

Working with India has reminded me it's not too late to be confident in my work. I've spent so much of my writing career thinking it needs to be kept on dusty bookshelves and hidden away in my Google Drive. India creates gentle but necessary pushes to introduce my work to the world.

Having India as a mentor is like hanging out with your favorite English teacher. We've spent a lot of time working on my novel featuring the reanimated dead lovers of Death themselves. In those moments I feel we're mirroring each other. We're both the audience our work needs.

INDIA CHOQUETTE

India Choquette (she/her) is a fiction writer. She also teaches creative writing and composition at the City College of New York.

MENTOR'S ANECDOTE:

Lilura is a creative force. They infuse their voice and worldview into everything they write, from poetry about Staten Island to a fantasy series about the reanimated dead who are haunted by plants and Death himself. Working with Lilura is a constant adventure, and whenever I give them a prompt, they return with something that is a complete surprise, yet 100 percent matches their personality. Lilura also has a desire for growth and devours feedback with the perfect balance: They take what works and leave what doesn't. They know themselves so well, and they are an excellent writer.

THE SEA BENEATH CAROLINE STREET AND TRUE LOVE COMES FROM

LILURA CHRISTOPHER

Content Warning: Gore

My home will one day be underwater, and it will be as if it never existed to anyone else. Where does true love really come from?

THE SEA BENEATH CAROLINE STREET

scientists say staten island will sink under
the global boiling will drown us first
but the island was already drowning
redlines bleed through our transit system
poured into our lakes
the residents of staten island
were born to be mermaids
we exchange body hair for scales and gills
legs for tails and fins
to drown is the island's birthright
sandy was the time to learn how to swim
but i'm a runner at heart
been pacing around in my mother's womb
i'm from an island that is a graveyard for some
i'm all scars, bruises, and sore spots
tripping over uneven sidewalks

sprinting past flopping bodies
running for my life, i make the stars seep out functioning streetlights
heavy feet cracking the perfectly paved streets of the south shore
when staten island sinks
the more memorable ones will watch
the sky aflame, our rude waters a-sheen and at my door
staten island is sinking
the north drowns first

TRUE LOVE COMES FROM

more than just the heart
it is the streams of marrow
leaking through withered bones
true love slips into my ears
it is a death rattle
soft, wet
it pulls my brain out and irons the wrinkles and creases
true love haunts the cave of my stomach
full of vampire moths infesting the pouch
the little messengers of love free from their cocoons
but not free from me
true love takes your heart captive
it twists the arteries into knots
and comes regurgitating out your mouth
a beating heart spit into a demitasse glass
go on now
drink it up

MAYA COLLINS

Maya Collins is a multimedia artist and poet who splits her time between Illinois and Pennsylvania. In her art and writing she explores love, identity, and community.

MENTEE'S ANECDOTE:

Working with Waeza has been so much fun. I have enjoyed writing and learning together. Waeza is easy to talk to, welcoming, and inspiring. I have loved getting to know her better through reading her work as well. She is both bold and vulnerable in her speech, something I aspire to.

WAEZA JAGIRDAR

Waeza is a senior at Lehman College studying media and communication studies. She resides in New York City and writes memoir and poetry. Waeza is a member of the 2024 Anthology Editorial Committee.

PEER MENTEE'S ANECDOTE:

Maya is a creative writer who likes to write nonfiction and poetry. Although I haven't known her for long, it's been a pleasure working with her. She is very kind and humble.

AN ANGEL AND A KEYBOARD

MAYA COLLINS

The psych ward is more than a harsh, white, dehumanizing space in some psychological thriller. It is a place that stores life. And with life, beauty.

This girl I met at the psych ward—we'll pretend her name is Angel. She is anxious and soft and sweet to talk to. We discuss bands and movies, books we love, and friends we don't see.

The others here are older, ranging from thirty to something like ninety. We're hardly in our twenties. Today, at the end of a meeting, she asks the tech to open the back room. It's the one with the keyboard.

All of us girls, we keep to ourselves. The men are always hogging the TV and watching sports.

We make fun of them, we sit with one another, we get bored. But today Angel got access to a group room, and she's promised us she'll sing.

The ladies shuffle in. She knows only one song, "The House of the Rising Sun." She pushes thick and gentle hair behind her ears. Her hair is strawberry pink, and the dye fades at the ends.

She has a small smile and a slight lisp. Notes are scribbled inside an old composition notebook. She props it up on the keyboard. Places pale hands on the keys.

Her voice is quiet for hardly a moment. It rises quickly, like a sun inside a time-lapse. She nearly yells. This gorgeous belt is let loose like a flock of birds. The skin of her face crinkles as she leans in to the high notes.

She sings like tears can pour. Like hearts can ache.

There is a fire in her eyes. In her lashes.

We sit around, watching.

The lady beside me struggles to speak at all, except to apologize and mutter. Now her eyes are wide. Now her eyes are spilling. "Oh, it's beautiful—sorry." Over and over, "It's beautiful—sorry."

An elderly woman sits across from me. She is fragile, a tender sort of thing. The day before she spent in silence, save quiet tears spent on a sofa.

Now she closes her eyes. Smiles, taps her foot, and nods.

The woman to my right is an alcoholic. She is small and blond. Wears weary eyes and weathered skin. She mouths the words to the song. This is one of her favorites.

When Angel finishes, we quickly ask for more. She says this is all she knows.

"We don't care! Go again."

I feel like a kid on Christmas. Like we haven't yet had breakfast and I'm sneaking another chocolate. "It won't spoil the meal, Mom—promise."

She sits back down and starts as before. Soft, then loud.

After she's done, her face is flushed. She looks around, beaming. She bounces with nervous excitement. We applaud and we applaud and three of the women give her hugs.

"You should go on *America's Got Talent*!" one of the ladies says. "You all missed out on a concert," another tells anyone who'll listen.

We were children on Christmas inside that psych ward back room. A room with a keyboard and an angel.

NICOLE COMLY

Nicole Comly is a senior communication and media studies major with a minor in English at Montclair State University. Nicole is a member of the 2024 Anthology Editorial Committee.

MENTEE'S ANECDOTE:

From our very first meeting in October, Jess has been enthusiastic and supportive. She's helped me define my career goals and plan for job applications this upcoming spring, in addition to providing feedback, editing suggestions, and overall encouragement for my writing. I'm excited to continue to learn from her and grow as the year progresses. I appreciate all of the support and guidance she's given me.

JESS FELDMAN

Jess Feldman is a special projects editor at *Travel + Leisure*, where she produces large-form projects for print and digital platforms.

MENTOR'S ANECDOTE:

Because I'm an editor for a magazine, fiction writing does not come easily to me. But since Nicole and I started working together, I've been able to slowly uncover the creative part of my brain that has been dormant for a while. Nicole's ability to capture unique, truly human moments with her flash fiction is unparalleled, and it's also a skill that does not come naturally to even the most seasoned writers. With each conversation or critique session, we grow closer, and I can't wait to be by her side as she continues to define her career goals and goes after them.

102, 103, 104, 105 WORD STORIES

NICOLE COMLY

Content Warning: Implied Violence

Here, you'll find four flash-fiction pieces that highlight moments of loss, love, and joy, written over the course of the past year. Short pieces to remind us that we're all human.

BOYS

The plaintiffs always looked the same, like kids who'd raided their fathers' closets, in baggy dress pants and shirts.

They'd tell their stories in a shaky way, filled with fear. Reverting to boys describing the monster they'd seen under their beds.

For a long time, that's what James saw as he presented their one mistake before the jury.

That was before he saw the bruised face of the girl he'd kissed on the forehead each night as he tucked her into bed.

Now he clutched her sleeping fingers. Watching the nurse tuck her in, he saw the true capability of a boy.

COLLECTORS

We're all collectors, accumulating pieces of others. Capturing an interest of someone's in a bottle, wrapping a laugh in a bow, nesting them on our shelves.

My favorites sit front and center, tucked behind sheets of glass, in golden frames.

That night, the grass poking up through your curls as your finger traced its way across the sky. To Venus, then the Seven Sisters.

Your smile in the city. The "you're a good writer" hidden in a string of conversation after you read one of my stories for school.

It's not often we realize when others change us—in these moments I knew.

THE BEST

I hit into him after he spins me, our hands still intertwined.

The jukebox hums while other couples twist around us, their eyebrows raised.

"Was that really necessary?" I ask, my cheeks hot.

"You're the best," he whispers, smiling against my forehead as he leans in to kiss it.

—

The radio on the bedside table buzzes the foggy but familiar tune from years before.

I've traded the dance floor for a hospital bed, my skirt for a paper gown.

He smiles down at me and intertwines our fingers, making our arms dance slowly.

"You're the best," I whisper, drawing his hand downward to kiss it.

KINTSUGI

[kin-tsoo-gee] *noun.*

The Japanese art of repairing what's broken by mending the areas of breakage with urushi lacquer or resin and powdered gold.

Ellis prefers glue to gold, mostly because it's at the bodega on the corner.

Anya and Ellis sit cross-legged on her carpet, each holding two torn pieces of a once-favorite photo strip, the off-brand Mod-Gloss still wet and sticking to their hands.

Ten minutes later, the pieces still separate, the glue still tacky, Anya sighs.

"If I had known—" she starts.

"I probably would've torn it, too," Ellis admits.

"If it doesn't stick?"

"We use tape. It'll be stronger now anyway."

SOPHIE DA SILVA

Sophie Da Silva is a sixteen-year-old writer from Houston, Texas, who explores her multicultural background through her poetry and upcoming first novel.

MENTEE'S ANECDOTE:

I first joined Girls Write Now unsure of what to expect, but then I met my amazing mentor, Angela. From our first meeting, we really clicked and quickly bonded over our love of Spotify and cute cafés. Angela has taught me so much about the writing process and the writing industry while giving me valuable feedback on my novel-in-the-making. During our pair sessions, we have learned greatly from each other—her in embracing creative writing and me in developing my editorial process. I am so happy to have finally met someone who supports and is invested in developing my writing journey!

ANGELA KAFKA

Angela Kafka is becoming comfortable with calling herself a writer and holds a deep appreciation for stories and people that challenge the status quo.

MENTOR'S ANECDOTE:

Sophie has consistently impressed me with her command of the craft. Her writing displays an advanced understanding of prose with a unique, powerful voice and natural tone. Alongside her incredible skill, she is just an all-around cool person! We spend most of our sessions laughing and talking about our latest inspirations. I've also learned so much through being her mentor; she's encouraged my creative writing by finding opportunities to bring me into hers and challenged me to dig deeper when she saw potential. I'm so proud of the poem we've created and the writing that's to come.

THE FIRST DECADE

SOPHIE DA SILVA

Sophie and Angela each wrote a poem to share their interpretation of the nuanced experience of girlhood. The poems work together as a whole, intending to move through a span of ten years.

i crave the taste of red nails
staying up late & long first dates
i'll take a slice of life not lies

where is my lotus flower?
is it lost in the mail
along with love letters i'll never send?
does later bring sinks
with short bangs & pen tattoos that live
  on my hands?

now i just lie on my bed
like salt in a soup
getting cold, waiting for better news
because i can't sit straight
& i can't even kiss a freckled face

i'll just let the walls
cry when i can't
water the flowers
so my peony soul won't die & dry out
from brain malfunction
or heat exhaustion

i need to recover from this
this angelic ache
my future half-baked
they call it chaos
i call it fate

boys never notice my perfectly painted nails
but girls do & always tell me
it's you and i for the rest of our lives

i will never forget all
the people that stayed
between then and now that i loved
friends partners and strangers
in my apartment & we're laughing at
  rachel's bad tattoo

i often try to just sit still
a leaf on a stalk
growing older, wanting less from others
& taking deep measured breaths
because i know i won't see you again

it takes more than time
to feel you won't
need to bleed
for a life you can cherish & trust that
it's self-fulfilling
with some dumb luck

it's always late in the afternoon
the stale fortune cookie
from my takeout says
by virtue of the present
there is no set fate

JILLIAN DANESHWAR

Jillian Daneshwar is a writer from Queens, New York. She mainly writes short stories and poetry, but loves experimenting with any genre and medium.

MENTEE'S ANECDOTE:

This is my third year with Marisa and Girls Write Now. I keep coming back not only because of the amazing workshops and opportunities, but because of my wonderful mentor. Never would I have been able to make it through college applications without her help. I am so grateful to be working with her. The amount of growth facilitated in these three years between the both of us has been incredible to experience. I hope that even after Girls Write Now we stay in close contact!

MARISA SIEGEL

Marisa Siegel is the author of *Fixed Stars* (Burrow Press, 2022) and a senior acquisitions editor at Northwestern University Press. Find her online at marisasiegel.com. Marisa is a member of the 2024 Anthology Editorial Committee.

MENTOR'S ANECDOTE:

Jillian and I have been working together for three years; it's been a tremendous privilege to see how she's grown as a writer and as a human through high school and to now help her prepare for college. Despite the chaos of senior year, poetry remains a priority for Jillian, and she continues to infuse every writing assignment with creativity at the sentence level. She blows me away.

WEEPING WISTERIA

JILLIAN DANESHWAR

All will wither eventually; enjoy it while it lasts instead.

sewn

embryo————————————————————succumb succeed
fallen—————o—————suffer
encased——fight
alone

tend

respirate / root in place / reach
higher / hear the birds / habituate
outward / over the ground / occupy
space / swing in the breeze / swallow
time / tiptoe through youth / trip

pluck

ripped from roots
you die
strung in water
you are alive
to all
believe such beauty
could not weep
until wilted petals
gather on leaves

***

SHREYA DARJI

Shreya Darji (she/her) is a mentee from southern New Jersey who loves to draw, read new books, and write articles for her high school newspaper.

MENTEE'S ANECDOTE:

My pair sessions with Ellyn have become the highlight of my week. After meeting Ellyn and getting to know her, I've enjoyed talking not only about writing, but also about what's going on in our lives. She always makes our pair sessions interesting by including writing prompts or readings of short memoir pieces. Ellyn encourages me to write in genres outside my comfort zone to improve my skills overall. At first, I was nervous because I was meeting someone new, but we have really forged a connection that I wouldn't have thought possible.

ELLYN MENDENHALL

Ellyn Mendenhall is based in New York City. She works as a copywriter for financial institutions and enjoys writing humor and personal essays.

MENTOR'S ANECDOTE:

Working with Shreya is such a delight. Her creativity shines in her writing—we have the best time brainstorming together. I've loved watching her set, and then reach, ambitious writing goals this year. One of my favorite projects was working together on our pieces for the food and culture zine. While our essays touched on different cuisines, we both wrote stories about our grandmothers. (They're the best.) Shreya is already a driven, talented writer, and I'm excited for everyone else to be as lucky as I am in reading her work.

THE REUNION

SHREYA DARJI

A story about realizing that having the courage to stray from the norm and not look for validation in others is one of the bravest (but most rewarding) things a person can do.

Mae needed a new computer. It was clunky, loud, and had so many folders she couldn't even see her background.

She didn't use her personal computer often, only to upload her science-fiction webcomics, and preferred to use the one from work: sleek, modern, and functional. Still, Mae realized that using your work computer to type up an identity reveal to your millions of comic readers might be a tiny bit unprofessional.

A cog in the machine of a corporate overlord, she dreaded becoming the one thing her teenage self swore she'd never go near. Well, more than one thing: being utterly broke. And that's what the job protected her from, so she compromised her beliefs for a stable life and some cash.

But her main concern now was the question for the ages: Is red or blue my color?

Mae had the exciting, glamorous opportunity to attend her college academic fraternity reunion. Months ago, she accidentally clicked "yes" on the RSVP form, and then had too much anxiety to say no. And now she scrambled to get ready in her hotel.

Her identity-revealing crisis would have to be left for later, as she hastily stored it in a folder named "Dad's Birthday 2013," which she hadn't opened since 2012. She looked at her watch . . . only twenty minutes until the reunion. If she left now, she'd arrive fifteen minutes late—which she feared was still too early for cheese plates and Bud Light with her old classmates.

Once she walked in, she found "Gamma Kappa Tau Academic

Fraternity Reunion—Class of 2015" on the digital marquee, pointing her to the Terrace View Ballroom.

She walked through slowly, with a phone in hand in case she needed to fake an emergency work call (there are many crises that only a director of operational synergy and logistical thinking can solve). It took five steps for her to see Scott and Adam.

Adam raised a beer, the same invitational greeting he often employed in the crowded, dingy bars. She found it comical to see him do it now, with fluorescent lighting and a Credit Suisse vest.

"Mae, it's been years! How is everything with InnoTech? Are they working you into the ground?"

Scott never hesitated to cut right to the business.

"Nothing new," she replied, even though she hadn't spoken to Scott since he'd called her for a reference two years ago. "How old are the kids? I couldn't believe how big they looked in your Christmas card!"

Before Scott could mess up their names, Adam chimed in, "Harry is the same age as Ella, so we've got a few playdates in the pipeline."

Before Adam spoke about playdates as if they were upcoming deals, he played lead guitar in a cover band. Mae remembered the Battle of the Bands where ThinkFast took home the grand prize.

"Do you still get into your drawing much? I doubt the *Daily Student* ever found a better cartoonist."

Scott added, "Oh, yeah, those were hilarious."

"No, not at all. You know how it is . . . I don't have the time for doodling."

Doodling? She couldn't believe she'd degraded an entire profession to try to fit in with these guys (who saw her do a keg stand). They covered all the topics in the next few minutes—partners, parents, mutual friends—and Mae excused herself to grab a drink.

"Mae! How are you?"

She looked up from her phone and saw a man she didn't immediately recognize, wearing a plaid vest over a button-down (a stark contrast to the bank logo vests).

"I'm Matt, from the *Daily Student*?"

Oh, right. Matt was the only other person involved with both the *Daily Student* and Gamma Kappa Tau. But Matt worked the student politics beat, so their paths didn't cross outside of organization-wide meetings.

"Of course! How are you?" Mae recovered quickly.

"All good, I'm writing now for the *Financial Times*; I left *Politico* in May."

"Wow, that's incredible. I didn't know you went into journalism after school."

"Oh, I didn't," he replied. "I started at a consulting firm like everyone else, but I kept writing and trying to publish pieces on the side. Eventually, one attracted interest from *The Independent* and I convinced them to let me try full-time."

Matt didn't even need a pseudonym to admit he was trying to do something different. Why couldn't she admit to these people how successful she was? Forget organizational psychology and the corner office. Original copies of her work sold on her site for tens of thousands a pop.

After downing the signature cocktail, she made her exit to the bathroom. She locked the stall door and pulled out her phone. It was time.

After ten minutes of combating the low speeds of complimentary Wi-Fi, she closed her eyes and posted it to her millions of followers on social media. Comments flooded in, notes of appreciation and encouragement as she sat in the stall at a reunion that she never wanted to go to. She felt welcomed, like her time had finally started, and she wasn't about to let that chance go.

AMIHAN DEL ROSARIO-TAPAN

Amihan del Rosario-Tapan is a soon-to-be graduate of Beacon High School in New York. She likes her coffee every morning, no sugar and no milk.

MENTEE'S ANECDOTE:

In every conversation with Faran, I come away with a new joke, clever connection, and insight. She challenges me through her many angled perspectives and pushes me to shape my writing and its style. Although she often asks me "millennial questions" (her words, not mine), she is also wicked cool and constantly introducing me to new media to engage with. I will miss our all-encompassing conversations when I graduate.

FARAN KRENTCIL

Faran Krentcil is a fashion writer and editor in New York City, and a professor of journalism at The New School. She often craves tomatoes.

MENTOR'S ANECDOTE:

Working with Amihan is a little bit like riding every express train in Manhattan. Her mind is so speedy, you often look up from a conversation and realize you've covered everything from a famous Renaissance art exhibit to some tiny tea joint in Midtown, and it all felt effortless. But I admire Amihan's ability to be kind even more than her ability to be brilliant. She's always looking out for her friends, peers, teammates, and the girls coming up behind her. I am frankly gutted that she is graduating, but thrilled that she is one step closer to ruling the world.

HOW TO GET RID OF FLOWERS

AMIHAN DEL ROSARIO-TAPAN

A story of my best friend and interacting with others through gifting flowers after a year of no contact. Created with the background of a pier and New York spring.

As we were climbing down the stairs of the 125th 1 train station, Isaiah and I paused at a sight under the stairs: flowers. Bouquets of multicolored roses in buckets lined the sidewalk, and when I looked at him I could see our minds were synced. We bought an assortment of pink, orange, red, and white roses and would hand them to strangers as we walked around.

I held the bouquet as he grabbed a white rose, our fingers complemented by rings with engraved stars, his silver, mine gold. We walked toward the pier, laughing about the last time we'd done this in middle school, when Isaiah had picked a flower and had given it to a middle-aged woman walking on the street. That was two years ago, before you had to keep a six-foot distance from everyone, when we still had school and had laughed when the principal told us hugging was absolutely unacceptable because of a faraway virus that was beginning to spread. Now, as the world began its reopening and we could, we would take inspiration from the smile the middle-aged woman had given us and pass out our flowers.

On a bench facing north sat a young woman with jet-black hair, reading a book. We walked toward her, and Isaiah stretched his arm out to give her our first rose. She looked up at us, confused.

"We're giving out flowers," he said.

She took it reluctantly and I thought she might try to pay us, but she only said thank you. I heard an accent peek through and was about to ask her where it was from, but Isaiah instead asked what she was reading. She tilted her book forward so we could see the lines of Arabic as she responded, "The Quran."

For every question I have, Isaiah has five more. *Chatty* is a word that has been used to describe both of us as little kids, yet when we're together we are often comfortably silent. We backed up and walked uptown, proud of our first success. Although it was spring, the air was still cold, as if winter was desperately trying to hold on despite the color of the branches telling it that it was time to go. The pier was lightly littered with people and our recipient was a little old lady with a full head of silver hair taking film pictures. She gladly accepted and asked us what we were doing while she poked the stem through a loop in her camera strap.

This time, I answered, "We're giving out flowers."

We walked back downtown, creating stories for each person we'd met. The woman reading the Quran had recently moved to New York and she prayed by the water every day. The little old lady with silver hair was born here and had recently discovered a love for photography after her husband's death.

We saw a tall man sitting on a bench in an army uniform, looking out to the water, so we gave him a white rose.

"Big man, little flower," Isaiah remarked as we walked back across the street, beaming. It was a heartwarming sight, the man holding up the flower that looked so tiny in his big hands, puzzled but smiling.

Columbia's science and technology building, all glass walls, towered over us. A family with two young boys sat in the grass off to the side of the building, and we inaudibly handed one to the boy closest to us. As we walked to hand one to his brother, we heard the mother yelp, "No!"

We turned around. The boy had put the flower in his mouth.

We laughed and walked on, back to Isaiah's, happily rid of the flowers.

SAANYA DHAM

Saanya Dham is a high school writer in South Florida, is a speech and debate competitor, loves health and wellness, and is a wannabe Carrie Bradshaw.

MENTEE'S ANECDOTE:

Through the Girls Write Now community, Ariana and I have been able to take super-cool classes on writing and develop our writing at the same time. We both bonded over our love for fashion, writing, and fashion writing. It has been extremely helpful to connect with someone involved in fashion writing and get a second opinion on all of my writing works. This short story that I wrote would not have been possible without Ariana's help and editing. I've been able to reach my personal goal of writing more frequently and uniquely.

ARIANA MARSH

Ariana Marsh is a Brooklyn-based editor who currently serves as the senior features editor at *Harper's Bazaar.*

MENTOR'S ANECDOTE:

Saanya and I immediately clicked over our love for fashion and fashion writing, which we got to further explore together in one of Girls Write Now's many community studios. We are both omnivorous when it comes to what types of writing styles we like to engage with, but our shared love for mysteries provided lots of conversation fodder—I've loved learning about new thriller authors through her. For her submission to the anthology, Saanya wrote her own brilliant short mystery story that has a voyeuristic and twisty plot, complete with a chilling kicker.

FOUR SESSIONS

SAANYA DHAM

Content Warning: Death, Murder, Violence

"Four Sessions" tells the story of a delusional and man-eating woman who finally sees a therapist. After going through four sessions of therapy, Paula the therapist goes on the hunt for her own therapist.

SESSION 1

I stood outside the mundane office building. Autumn leaves fell all around me, reminding me that I now live in Asheville, North Carolina, not Florida.

"Michelle? Hi, I'm Paula, your new therapist. It's nice to meet you, come on in," Paula greeted me. She began by asking about my work and family life.

"I'm a chemist, I work over at UNC Asheville."

"Do you have a significant other?" Paula questioned.

"No, I just broke up with my boyfriend," I answered, annoyed. Paula asks why. "Jane, my sister, would tell me to." This lady asked why again, what a stupid question. "That's a stupid question," I voiced my thoughts.

"What would you like to talk about?" My therapist finally asked a good question.

"I don't know, honestly. I only came because of Janey."

"Would you like to talk about your sister?"

"Oh, Janey, such a sweetheart. The best sister and friend."

Paula and I discussed some more things that will remain between us, things you guys won't be hearing about.

I ended the session with a question: "So, Paula, what do you think is wrong with me?"

"I would refrain from saying something is 'wrong with you,' but we should work on your lack of remorse and empathy toward men, your attachment to your sister, and your impulsivity." Paula's answer pissed me off.

SESSION 2

One more session with Paula couldn't hurt, so I didn't cancel my next appointment. I waited outside the haunted building for five minutes. I felt the glass on the tall structure in front of me laugh at me. Paula stared at me patiently, as if she could sit there for hours until I broke. I won't break, though, no one can break me.

"What did you do this past week?"

"I was supposed to get drinks with this guy, but he canceled on me at the last minute. Said something about his dog needing to go to the vet. What a bad excuse, right? Anyway, I burned his car down and smashed it with a baseball bat. That's what he deserves for being a trash guy. Imagine how he's treated other girls. I'm just avenging them." Paula didn't react; she looked up from her clipboard, cool as a cucumber.

"Do you do things like this often?"

"When they deserve it, yes."

SESSION 3

I headed into the building at 6:20, no longer lingering in the parking lot where the office building mocked me.

"Paula, I have some news that will excite you. I met someone. He's super-sweet and respectful. I think things will end better than they have." For the first time, I sense an emotion in Paula, and it's nervousness.

"Are you sure you're ready for a new relationship? It seems like you've spent the past year serial dating and heartbreaking."

"That won't happen with Ryan; he's a good guy." I quickly changed the conversation. "I think I'm going to move apartments, yeah, let me text my real estate agent."

"That was a quick decision."

"I don't want to live at The Cascade forever."

"I understand, but it seemed to be an impulsive choice."

"I was trying to change the subject, which a good therapist would've been able to detect."

"What're you going to do after the session?"

"I have plans with Ryan, your favorite person. He's honestly not a big deal. I'm thinking more about Jane's birthday tomorrow."

"How are you planning on celebrating her birthday?"

"I normally spend the day at her grave, saying all the things I would tell her if she were here. I miss Jane, she didn't deserve that ending."

"Do you feel like you did her justice with Doug?" Paula questions. I'm going to be honest; I don't know the answer.

SESSION 4

This Tuesday at 6:15 p.m., I rushed into Paula's building. I banged on the wooden door that read "Dr. Paula Agard—Occupational Therapist."

"Michelle! You're early, no problem, come on in," Paula welcomed me in, no surprise shown on her tan face.

"Paula, he is a dirtbag. You were so right," I announce.

"What happened?"

"I saw a text from another girl on his phone!"

"Michelle, you're overreacting. There's no proof that he's cheating on you. You're applying your past experiences to a different situation." Paula scribbled on her clipboard furiously.

"What aren't you understanding? All guys are the same."

"You have this idea that every guy is like Doug and is harmful, but that's not true. You have a pattern of going overboard in these circumstances. Are you going to be okay?"

Later that night, Paula lay across the brown couch in her office, resting her head on a bundle of throw pillows. She scrolled through the news on her MacBook, occasionally pushing her glasses up. Suddenly she shifted to an upright position. The news article on her screen read "10 DEAD BODIES FOUND IN THE DUMPSTER OF THE CASCADE."

"Oh, no, not again," Paula's words echoed throughout her corner office.

VALENTINA DI-MAJO

Valentina Di-Majo is an aspiring high school writer, an avid reader of poetry, and a lover of all things Vincent van Gogh.

MENTEE'S ANECDOTE:

Working with my peer mentee, Najma, has allowed me to grow as a young writer and individual. We instantly connected during our first session, sparking hourlong discussions regarding the Renaissance, public health, diversity, and culture. Using Najma's constant support and mentorship has allowed me to expand the scope of my creativity and approach writing from a fresh perspective. Her eloquent use of words and her unique skill for rhyming influenced my piece, "Cartagena's Esmeralda."

NAJMA DARWISH

Najma is a nineteen-year-old writer from Minnesota who is currently working on getting her public health degree.

PEER MENTEE'S ANECDOTE:

Working with Valentina has made a tremendous difference in my writing journey. She has given me great ideas and a new way of looking at things. With her help, I have also been experimenting with various unique forms of poetry! Valentina's style is distinct—she is not afraid to touch on concepts that might be deemed uncomfortable, which has inspired me to be bolder in my own works as well. Being her mentee has given me the confidence to take creative risks. I'm truly grateful for the growth she has helped me achieve.

CARTAGENA'S ESMERALDA

VALENTINA DI-MAJO

Colorful scenery and diverse, priceless botany emulating pure gemlike beauty engulf all who visit Cartagena, Colombia's largest mine of esmeraldas.

As I walk with Tío Jorge underneath the scorching heat,
We pass vibrant houses of *turquesa, rosada,* and *azul,*
Brittle with age,
And vibrant with beauty,
With white balconies, ornate with *orquídeas moradas*
And hanging flags of
Yellow, blue, and red

We pass the cobblestone streets,
Bustling with street vendors,
Talented musicians,
As their cinnamon-colored fingers pluck at the *guitarrón,*
And their callused hands sway to the rhythm of the *tambores*
Graceful dancers,
As their ruffled dresses extend like a bird's wings
And their elaborate, beige *sombreros* tip toward *el cielo*

"Mi niña,"
Calls a woman,
Of coffee-bean curls,
And golden skin
I turn around as she extends a mango toward me,
Having picked it from a woven basket at her feet
Green, like an *esmeralda*

But a deep, rich orange at the tip,
With specks of magenta scattered like paint across its sides

"Toma este mango,"
She said with a small, toothy grin
As I gingerly received it,
My fingertips sticky with glistening sap

"¿Cuanto es?"
I asked as Tío Jorge looked behind,
Aware that I am not at his side,
He raises his hand, covering his sooty eyes,
Gesturing to a *panedería* close by

The woman closes my fingers around
The mango,
Her hands warm and rough and wrinkled,
Like the roots of an aged tree

"La esmeralda de Cartagena no tiene precio"

GLOSSARY

SPANISH	ENGLISH
Azul	blue
El cielo	the sky
Esmeralda	emerald
Guitarrón	big guitar
Mi niña	my girl
Morada	purple
Orquídeas	orchids
Panedería	bakery
Rosada	pink
Sombreros	hats
Tambores	Tambor drums
Turquesa	turquoise

EXPRESSIONS

SPANISH	ENGLISH
"¿Cuanto es?"	"How much?"
"La esmeralda de Cartagena no tiene precio"	"Cartagena's emerald is priceless"
"Toma este mango"	"Take this mango"

FREDA DONG

Freda Dong (she/her) is a high school senior who enjoys writing poetry and short stories. She hopes to study astronomy in the future.

MENTEE'S ANECDOTE:

I've been working with Jen for three years now, and it's been a blast! We can talk about a variety of topics, especially concerning education and writing. Some of my favorite moments are when we manage to meet up in person and grab a coffee, talking about anything and everything. Jen really helped me improve a lot as a writer. We worked on things like forming more concrete imagery, ensuring that a piece of writing flows smoothly, and combating writer's block and creative burnout. I'm thankful to Girls Write Now for giving us the opportunity to meet and grow.

JEN STRAUS

Jen Straus received a B.A. from Barnard College. Her current writing focuses on disability, grief, and identity. She is at work on her first novel.

MENTOR'S ANECDOTE:

As Freda's mentor over the last three years, I have watched her grow into an ambitious and thoughtful young adult. It has been an honor to watch her development as a writer as she honed her voice, experimenting with new genres and learning to fine-tune her writing through revision. From our earliest meetings, I have been impressed by the vulnerability of her writing, and I can't wait to see what's in store as she heads off to college. I hope this is just the start of a lifelong bond, with Girls Write Now as the wonderful foundation of our friendship.

RAIN

FREDA DONG

The thoughts of a student on a rainy day.

it *clinks clacks pit plat splats* against your umbrella, muting the world in shades of gray, sending you afloat to an inner void. the melody trickles into your slowing thoughts, the beats and rhythms lulling you into a rare calm. you breathe in the fresh, cold leaves and release the franticness, the suffocation from your repressed emotions and unspoken anxiety. catch a droplet on your tongue and taste the metallic acid and dust, letting it circulate throughout your body—

and then it suddenly starts pouring and thundering and you think *oh no not this again*. the wind roars as it pushes against you, threatening to blow you away, like a dandelion unable to keep itself together, and you lower your umbrella as if it's a shield that can defend you against angry swords sent by the wind to cut into your skin. the chill seeps in and the puddles soak your shoes, and you feel and hear the *squish squish* of your mushy wet socks, numbing your senses as you miserably trudge on in the storm

until you reach the station, where you shake off and wrap up your umbrella and grimace as water falls on your soaked shoes. you wait for the train, watching drips fall from the ceiling onto the tracks, hoping it doesn't cause another fire, until the train comes and you join a car filled with a sea of tired, groggy, wet people who do not want to go to work or school at 8 a.m. you stand on the slippery floor because the seats are filled with water and the other people are wet, too, and the entire car is a wet cat, and you don't want to get even wetter and the train runs and creaks and groans and pierces your ears as you wait for your stop, then you transfer and wait and get on the second train and repeat the cycle again

and midway on the stairs, you open up your umbrella once more and you step out of the station, the storm calmed into a drizzle. it always amazes you how the moment you look away things change, yet when you stare at something, time tricks you into thinking it remains stagnant, like seeing the sun setting, or the stars moving when it's actually the Earth rotating, or the tides changing, or the clock ticking, ticking, ticking,

ticking,

ticking like the rhythm of your thoughts, always subtly moving, a never-ending constant on the inside, as you exist through your days disconnected from the world, except when the rain comes and forces you to feel—

so you surrender and offer your palm to the gods, to the dragons swimming in the cloudy skies above, and they bless you with a soft droplet in your hand. you close your umbrella once more and walk in the mist, the drizzle slowly coating your jacket into a slightly heavier, darker shade

as you amble and feel and smell the petrichor and the rain, soaking in the tranquility even in your wet socks until you finally reach your destination, ready to start another day.

ILANA DRAKE

Ilana Drake is a junior at Vanderbilt University majoring in public policy studies and English. She has written for numerous publications.

MENTEE'S ANECDOTE:

Through working with Linda, I have gained not only mentorship, but also friendship. This year was our first year working together, and we automatically clicked through our love of nature and the writing process. I have enjoyed our walks and talks, and our Zoom calls are always the most uplifting part of my day. I have watched Linda's persistence and determination through seeing her writing, and I am so grateful to Girls Write Now for making this match.

LINDA MARSHALL

Linda Elovitz Marshall is the award-winning author of almost thirty picture books, including *Brave Volodymyr: The Story of Volodymyr Zelensky and the Fight for Ukraine*. You can find her work at lindamarshall.com.

MENTOR'S ANECDOTE:

As a first-year mentor with Girls Write Now, I was paired with thoughtful, talented Ilana Drake. On walks, on the phone, and on Zoom, we've shared writing and family, politics and problems. Our different generational points of view are helpful, aiding discourse and deep thinking. Ilana has even provided insight into what my own college-age grandchildren might be experiencing. I wish everyone could have a mentor . . . and that someone had mentored me when I was young. What an amazing growth—and friendship—experience this has been. Thank you, Girls Write Now, for giving me a new friend! Write on!

DELICATE

ILANA DRAKE

I composed this piece following the October 7 attacks by Hamas on Israel and in the aftermath of the families' suffering.

the way she clutches
a handkerchief as she
exits through the wooden
door, the way she clutches
her hands as she realizes
that fires have erupted at
home

and a heart melts into
itself on the other side of the
world, a heart is interconnected
to other hearts, beating
at the same time, beating
and praying

and she recites prayers in the
distance as two little boys
play with dice, as two little
boys notice the aroma from
herbal tea in the small kitchen

the way she latches on to
her phone, checking WhatsApp,
reading the news, as she pretends
she is in the present, as she grabs
baklava from the fridge and knows

her tears are about to fall, tears that
could fall for miles and miles across
the land

but she puts on a smile.

SALMA ELHANDAOUI

Salma Elhandaoui, a student at Vanderbilt University, is majoring in neuroscience and computer science. Her hobbies include singing, painting, writing poems, and engaging in conversations.

MENTEE'S ANECDOTE:

It's no surprise that Ashley and I can talk forever if given the chance. Every meeting is layered with intriguing topics, allowing us to expand on our points of view. Throughout the year, we have shared our film recommendations and discussed many films and songs. I would call this "The Incredible Never-Ending Journey" because of how much we have learned from each other through our fun chats. One day we could be reading lyrics to "See You Again," while another we might talk about music bands we enjoy listening to. Every meeting is unpredictable and a true joy to attend.

ASHLEY ALBERT

Ashley Albert holds an MFA in fiction writing from Hunter College and has worked in trade book publishing for more than eight years.

MENTOR'S ANECDOTE:

When Salma has TV and movie recommendations, I know she is onto something powerful. Pun intended! Our discussions about Korean thrillers and TV dramas this year have been a natural tangent from our obsession last year with the Stanford Prison Experiment and Salma's piece about an intergalactic war and a fascist AI regime. We love to find connections among history, psychology, and art, especially those related to inequity, injustice, and crime.

SYMPHONIC SKYSCRAPERS

SALMA ELHANDAOUI

In the mythic glow of the American Dream, where aspirations gleam like beacons in the night, this poem delves into the journey of one immigrant family with grand visions of opulence and quiet resilience.

In the mythic glow of the American Dream,
I carved my visions, chiseled dreams
of mansions rising like empires,
chauffeurs steering through avenues
lined with prosperity, a personal chef
conjuring opulence in culinary alchemy.

But reality, a stern sculptor, reshaped
my dreams in the crucible of truth.

In a small Moroccan town, my father's three houses
stand as monuments to a high-class existence,
but across the ocean, in the image
of New York's skyline, the myth unravels.

Here, where rents soar like skyscrapers,
and inflation whispers through
the canyons of economic disparity,
my father, a chef in a high-class hotel,
serves dishes of ambition, but the feast
of wealth remains elusive.

Twenty years of toil, the American soil
bears witness to his labor, a testament
to resilience etched in the lines of his brow.

The mansion I envisioned, a mirage
in the desert of aspirations, dissolves
like sand slipping through eager fingers.

Yet, in the face of unmet expectations,
the American Dream weaves a different tale.

Not in the gilded halls of affluence,
but in the corridors of opportunity,
where social mobility, a subtle alchemy,
transforms lives in quiet revolutions.

My father, a silent architect, not of mansions,
but of a better future, builds bridges
of education, ambition, and hope.

Chauffeurs may elude our grasp,
but the journey of progress is navigated
by the wheels of determination.

A personal chef, not of decadence,
but of resilience, serves a banquet
of hard work and dedication.

In the currency of dreams, wealth
is not measured in gold but in the sounds
of accomplishments, the strides
toward a horizon of possibilities.

The American Dream, a chameleon
shifting in definition, transcends
the confines of material opulence.

It is the rise from the dust of circumstance,
the ascent fueled by effort, the summit
reached through the footholds of persistence.

My father, an immigrant artisan,
sculpts his story on the canvas
of opportunity, an embodiment
of the American Dream redefined.

The American Dream, not the grandiose
spectacle of excess, but the quiet victory
of goals achieved, of obstacles overcome.

In this land of dreams, where the skyline
touches aspirations, my father's journey
is a testament—a living verse
in the epic poem of the American Dream.

FELECIA B. FACEY

Felecia Facey is a first-year student at John Jay College of Criminal Justice, currently pursuing a degree in law and society with a minor in psychology.

MENTEE'S ANECDOTE:

Working with Allahna has been a pleasure. She is an engaging writer and a creative thinker. Her writing exudes life, with a knack for sensory details and language that captivates the ear and the mind. We haven't known each other long, but we bonded over our common interests, including our love for poetry and Pinterest. Listening to her work transports me into a world filled with imagery from her words. Allahna has the potential to spellbind people with her poems. She is inspirational, and I wish her all the best. I am excited to continue this journey with her.

ALLAHNA JOHNSON

Allahna Johnson is a high school senior and future social worker! She writes to start conversations and to make the world a more empathetic place.

PEER MENTEE'S ANECDOTE:

When I first met Felecia, I was excited and wanted to establish a professional environment in which to share work and bounce ideas off each other. While this has all remained true, I have come to find that despite being a part of different walks of life, we share various similarities when it comes to our interpretation of other pieces, the themes we explore in our writing, and how poetry aids us in our daily life and managing emotions. Felecia is passionate, witty, and truthful, and, despite being a peer mentee, is someone I look up to greatly when navigating the Girls Write Now world.

CUTTING TIES

FELECIA B. FACEY

Relationships can feel toxic like a snake bite and binding like a contract.
Learn to use a cutter. My tool of choice is words.

Watching *you* watching me.
I feel like a doctor about to make their first incision.
With steady hands holding a scalpel
And the intent to make you *bleed.*

You built bonds,
Out of false promises and blatant lies
Telling stories of you as a helpless victim
Only to cut corners and accuse me of *fuckery*

Knowing damn well
You have a knack
For owning the *dirt*iest laundry

Counting on my demise,
like a gambler with cards.
But I will go all in
And gladly watch you *fold.*

You prayed on my downfall,
like a devoted priest.
Lit candles and blew them out
As you *envisioned* my sinus rhythm.

You've lived this life a lot longer
I thought you'd have known better by now.
But I gotta be playing teacher
Because apparently, you still *got* lessons to learn.

Lesson #1: You are a wound that will leave no scars
When we cut ties,
Don't bother circling back to spew more lies
You can write R.I.P. next to my name.
Best believe *I ain't gon have to die*
Before *I rest in my peace.*

Lesson #2: Be careful what you wish for
You wanted to see me unhinged,
Now you can't close the door to your skeleton closet
Hope and pray that one day,
I don't pick one out to try on just for size
And bring bodies out of graveyards
That you *left for dead*

Lesson #3: *Wa Sweet Nanny Goat A Go Run Dem Belly!*
Seeing as to how you *wear hypocrisy like a second skin*
You might have forgotten that proverb from our roots
So let me reiterate
That smile will soon be turned upside down :)
I won't let you have *my* cake and eat it too!
I will set fire to every bakery before I let you

Lesson #4: Remember,
Time is longer than any rope
You have *twisted and twined*
To hang me out to dry

It seems Mother taught you no *manners,*
So I've kindly offered you a hand.
I've been guiding you for some time now.
Now it's time to *let go of my hand*!

My life won't be a circus
For *you* to play tricks in
Or run in and out of
Like a track field

We have reached a dead end . . .

ANGELINA MARISOL FREYRE

Angelina Marisol Freyre is a writer who also enjoys volunteering to teach and playing Minecraft. Her goal is to make an impact on people's lives.

MENTEE'S ANECDOTE:

Collaborating with my mentor, Ashley, has proven to be an enriching journey filled with unwavering encouragement, profound understanding, and a steadfast dedication to my personal and professional development. Throughout our shared experiences, Ashley's unwavering support has become the driving force propelling me forward, and her infectious optimism consistently illuminates the path to innovative solutions in the face of challenges. Ashley's genuine care has not only fostered a nurturing work environment for me, but has also significantly eased every stage of my creative process, contributing to an atmosphere where each step feels like a natural progression in my growth and accomplishments.

ASHLEY R. SOWERS

Ashley specializes in content and brand strategy, with passions in culture and medicine. She plans to leverage her marketing experience to support her entrepreneurial goals.

MENTOR'S ANECDOTE:

Working with Angie this year has been such a pleasure. I am fascinated by the stories she tells in her writings. They are universal topics I myself relate to, yet she finds such a unique way to articulate the different concepts she and her characters grapple with. My role as Angie's mentor is to support her in understanding how valid and necessary her unique voice is and how to harness the strength of her differences. I feel lucky to play even a small role in encouraging her to continue building her own world—in writing and beyond.

WAIT FOR IT?

ANGELINA MARISOL FREYRE

My goal with this piece was to capture how no one mentions to young people how much hard work it actually takes to get to the big dreams they're encouraged to make and carry out.

I sit and I wait for my day to come.
These puzzles are old and must be tired.
I piece them together all day with a hum,
Yet I take them apart when I don't feel inspired.

One day maybe I could join the rest of you,
I know my happy ending is ready for me.
How to get there though, I don't have a clue.
I don't need to, right? I'll just wait and see.

You all have amazing lives,
Big families and great careers.
All without making any big strives,
How fast did everything just appear?

I wonder how long all of you waited,
Were you too waiting around to be found?
I know my destiny was already created
I hope, like everyone's, it is just as profound.

Not to worry, I'm really good at waiting!
In my room, I stay still 'til my amazing future arrives.
I do nothing except wait here with my toys, anticipating . . .
Wait, should I trust my future's simply coming from the skies?
What am I supposed to do now?

VICTORIA GAO

Victoria Gao is a published writer and artist from New York City who enjoys building worlds in her fictional stories.

MENTEE'S ANECDOTE:

Writing with Tracy during our pair sessions has been an enlightening experience. Tracy always brings thought-provoking excerpts and writing exercises that rejuvenate my creativity and cause my ideas to bloom like wildflowers in a meadow. With her vast knowledge of literature and keen eye for detail, she has provided valuable advice on how to add depth to characters in concise short stories without losing sight of the bigger picture and purpose of the story.

TRACY MORIN

Tracy Morin is an award-winning writer and editor with twenty-plus years of experience in print magazines. Her creative work includes memoir / personal essay, fiction, and photography.

MENTOR'S ANECDOTE:

Victoria is such an impressive student, with interests that range from music composition to app creation. Honestly, I can't even wrap my head around most of the super-advanced projects she is tackling in college as a computer science major! But I do know that she is asking big, brave questions through her writing, which incorporates thought-provoking themes inspired by her tech background. She possesses a rare combination of STEM savvy and artistic passion, with a talent for both the analytical and the creative. She always shows up to our meetings with a positive mindset, willing to learn and challenge herself.

IMAGINEATER

VICTORIA GAO

In a futuristic society, ImaginEater is a gadget that conjures food for people to consume without adverse health impacts, but Quasara discovers that unanticipated uses of ImaginEater can have serious repercussions.

Quasara slumps onto her couch with a thud, the fatigue of hours spent on her feet and flashes of the frowning faces of department store customers washing over her. The interactive screen on the wall in front of her flickers to life, abruptly interrupted by a thirty-second ad. An exasperated groan escapes her lips as she watches, her eyes narrowing at the sleek figure of a fitness coach.

"Hello, health enthusiasts! I'm Bliss Wellspring, your guide to tackling your healthy eating goals. Introducing the ImaginEater!"

A circular wireless sensor drifts up from the table and hovers in the air around Bliss's head.

"With just a thought, you can summon delicious food to a table in front of you, allowing you to savor every flavor without the guilt or weight gain. I'm imagining a buttermilk crispy chicken sandwich paired with corn on the cob and a strawberry-banana smoothie."

A chicken sandwich and corn appear on the plate in front of her and her glass fills. She takes a quick sip and bite of tender, juicy chicken.

"Mmmm," she murmurs.

She flashes a smile at the audience and announces, "Now, the ImaginEater is available for a limited-time offer of $49.99!"

Quasara pauses the ad and sits straight up. She notices the empty cold meat cans, their centers dented by her bare hands, and jagged edges of family-size popcorn bags on the floor. Hand-to-mouth motion has become a habitual response, closing the distance between her life as a new college graduate barely making ends meet and her dream life as the owner of a sustainable business. She purchases the ImaginEater with a few quick taps and hopes its arrival in two weeks will be the game-changer that helps her gain more control over her life.

For the next week, Quasara commutes to work at the department store with a spring in her step. But one morning, she encounters a male customer on crutches who repeatedly screeches, “Excuse me, is anyone working here today?” at a checkout counter.

When Quasara walks over, he says, “I’m here to return this product.” Quasara’s heart sinks when he puts the ImaginEater box on the counter.

“May I ask what’s wrong with the product?”

“After using the ImaginEater to fill a glass with water, I thought I could make it fill a twelve-foot-deep swimming pool. I saw the pool fill, dipped my toes into the pool, and felt the cool water. But after jumping in, I hit the bottom of the pool and twisted my ankle.”

“So the ImaginEater only simulates water? What did you see when you were in the pool?”

“I saw water surrounding me and the water level was above my head. I thought I was drowning and couldn’t float to the surface.”

“I’m really sorry about your bad experience with this product. Let me process the return.”

The point-of-sale system suddenly beeps. Quasara’s manager arrives and opens the product’s box. She turns on the ImaginEater and attaches a device to read its data.

“Unfortunately, you can’t return this product because you still have an active session associated with this device,” the manager says. “I can’t erase the ImaginEater’s data because you didn’t finish all the food conjured by the ImaginEater.”

“What? I have to finish drinking up all the water in my pool before returning this gadget?” The man narrows his eyes.

“Maybe you can reach out to the manufacturer for help with the product defect?” Quasara’s manager suggests.

“I already filed a complaint about my incident and got no response. What a waste of money.” The man sighs and marches away from the counter, leaving behind his ImaginEater.

Quasara brings the ImaginEater home and uses its barcode to connect with a customer service representative from ImaginEater in an online live chat. She asks, “Why won’t the ImaginEater let me conjure up more food after it simulated gallons of water? Is my ImaginEater defective?"

"The sustainability feature of the ImaginEater forces users to finish their food after they generate a large quantity of food," the representative types back.

"But I didn't expect the pool to fill with that much water. Is there a feature to get rid of the food that I generate?"

"Why would you simulate water to fill a swimming pool in the first place? There is no undo feature. You can just drink up all the water gradually (the condition of simulated food remains fresh, like the state it was in when it was first simulated) or in one sitting (you won't feel full from drinking simulated water that isn't actually entering your physical body)."

Right after sending that message, the representative ends the chat session. Quasara decides to cancel her ImaginEater order. She tries to restart a live session to chat with another representative, but the reloaded page says, "You have already chatted with a representative and your issue is resolved."

ISABELLA GEORGE

Isabella George (she/her) is a high school senior who loves listening to music, playing with her cats, writing, reading, and anything literary.

MENTEE'S ANECDOTE:

Christine, my mentor, is a beacon of support for me. She always has great feedback and assures the quality of my writing. Her encouragement fuels my passion for writing; with her guidance, I've grown both as a writer and as a person. In her, I've found not just a mentor, but a source of inspiration that propels my pen forward. I am forever grateful to Christine and the year and a half we spent as a pair—she is the best mentor I could ever ask for.

CHRISTINE MOORE

Christine Moore is a marketing director who has lived in Hoboken, New Jersey, for twenty years. She has been a mentor with Girls Write Now since 2021.

MENTOR'S ANECDOTE:

Working with Isabella has been amazing—I truly feel as though I'm witnessing the emergence of one of the great writers of the future. Isabella's pieces span genres and regularly amaze me—she is wise beyond her years in her observations of human relationships, both with others and with ourselves. I get incredibly excited every time she shares a new piece with me, and I have been honored to celebrate her writing accomplishments over the past year and a half. I cannot wait to see what Isabella does in the future.

IDENTITY ECDYSIS

ISABELLA GEORGE

This letter explores my journey of navigating the challenges of embracing my asexuality, breaking free from societal expectations, and finding solace in a new identity while shedding my old one.

Dear No Name,

Your name, a delicate trinket of consonants and vowels, carries the weight of history—chosen by your mother, passed down like an heirloom. A queen had it first, then your great-great-aunt, and, at long last, you. You admired it back then, when you were the queen of your namesake, gracing every single particle of stardust with your smile, stuck on a self-imposed leash between your mother's legs, stumbling and fumbling within your castle, yours. It was your name, your definition, and your perfection—that was the beautiful, oh-so-wonderfully beautiful, part.

I'm sorry, No Name. A name that once felt like a castle to you is now left out in the rain, rusted and weathered, until it becomes unrecognizable—now a prison of expectations, a chain to this oversexualized society. I'm sorry, but the name you once cherished has crumbled, picked at like a scab, and replaced by a new one forged in the fires of high school corridors and secret meetings. It is a dead poet's name, resting now between my shoulder blades, a tattoo of ecdysis etched into the creases of my epidermis. The acceptance of this new identity arrived gradually, a name that is alive and well suited, draped around my collarbones like a familiar cardigan, offering warmth and comfort.

I'm sorry again for leaving you behind, killing you gently with fingers once intertwined, lips numbed by unwanted kisses, and a struggle to understand desires that did not align. Ghosting messages—a silent plea for freedom, but they persist, a love unreciprocated. Is it fate to endure this until death? Don't misunderstand me; I love and yearn to be loved, intertwining hands as we walk across the sidewalks of time. But I haven't any desire, need, of a lover; coming together as one for all of eternity. Why crave physical intimacy when emotional connection creates a more profound, eternal bond instead? Does that make sense, No Name? I can only hope that you understand it, even if others don't.

I ponder and grieve the selfishness of not falling in love and the selflessness of pretending, grappling with the remnants of societal norms that insist on scripts I can't follow. I hope for someone to intervene, to save me from a path that feels increasingly stifling. But eventually they, my wardens, leave this prison, carrying with them the weight of misguided assumptions and tears of frustration and freedom, my kingdom come. The chains of expectation are shattered, setting me free at last. Perhaps I yearn for love, but that love doesn't define me; it never will.

So, No Name, I say hello to the person I have become, marked by the scars of growth and self-discovery. You make it through, altered by the journey yet still tasting of stardust. The queen in this story, the survivor of a war, is reshaped by the storms of identity and love.

As the night falls, No Name, I send you love from the queen you once were, acknowledging the challenges and celebrating the triumphs of the journey. May you rest in the quiet acceptance of the person you've become.

With love,
New Name

MAGGIE GOTTLIEB

Maggie Gottlieb is a high school student and an aspiring writer living in Brooklyn, New York.

MENTEE'S ANECDOTE:

Working and spending time with my mentor, Meredith, has been so exciting. I never thought I'd ever sit down with a published author, yet now I've done more than just talk to one; I've also become friends with one. Meeting with Meredith after a long day of school has been reinvigorating, and it leaves me with so much excitement to share once I get home. Recently, we've been working on writing a comedic murder mystery play, which has been fun since it has so many twists and turns I don't even know the answer yet.

MEREDITH WESTGATE

Meredith Westgate is a Brooklyn-based writer and the author of *The Shimmering State*. Her short fiction and nonfiction have appeared in *Epiphany*, *Joyland*, *LitHub*, and *No Tokens*.

MENTOR'S ANECDOTE:

Working with Maggie has been such a treat. She has a wide range of interests and writing skills across different genres, which have been so exciting to play with. We've worked on everything from poetry and short stories to, my favorite so far, a murder mystery play that is becoming a total web of eccentric characters and circumstances—shaping up to be a real whodunit!—and the perfect kind of project to have fun collaborating on, brainstorming, mapping, and sharing a laugh.

ONLY THE BEGINNING

MAGGIE GOTTLIEB

Reflections on the world around me.

RED MOONS

Face each other
On a landscape dug so many times

Red Moons multiply

As silver
Cuts into tilled land
In the shadows of a drive

Let red moons gloss
'Til only silver shines

REBIRTH AFTER PHILLIS WHEATLEY

Burning sand does turn to ice when warmer
Day meets with night, subtle light transformer.
Sky holding suns, with the wind wonder blew,
To find a long-gone song of times anew.
From salted sprays of seas to mountain range
Land grows and falls beneath with steady change.
Steps carry across the grain where dancers
Fell upon their legs, ring voice of chanters
Who find no ear to lay their claims of love.

Once wingless birds now find their flight above
In sky, once so broken, has at last healed.
Scurry small mice who now revel in field
Filled with decay as rain do wash away.
No mourners stand when all have disobeyed
Green returns to stolen, concrete covered.
Bursting spring causes gray world to recolor

LITTLE SECRETS HIDDEN

In whining winds and breezes
Roses flower for one reason
As rains begin to break
Upon the sweetest sunshine
Laughter not too far away

WORDS

Always running
Even when I think of
Nothing

Words never ending
Forever sending
Never said

Words lost
Words found

Words
Just lines
Just sounds
My way of
Being

PRESENT AFTER AMANDA GORMAN

We have turned our backs
We quit the fight
Intimidated by this plight
We know that as we sit
The storm thickens
And those who come next will never know
What it feels to have snow settle where our dirty steps are left
We pretend not to notice these cold winds that sting our faces
We make no changes
The storm continues to grow
Our gift to them will be all we know

SWALLOW

A bird. From beak to tail
A bright, shiny blue

Cappuccino in hand
Turning stools
By big windows
Cars driving by

I await your arrival

So I may leave
To hide more than I speak
To come back next week
Little bird on the door
Welcome me

THE BIG WIDE BLUE

Sandy structures crumbling
With waters touch

Too cold

Wade in
Dive beneath
Tides pull gently at my feet

Cold feels warmer
Where waves collide

On the horizon
The line between
Sea and sky
The end of sight
Only the beginning

LAUREN HACKE

Lauren Hacke loves to explore all kinds of creative expression. She lives in Colorado, where she enjoys archery, collecting fossils, and listening to classical music.

MENTEE'S ANECDOTE:

Jana is an outstanding mentor and a rock of support for my writing. I'm grateful to have a kind mentor who cheers me on and motivates me to write beyond my comfort zone. She encourages me on paths that open my eyes to new ways of writing that I have never considered before. Her advice has helped my writing dreams come true, and I have gained more confidence in my creativity thanks to her. I can't wait to see what new, exciting ideas we will bring to life and what journeys we will embark on together in the future!

JANA KASPERKEVIC

Jana Kasperkevic is weekend director of platforms at NBC News. She loves exploring how people consume news. She lives in Brooklyn, New York.

MENTOR'S ANECDOTE:

Lauren's passion for the world around her and her writing inspires me every time we chat. She is a great leader who thinks about the future and sees the world as it could be if we all tried a little harder and invested in our shared future. Seeing the world through her eyes has pushed me to be braver, to take risks in my writing, and to make changes, small and large, to my life that could help save our planet. I hope I have offered at least a fraction of the guidance and inspiration that she has given me.

HOW TO DANCE ON BROKEN GLASS

LAUREN HACKE

How have girls and women risen up against oppression throughout history?

Her glass slippers were bound to shatter by midnight,
if she danced at all in the way shoes were meant to be danced in.
  When a crack from a waltz spiderwebbed into a million shards of choices,
she had no choice but to embrace crimson soles.

She sprinted on shattered glass that scratched and scraped her,
  Nipped at her toenails, shaving them straight,
Stabbed the longest shard up her heel.

She begged for new shoes,
  But they choked her feet with slippers better fitting a baby,
Bent them, bound them into crumpled lotuses.

Crippled as a crone,
She became a pile of pink petals shriveling,
  In a desert refracting all the light she could not find.

She preferred the pain of movement,
  Peeled the shoes off of her shrunken feet,
Figured out how to stand again.

She trained herself to jump on the tip of her toes,
With the grace of a doe bounding away from its hunter.
  She couldn't let the wound he had inflicted slow her down.

Sometimes she only hopped on one foot,
so that the other had a chance of healing,
Pirouetting for a production no one would ever see.

She danced on the glass for so long,
Calluses hardened into a shield.
Toes and glass chiseled away at each other,
Eroding small crystal pebbles into dust.

Ribbons of pink skin hung off of her ankles,
Yet she balanced en pointe in triumph,
Twirling to the slowing tempo.

She held her breath,
wondering if there would be a standing ovation.

FIONA HERNANDEZ

Fiona is a recent graduate from the University at Albany with a degree in journalism. She enjoys reading memoirs, writing, and singing.

MENTEE'S ANECDOTE:

Leonora and I met last year when I was applying for jobs and was a part of the Girls Write Now Career 360 program. I remember feeling so nervous and anxious, but Leonora inspired me to continue sharing my story and what makes me unique. I'm so happy to be working with her again this year and facilitating community studios together on memoirs. I love being able to talk with her about writing and my goals!

LEONORA LAPETER ANTON

Leonora LaPeter Anton is a freelance writer who spent thirty-six years writing news, long-form, and investigative stories for five newspapers, including the *Tampa Bay Times*.

MENTOR'S ANECDOTE:

Fiona is a dynamo of creativity and ambition. I'm just trying to keep up. Her versatility and eagerness make her an ideal mentee because she's always exploring new paths. I'm learning new things as she writes stories for the anthology and applies for jobs, scholarships, and opportunities to help other mentors and mentees. I'm really proud of Fiona.

HOW WRITING MADE ME A BETTER PERSON

FIONA HERNANDEZ

The author writes this piece to reflect and discuss how writing has been an integral part of her life. She looks at how she began writing and how she changed.

Writing has always been an important part of my life, but my love for it started when I fell in love with reading. Growing up, I had a horrible speech impediment that made me not want to speak to others and afraid to speak publicly. But every night before I went to bed, my mom and I read lots of stories to practice my speaking.

At age six, my mom and I read the whole series of Amelia Bedelia and Junie B. Jones. I loved how reading allowed me to escape into worlds filled with comedy and entertainment. Every time I read Junie B. Jones, I was drawn to this first-grader who was a huge risk-taker. She even took a raccoon to school. Or in *Teach Us, Amelia Bedelia,* where Amelia, a hardworking housekeeper, became a teacher who juggled lots of things at once.

Reading all these stories inspired me to write stories. Writing became an important part of my life. I wrote about witches and fairies in other worlds. I wrote about characters who were ambitious, looking to explore and venture into an unknown future. Writing influenced me to want to be like this. It changed my beliefs, morals, and my way of thinking.

Once I moved away from writing fictional stories, I started writing in my diary when I was eight. I used to keep my journal entries short, talking about how my days went, what I learned at school, when my mom would take me to the park or the library, or when I went to hang out with friends. But then it grew to my sharing emotions, thoughts, and feelings, like when I was in high school after freshman year and struggled through the drama of fake friends, gossiping, and cliques.

When I had just started college and was taking classes and making friends, I found myself in the midst of the pandemic and suddenly had to move back home. I was stuck in isolation and was glued to a computer screen all day. But it was writing that helped me along the way. I wrote all day in my journal about my feelings, my questions, and my worries.

One day, I was alone on a rainy cold morning, and I turned the news on. All I could see were so many people losing their loved ones and struggling to pay the rent, get groceries, and find a job.

"They say that everything happens for a reason," I wrote. "But it's a time like this where I feel really, really lost, and I don't even know what is happening. I can't seem to process it."

But writing also allowed me to share the good times in my life. I look back at some of my memories, like spending the summers with my family in Cape Cod. Every day we went to the beach, where I would sink my toes into the sand and pick up seashells by the shore. Or the fun moments when my family and I moved into our home in Yonkers in 2010 on a cold January day, the sun shining through the windows. We spent our summers at Yankees games, and even went to see *Mary Poppins*, the first ever play I saw on Broadway in New York City.

I have always sought comfort and found my voice in writing. Writing helped me share an important part of who I am, and it helped me learn more about myself. It showed me the importance of taking risks and taking advantage of opportunities. As I look back, it taught me to be humble. It taught me important values that I could think and dream about. It helped me become more resilient and gave me perspective on love and respect. It taught me that life can be simple, life can be whole, but it changes constantly.

As I wrote more about myself, I read memoirs of women who learned important lessons during difficult times. I was inspired by *Aftershocks*, where Nadia finds out about her cultural background, and her multiracial family's story growing up with an Armenian American mom and a Ghanaian father. Another one I read was *Call You When I Land*, about another woman taking some time to travel, choosing not to marry, changing her career, and moving her life in another direction.

How did writing make me a better person?

Writing was like my friend, my mentor. Writing was always there with my ups and downs. I now realize why people say writing is very therapeutic. No matter what, the words always stayed on the paper. They listened to my emotions, my biggest fears, and some of my biggest regrets. Writing showed me my passion in life. It allowed me to be honest with myself, reflect, and learn how I can overcome. I've learned the value and importance of writing, and, most of all, I've learned how it became a part of me. Long after I overcame my speech impediment, my diary kept all of my feelings, my questions, my worries, and, most of all, my hopes, dreams, and aspirations.

KAYAH HODGE

Kayah Hodge is a digital creator in marketing at Macmillan Publishers. She is a multimedia artist, innovator, and food blogger. Kayah is a member of the 2024 Anthology Editorial Committee.

MENTEE'S ANECDOTE:

Elissa and I share an introspective and easygoing nature that balances so well. I love our conversations about holistic health. Elissa reminds me that pouring into myself and giving grace is crucial for generating powerful, inspiring art. I often leave our conversations feeling fulfilled, grounded with action steps, and guided by intentional and thorough feedback on my writing. I'm genuinely grateful for all of the motivation, support, and encouragement she offers consistently.

ELISSA WEINSTEIN

Elissa Weinstein is a goldsmith and a writer. She is currently at work on several new designs and a collection of genre-bending writings.

MENTOR'S ANECDOTE:

Working with Kayah this year has continued to be nothing but a joy and an ongoing Spanish lesson for me. Her dual-language poems—especially the ones about food and cooking—are mouthwateringly juicy and instructive. In our conversations, I am always impressed by her commitment and dedication, whether it be to work on writing, self-growth, career, or service to those in her community. Did I forget to mention that she's also funny? In addition to the serious work of writing and editing, we find plenty of opportunity for laughter; so enlivening! Works wonders on the soul.

FOOD FOR THE SOUL

KAYAH HODGE

Flavor, cookery, and presentation are the vehicles of culture, identity, and creativity. I'm extremely blessed to be loved with enough provision to experience finger-lickin' meals.

On the grill
coal chars BBQ,
sweet corn, and steak—
sizzling over a flame
brighter than the sun
roasting our skin.
An ice-cold drink
soothes my insides like
bass and drums
heal the soul.

In the kitchen
gandules dance con
sofrito y adobo en arroz
to chisme from
long-distance phone calls.
Mis tías y tíos
weave between languages
como agua en el río.

Licking my fingers:
a gesture of savor

Jiggle in my step:
a rumble of power

Stretch marks on my thighs:
a blessing of abundance

Loosening my waistband:
a sign of provision

MIN HOLLWECK

Min Hollweck is a junior in high school and a lover of essay writing, pomegranates, and rewatching sitcoms.

MENTEE'S ANECDOTE:

I've really appreciated working with Cindy, and just getting the opportunity to know her as a person. Right when we first met, I felt like we had so much to talk about, even just little things going on in our lives. I've been able to actually work on developing ideas with her prompts and the way we are just able to talk everything through.

CINDY M. DEL ROSARIO-TAPAN

A journalist by training, Cindy M. del Rosario-Tapan is a Harlem-based writer who loves stories of all shapes and sizes.

MENTOR'S ANECDOTE:

Working with Min is akin to watching a modern-day Renaissance woman. From diving, to gymnastics, to juggling all her rigorous academic work, I've loved getting the chance to support Min on finding her voice. She has a natural gift for setting scenes and capturing emotions through her words, and it's been an absolute dream to accompany her this year.

LESSONS IN POTTERY AND GROWING UP

MIN HOLLWECK

This piece was created to honor my childhood spent with my grandmother!

In the garage with my grandmother, the summer humidity hangs thick, almost foglike, in the air. I watch the dusty garage fill with the smell of clay and the hum of the cracked pottery wheel as she effortlessly materializes a pot. In my own attempt shortly after, the clay folds in on itself, drowning in the muddy water and crumpled layers of what can be described only as a mess. This afternoon spent in our garage was the first of many pottery lessons, something my grandmother had been talking about for years and years before.

I was born sixty years after my grandmother. We share the golden pig as our zodiac sign, the special thread between us that she never fails to mention. I spent much of my childhood reading past my bedtime, thanks to the light thrown up on my walls through the star-shaped cutouts in the pig-shaped night-light she made me. Besides attempting pottery in the garage, we would often spend the endless summer days in the library. Racing through the unrelenting July sun to reach the air-conditioned sanctuary of the Queens Public Library, my grandmother encouraged me to read and keep reading. We would load her grocery cart with books and drag them home, rattling and creaking over the uneven sidewalk the entire way back.

Long after the first time my grandmother attempted to teach me how to make a bowl, I was the one showing her how to do math problems and editing her emails. She often thanked me with the title of 선생님 (seonsaengnim), which is "teacher" in Korean. I remember feeling a certain unease at this, the idea that *I* was now the one who could teach, that I couldn't just rely on her, that I was getting older. I was afraid to grow up, to lose the childhood feeling of eternal summer breezes, soundtracked by the chirp of crickets and warped singing into the fan. I didn't want her to get older, either, to be faced with the idea that one day she wouldn't be the one caring for me. I was grateful for how things felt *easy*, the way life was an endless stream of cut fruit and dreamlike sunsets. I hated feeling like the one in charge, the one who talked to cashiers and checked the map before we left the house. I didn't want to think about *real* things, and I resented how it felt like we had switched.

Now, as I actually have gotten older, my family doesn't rely on my grandmother so heavily. Even though I don't see her so often, she is with me every single day. I eat the food she brings over to our house, the seemingly never-ending supply of glowing red pomegranates all because I said they were my favorite that one time. I wear the necklace with her birthstone every day, and turn on that pig light every so often. More important, I try to create. This is what she taught me, and what holds us together no matter what, the link through the universe: our sameness that began with the golden pig.

Throughout my childhood, my grandmother fed me with creativity: all those trips to the library, where only I was reading; the times she insisted we visit the museums in the city, even when I was the one navigating the subway for the both of us. Even as I get older, and become more and more of the teacher, I remember her creation. The watercolored cards, with scrawled Korean I am barely literate enough to understand, the ceramic strawberries and slices of cake gifted on birthdays, all remind me that appreciation and joy for life aren't lost through age. Getting older doesn't mean you have to remain only the teacher, or be the one who knows all the time. I can hold on to a certain whimsy for everything through making *something*.

STELLA Z. HU, AKA TWIG

When reached for questioning, self-described "crazy little space elf" Stella/Twig, who hasn't been seen outdoors in twelve months, said, "I'm not telling you squat."

MENTEE'S ANECDOTE:

One night, on the way back from the library, we searched for a place to get stamps and ended up tracking down this tiny room on the side of an apartment building that turned out to have run out of any. Good times.

EMMA WINTERS

Emma Winters (she/her) is a writing and communications professional. She lives and works in New York City. Careful, she's also a boxer.

MENTOR'S ANECDOTE:

I love going to the library and eating pizza with Stella. It's on my bucket list to try every specialty slice at La Vera Pizza. Stella gets cheese every time. My pizza taste is about the only way I'm more interesting than Stella. Otherwise, she's the one who keeps our time interesting, unique, and exciting.

THINGS I WISH TREES COULD DO

STELLA Z. HU, A.K.A. TWIG

You ever just . . . Think?

Shoot fireworks from their branches in any direction whenever they felt like it. It would cause mass chaos, and it would be hilarious.

Speak, but only to shout completely random things like "PEE IS STORED IN THE MIRRORPANTS WORLD" or "THE CATFISH IS ON THE ROOF." See above.

Smack billionaires on the head when they come near.

Smack bigots on the head when they come near.

Actually, just sense when anycreature who's a garbage human being comes near and smack them.

Grow leaves in all different colors because pretty.

Have wood in all different colors. See above.

Sing. I just think it'd be cool.

Communicate with people in their dreams when people sleep under them, whether to offer wisdom or to make fun of your hair or to just talk about whatever the heck.

Get up and walk around if they're bored, then maybe put their roots back in the ground somewhere else.

Put their roots through solid concrete and, like, anything else.

Communicate with animals, and respond to anything they say out loud in human languages at high volumes.

Scream uncontrollably at inhuman volumes when you chop or uproot them.

Create weirdly shaped unidentifiable objects out of their sap and just drop those.

Make fun of people, but only when those passing by are not the people they're making fun of and don't know the people they're making fun of, and only for things no person would ever make fun of another person for, like having eyes, or blowing their nose, or walking forward instead of backward.

See, but only in colors that humans can't see.

Absorb anything made from wood that you place near them and use it to become bigger and stronger trees.

Make phone calls, but just to tell you something weird as frick that you'll be thinking about for the rest of your life, and then hang up.

Shake and wiggle and pulse and sort of stretch up and down like they're bouncing and wave their branches all around when somecreature plays music aloud around them that happens to go hard enough and/or be unhinged enough.

Poop.

Put weird urges in the heads of some people, like to drop everything and start tap dancing on the spot.

Drop fruit on your head on purpose if they think it will be funny.

Place leaves or flowers in your hair.

Tell you what you need to hear most.

Pat children on the head.

Pat anycreature who is internally on any level a child on the head.

Spit sap all over passing cops.

ANGEL JACKSON

Angel is a high school senior from Guilderland, New York. She currently works at her local library and enjoys listening to music, running, and reading.

MENTEE'S ANECDOTE:

Every other Saturday, I can expect to grow as a writer with the help of my mentor, Molly. It's not only about the writing, though. You can catch us discussing our plans or the latest world events; whatever it is, we find a way to talk about it. I am more confident in myself as a writer because of Molly. She is the most motivating and truthful mentor that I've had in my life. I will carry the advice she gives me into my adult life and continue to flourish as a writer because of her.

MOLLY COYNE

Molly is building a joyful life in Brooklyn, where she fills her days with people she loves, good books, and crafts beyond her skill level.

MENTOR'S ANECDOTE:

My Saturdays are always better when they start with an Angel meeting! Angel's interest in learning and commitment to writing brighten my day every time we meet. She is eager to explore different techniques and styles; I always love hearing about what she's been working on since we last met. It has been amazing to see her grow as a writer—I can't wait to see what her future holds!

ANGEL JACKSON

This is a piece about my upbringing so that others will know who I am.

I am from plastic barrettes,
from Oil Sheen hair spray and glycerin
I am from the gravel above the back-deck patio,
gray and rough, like the bark from an oak tree.
I am from the transvaal daisy,
the zanzibar gem
that is easy to grow,
a favorite among houseplant growers.

I am from baked macaroni and cheese and eczema
from Xina and Salina.
I'm from the I-know-I-cans
and pass-it-downs,
from speak up to speak more.
I'm from He gave light to my soul
with a new unicorn
and ten prayers I often say myself.

I'm from St. Peters and the Jacksons,
yams and ginger ale
From the extra finger my father was birthed with
to the mark on my brother's forehead from
falling on concrete
outside on a sunny day with my mother.
I am from the leather double-sided
photo album under the coffee table,
filled with the memories

of those before me,
and, one day, after me, too.
Those moments are snapshots
of who I know I am.
I am a Black girl who loves to write.

WAEZA JAGIRDAR

Waeza is a senior at Lehman College studying media and communications. She's passionate about advocating for human rights through her writing. Waeza is a member of the 2024 Anthology Editorial Committee.

MENTEE'S ANECDOTE:

Maya and I first connected through messaging on Slack, where we bonded over our shared passion for writing. Despite not knowing each other for long, Maya's warmth and enthusiasm for storytelling shone through in every message. As we exchanged ideas and drafts, I quickly discovered her talent for both nonfiction and poetry. Maya's kindness and humble demeanor made it easy to collaborate and share feedback, and our writing relationship blossomed from there. I'm grateful for the opportunity to work alongside Maya and look forward to seeing where our shared love for writing takes us.

MAYA COLLINS

Maya Collins is a multimedia artist and poet who splits her time between Illinois and Pennsylvania. In her art and writing she explores love, identity, and community.

PEER MENTEE'S ANECDOTE:

Working with Waeza has been so much fun. I have enjoyed writing and learning together. Waeza is easy to talk to, welcoming, and inspiring. I have loved getting to know her better through reading her work as well. She is both bold and vulnerable in her speech, something I can only aspire to.

HAYAT

WAEZA JAGIRDAR

This poem reflects the resilience of the Palestinian people, who are struggling for justice, dignity, and peace.

Hayat:

Hayat means life.
To live doesn't mean to breathe.
To live means to follow the path chosen for you.
To live is a rarity.
Our hayats are gifted
For what seems like a fleeting moment,
And we strive to make the most of it.

The bitter taste of life,
The bitter taste of death.
And we strive
To forget
that death is unavoidable.
But sometimes hayat is stolen from us,
And though this may be predetermined
As to how we depart from this world,
It is unjust.

It's been seventy-five years and one hundred and twenty-eight days.
And we're all drained from pleading for a ceasefire.
We're tired of having to justify why Palestinians deserve basic decency.
We're tired of having to explain the essence of being human.
We've already lost thousands of lives and we're still losing people.

We are tired of explaining what humanity entails.
Nobody deserves to live in conditions
where they have to write their parent's name on themselves
just to know which family they belong to, in case they pass.

Palestinians deserve their inherent rights,
alongside all the nations that have stood in solidarity with them, like Lebanon and Yemen.

This isn't a "war" or a "conflict."
This is a genocide. Period.
To call this a war is simply unacceptable.

I stand for humanity, which means I stand unequivocally with the Palestinian people and their fight for liberation.

We stand united, unwavering in our resolve,
For justice, dignity, and peace to evolve.
With every heartbeat, with every breath,
We continue the struggle, defying death.
Palestinians deserve their rights, it's true,
And with unwavering support, we'll see it through.

I stand with the Palestinian people and their liberation.

ISABELLA JAPAL

Isabella (she/her) is a full-time arts and culture journalist based in New York City. This is her second year as a mentee with Girls Write Now.

MENTEE'S ANECDOTE:

Kiki has been my cheerleader since day one, even while I was suffering from perpetual writer's block. I can always count on Kiki for honest feedback and advice whenever I'm feeling lost about any topic. She was the first person I called when I almost got pushed into the subway tracks one night, which my mom still doesn't know about. (Sorry, Mommy!) She is like the older sister I never had. This may be the last year I'll be working with Kiki through Girls Write Now, but I know I have made a friend for life.

KIKI T.

The Year of the Dragon is Kiki's time to break out and try new things—including releasing her first ebook, titled *Letters to a Young Poetess*, which is heartwarming, inspiring, and only sixteen pages. It consists of letters written to her mentee during their year of zooming in the middle of the pandemic, answering all questions about writing, life, and beyond. Kiki is a member of the 2024 Anthology Editorial Committee.

MENTOR'S ANECDOTE:

I love that Isabella is answering questions she had about the direction of her life from the start of our pairing. She has persevered and made her dreams a reality. Isabella applies what she learns to her talents, creating opportunities and making the most of the ones that come her way. Her strength, confidence, and humor have only grown. Isabella has magnificently stepped up into who she is and what she wants to be.

TEMPERATURE CHECK (EXCERPT)

ISABELLA JAPAL

An excerpt from Temperature Check, *an adult thriller featuring Kara, a twenty-two-year-old recluse whose life is changed overnight when she is the subject of a viral video, which creates a domino effect of events.*

I put on thick corduroys and a wool argyle sweater, grabbed a blanket and my clunky black plastic sunglasses, and headed to the park. My mother said the sunglasses made me look like I belonged on the short bus the first time she saw them, proceeding with the hearty squawk she made when I knew she was particularly tickled. I stopped wearing them for two days after that comment. Then I realized that the glasses made me feel safe—not only from the pulsating rays of the sun, but from the eyes of others.

I made it to Central Park around 11:30 a.m., just before peak day-break and before the typical crowd began to gather. At this time it was other unemployed folks like myself, and touring groups of pimply blond high schoolers from Scandinavian countries toting bags from the Times Square Foot Locker or Zara, laughing and gossiping among one another while their gray-haired chaperone sheepishly herded them along. The stay-at-home wives of Wall Street's finest pushed strollers along the park's perimeter and competed with other thin, box-shaped women and their tiny white and brown dogs to see who could complete the six-mile loop the fastest, their Caribbean nannies doting alongside them. Chinese grandparents gathered for tai chi. Frazzled young women and the occasional young man led groups of preschoolers through the park, all linked by a stretchy length of rope as if they were being guided on a safari.

I moved to New York City last year at the age of twenty-two. I had spent the last four years slowly cracking at my associate's degree at the county-wide community college, splitting my time between the classroom and my movie theater job, where I swept popcorn from under mauve velvet cushions and picked at Subway sandwiches while my coworkers smoked weed in the neighboring church parking lot.

I lived in a studio in Harlem, paid for by my mom. "Just until I can find a job," I explained to her, even though we both knew my effort in applying to jobs would be minimal and she had more than enough money funneled away to support us until either one of us died. I lived on the fourth floor of a walk-up, with hallways so long and narrow I questioned how any of my furniture would get inside. Old R&B tracks, slamming car doors, and whooping shouts and laughs floated up to my window from the street below, filling the air around me like a hug.

The ritual begins as follows: I wake up at 8 a.m. on the dot after a blissful and deep sleep ranging anywhere from ten to thirteen hours. I had done away with my alarm clock after graduation and figured this was my body's natural resting point. I spend the next hour preparing for the day ahead, beginning with a series of stretches—child's pose into downward dog into a forward bend into tadasana, then eagle pose back into child's pose, repeated three times and topped off with another forward bend. I have a glass of water, brush my teeth, and cook breakfast. Two fried eggs, multigrain toast, and a banana. No coffee or tea.

I sit at the round table in the corner of my apartment, about ten feet away from my bed. I stare out the window and make my way through breakfast, observing the children walking toward the subway station for school, the grandmothers walking their dogs, the men and women in uniforms heading to work.

Of course, I made exceptions to my rules. Weekends, for one, were a no go. Too many sunbathers, picnickers, Bluetooth speakers, and eyes. Rainy days were out of the question, too. I never understood people who enjoyed rain.

I'm not sure when the idea for my project first came about, but it felt like a good use of time. *I'm soaking in vitamins,* I told myself. This is nature's SAD lamp. A DIY sauna, if you will.

I made a habit of planting myself in the middle of Sheep Meadow in the heaviest clothes I could wear without effectively passing out on the subway or the sidewalk. Never on rainy days, though, I wasn't crazy.

I sat in one spot, facing the twin peaks of the San Remo. I let the sun penetrate my soul. I baked in my clothing, beads of sweat traveling down my body and collecting in cool layers between my rolls of stomach fat. I questioned my existence, softly cursing and moaning aloud.

Then the earth would rotate and the sun rolled down from its mantel. The trees and skyscrapers cast long shadows across the park, starting small, then gradually stretching forward, and the sweet relief of the shade fell over me. It felt spiritual. I felt cleansed. It felt like I had survived.

Until I didn't.

SHEYLA JAVIER

Sheyla Javier is a writer from Queens. She is a junior at Hunter College majoring in English with a creative writing concentration.

MENTEE'S ANECDOTE:

This was my first time being in a peer-to-peer pairing, and working with Sophie has been a fun journey. She is such a light and loves to write fantasy, which I admire so much! She has also taught me the importance of advocating for the things you care about in this world.

SOPHIE MYERS

Sophie Myers is a fairy tale enthusiast, a fairy tale and poetry writer, a researcher into queer and BIPOC communities, and a student activist.

PEER MENTEE'S ANECDOTE:

Working with Sheyla has been a great experience. She brings a wonderful energy, creativity, and competency to her writing and to our meetings, and I look forward to seeing her continue to flourish.

WHY I WRITE

SHEYLA JAVIER

A piece that encompasses why I do this in the first place.

I write because I have so much to say
there simply aren't enough words in the English dictionary
I write because a picture is worth a thousand words
yet a thesaurus contains way more I have yet to use
I write because a tsunami of intensity flows through my veins and
a whirlpool of emotions circulates at the frontal cortex of my brain
I write because sometimes I fear being too much like this, or not
enough like that
mapping similes and metaphors of poetry and prose
I write because I'm an overthinker
in an attempt to better understand my thoughts
I write because I'm passionate about the things I care about and
if you let me, I could speak forever
I write because I'm an observer and
curious about the state of our world
I write for the immigrants who paved the way
to get to where they are today
For my parents, grandparents, great-grandparents, and ancestors
who didn't receive the opportunities I did
For Latina girls, Black girls, and those who despised their natural hair
For broken families trying to make ends meet
For the support system I've built who remind me—
I don't have to do it all alone
For teachers, for educators, for those who have created safe spaces
and helped me get to where I am today
For those who believed in me, way before I could

For friends, for acquaintances, for everyday people
and those who smile when eye contact is made
For those I sit next to in classes
and those who remember the little things
I write for the vanity of existence—
For lights that don't go out
For stories that don't end

MEGUMI JINDO

Megumi Jindo is an upcoming college freshman at Swarthmore College who hopes to wield words to inspire and mend the world.

MENTEE'S ANECDOTE:

Wow, I can't believe it's already been three years with Girls Write Now. Even when I someday move on, there is one thing I will never forget: the unbelievable support system, starting with my mentor, Maddie. To think, our first interaction on Zoom was filled with the anxiousness of "Will we really fit together?" Now when we meet, we can talk endlessly about whatever is on our minds—it's such a turnover. I am so grateful for her knowing me so well, for always finding the right words of wisdom, and for all the sweet hugs and letters. Maddie, thank you.

MADELINE WALLACE

Madeline Wallace is a New York City transplant—but a Midwesterner at heart—who works in publishing. Madeline is a member of the 2024 Anthology Editorial Committee.

MENTOR'S ANECDOTE:

I met Megumi when she was fifteen years old, and was immediately struck by her thoughtfulness, passion, and perseverance. These qualities have only blossomed and cemented as she's grown into the eighteen-year-old she is today, about to head off to the college of her dreams. Working with her has been an incredible honor. She's given as much to me as I hope I have to her, bringing vibrance, laughter, purpose, and presence to my life. It's been a joyful three years, and I am forever grateful to Girls Write Now for bringing us together.

EVERYTHING TURNS KIND OF COLD

MEGUMI JINDO

When the world becomes something like hopeless.

i wish the world would go dark for once
forget and forget
i'll let you rot
the people can forget you
they can weep about you
but it won't ever bring back what you hated
biting into bread too hard—rotted.
god, everything is rotted.
desecrated.
avenged.
leaving anything to your mercy was hard, wasn't it?
a little too soft to be
stifling their cries and staunching their hunger
how much strength it must have took to become invincible
raking destruction at your core
this is what the hose is for:
(what you're for)
to flood everything away
when everything's in the way
everything is in the way
everything.

ALLAHNA JOHNSON

Allahna Johnson is a high school senior and future social worker. She writes to start conversations and to make the world a more empathetic place.

MENTEE'S ANECDOTE:

When I first met Felecia, I was excited and wanted to establish a professional environment in which to share work and bounce ideas off each other. While this has all remained true, I have come to find that despite being a part of different walks of life, we share various similarities when it comes to our interpretation of other pieces, the themes we explore in our writing, and how poetry aids us in our daily life and managing emotions. Felecia is passionate, witty, and truthful, and, despite being a peer mentee, is someone I look up to greatly when navigating the Girls Write Now world.

FELECIA B. FACEY

Felecia Facey is a first-year student at John Jay College of Criminal Justice, currently pursuing studies in law and society with a minor in psychology.

PEER MENTEE'S ANECDOTE:

Working with Allahna has been a pleasure. She is an engaging writer and a creative thinker. Her writing exudes life, with a knack for sensory details and language that captivates the ear and the mind. We haven't known each other long, but we bonded over our common interests, including our love for poetry and Pinterest. Listening to her work transports me into a world filled with imagery from her words. Allahna has the potential to spellbind people with her poems. She is inspirational, and I wish her all the best. I am excited to continue this journey with her.

GREW THROUGH JAZZ

ALLAHNA JOHNSON

This piece shares the story of a young woman who was influenced heavily by jazz throughout her life and details her understanding of jazz through a Black perspective.

I grew up on Jazz
The depth of the trumpets runs through my bones
The freedom of my people through my bloodstream

Such a liberating sound from those in the shadows
Harlem doesn't know what's coming
A certain kind of whimsy from a certain kind of sadness
And a certain kind of pain worth singing about

That's the key to Jazz in NYC
Have a passion just waiting to come out

The brown skin on my body matches that of my father's bass
The strings pull straight like my hair on that hot comb

Between my mother's legs, or by the kitchen sink
While my father stayed and played like a metronome

Consistent in his love for Jazz
And consistent in his love for me

He preached on and on about the rhythms and blues
And on and on about family

We sang together in church on Sundays
And the radio had its own chair at dinner

We took in the nutrients prepared by my mother
While my father fed our soul's despair

With the depth of trumpets pumping my blood
And chilling Harlem with the most desperate cries

Of the people whose beauty was pushed to the back
And whose music was a way to survive

On plantations and speakeasies
Through the ghettos of today
Rhythms are what keep the rage at bay
A vessel for the beauty of my people and me
And in my heart a vessel for my family

So I grew up on Jazz
And the depth of the trumpets runs through my bones
The freedom of my people through my bloodstream

TASHINA JOHNSON

Tashina is a sixteen-year-old aspiring author. When not writing, Tashina enjoys obscure horror flicks, obsessing over stray cats, and burning her fingers on baking pans.

MENTEE'S ANECDOTE:

In a beautiful way, Elle is like my superpowered writing fairy godmother! It simply cannot be put into words how essential our pair relationship has been to my writing journey these last two years. Being a junior in the international baccalaureate program, imposter syndrome is something I struggle with daily. With my mentor's help, however, I've fully realized my potential and the importance of my voice. When we're not talking about writing, it's so fun to gush about my interests with her, whether it be books by BIPOC authors, horror movies, or underrated creative publications online! There's never been a dull moment with Elle.

ELLE GONZALEZ ROSE

Elle Gonzalez Rose is a YA author and producer. She's the author of *Caught in a Bad Fauxmance* and *10 Things I Hate About Prom*. Elle is a member of the 2024 Anthology Editorial Committee.

MENTOR'S ANECDOTE:

Working with Tashina has been an absolute delight! Our sessions are always so fun and engaging, and have helped me nourish my own love of writing. I'm so lucky to be able to work with such a bright, talented, and motivated young writer, and I have no doubt Tashina and her words will take the world by storm someday soon!

THE MORNING, THE EVENING, THE EIGHTH DAY

TASHINA JOHNSON

Love and tragedy at the dawn of the world.

Somewhere in Eden, the serpent lies waiting
Still seething, doubtless, from The Fall
Tomorrow, He will wrap himself 'round my
    fragile chest, and squeeze my stuttering heart
Tomorrow, the gates to paradise will close for the final time,
    the bare world all before us
Tomorrow, my love and I shall run naked throughout
    the woodlands
The weight of mortal lives
    heavy on our feet

And that is the damning curse of humanity
The pervasive urge to rebel
To lick the serpent's tongue
To become like the Father, holy
And the fruit of knowledge is heavy in my naked hand
And the serpent says, "You shall not surely die."

Today, Hyacinth, the beloved,
    drops violet petals upon the flower bed
Today, the young Menelaos loves Helen,
    the fair-haired
Today, the Tigris makes leaps toward paradise,
    desperate in its longing

Today, the citharist makes calls to
the lifeless things
With his song, he puts death on its heels

Today, I see my love beside me,
surrounded still by the quiet beauty of the earth
By the dew-tipped grass heads, the water striders, the lightning bugs
By the grand meadows, and the cattle and
the beasts within them
By the box trees, and the killing oleanders, and the humble plant with
the bell-shaped flowers
By sultry June nights and the dearest sunrise
and the four heavenly streams that flow still in the hereafter

He is bathed in swelling summer's sun, the
light like gold on his skin
I worship him to show my devotion
I devour him to show my love

NYLA JONES

Nyla Jones (she/her) is a recent English graduate from Howard University who now works in the advertising department at Paramount Network in New York City.

MENTEE'S ANECDOTE:

Jaime Brockway is my mentor this year, and I think we are a great pairing. It is my first time at Girls Write Now and Jaime has helped me navigate my voice and my writing style since the beginning, whether for graduate school applications or a five-minute prompt. We live in different time zones and have crazy schedules with our jobs, but we always make time to meet virtually at least once a month and have a discussion about our lives, giving us time to truly learn about each other outside of writing.

JAIME BROCKWAY

Jaime is a third-year mentor with Girls Write Now. She has years of experience copyediting for New York City magazines and major publications, businesses, and agencies.

MENTOR'S ANECDOTE:

Even through the video screen, across two different time zones, Nyla's good energy is palpable. She has only good vibes! Since our first session, it's a delight to get to spend time with her and listen to her experience of finding a balance between starting her first full-time job and following her passions after college. Her dedication to her craft is impressive and inspiring, and she has a great voice and a strong imagination that shines through in her creative and fantasy works.

ODE TO POPCORN

NYLA JONES

This poem was written when I saw everyone around me succeeding, as I felt stuck.

Oh how I love your kernel
Seeds so hard and small
Turning into a tasty, buttery treat
Enjoyed by one and all

You've taught me much
More than you will ever know
Learning from your unpopped cousin
A lesson on how to grow

Some people seem to think
That we all bloom at the same time
But you have shown me
Life isn't a straight line

This longtime fan-favorite snack
Did not start out on top
Taking its own pace to fulfill its destiny
Until you hear a definite pop!

NANDINI KALANI

Nandini (she/her) is a freshman in college with a fervent love for cinematography, traveling, piano melodies, and the occasional indulgence in a well-crafted passion fruit gelato.

MENTEE'S ANECDOTE:

Thainá is an exceptional and imaginative individual. Our shared enthusiasm for civic engagement and social justice has strengthened our bond as college freshmen, guiding us through the whirlwind transition from high school to university life. Delving into political science, advocacy, and activism work together, we've found solace in navigating a male-dominated field as empowered women. It's a joy to connect with someone who shares so many common passions. Through our collaborations, I've cherished the opportunity to learn, grow, and laugh alongside Thainá, finding inspiration in her unwavering dedication and vibrant spirit.

THAINÁ THEODORO

Thainá is a twenty-year-old student at Grinnell College majoring in political science and gender, women's, and sexuality studies.

PEER MENTEE'S ANECDOTE:

While we were discovering our shared passion for political science, we stumbled upon a writing project that intrigued us both—the Anthology. Despite the busy schedule of midterms, assignments, and readings, we relied on each other to discuss our vulnerabilities and learn from each other. Our desire to enhance our knowledge and gain practical experience through internships further fueled our interest in the project.

JOURNEYS OF DISCOVERY: EXPLORING EUROPE'S HEART AND SOUL

NANDINI KALANI

Embark on a poetic voyage through the streets of Paris, Prague, and Berlin, where each city becomes a canvas for self-discovery amid the beauty, history, and vibrancy of Europe's cultural tapestry.

"WHISPERS OF PRAGUE: MUSINGS BY THE VLTAVA"

in prague's winter hush, a silent ballet unfolds,
as swans glide gracefully on rivers of gold.
moonlight bathes the city in a soft, silver glow,
casting shadows that dance with secrets we know.
underneath the yellow streetlamps' gentle hum,
i ponder the mysteries of life, where we've come.
in the stillness of night, in nature's embrace,
i find solace and wisdom in this quiet space.
each swan a symbol of grace and of might,
navigating waters, a beacon in the night.
their journey mirrors mine, a quest to find,
meaning in moments, in the depths of the mind.
as the moonlight weaves tales of love and of loss,
i embrace the beauty of life, its tempests and gloss.
for in prague's winter silence, I come to see,
the interconnectedness of nature, of you, and of me.

"PARISIAN REVERIE: A LOVE LETTER TO THE AVE OF CAMOENS"

in paris, where the lights softly gleam,
and the eiffel tower stands tall in a dream,
i find myself lost in a world of art,
where creativity and passion impart.
through quiet streets, i wander alone,
in the gentle rain, i find my home.
books and laughter fill the air,
molière's wit, beyond compare.
in montmartre's embrace, i am free,
among artists and poets, i see
the beauty of expression unfurled,
in every stroke, in every word.
the rain whispers secrets untold,
of renewal and stories yet to unfold.
in paris, i find myself anew,
in the love of art and skies of blue.
this city of light, this city of dreams,
where the soul finds solace, it seems.
in paris, I discover the artist in me,
and in its embrace, i am truly free.

"ECHOES OF REBELLION: BERLIN'S CREATIVE PULSE"

in berlin's streets, where history breathes,
graffiti whispers tales of rebels and thieves.
on the wall, bold strokes tell stories untold,
of freedom sought and truths bold.
amid the chaos, i find my voice,
in the riot of colors, i make my choice.
to paint my dreams on life's canvas wide,
and let my spirit soar, no longer to hide.
music pulses through the city's veins,
a rhythm that echoes through joy and pains.

in its melody, i find release,
a symphony of self, a moment of peace.
berlin, a sanctuary for the creative soul,
where passion ignites and dreams take control.
in its embrace, i find my muse,
and in its chaos, i find my truth to choose.
for in the rebellious graffiti's sprawl,
i see reflections of myself, standing tall.
a rebel with a cause, a dreamer at heart,
in berlin's embrace, i find my art.

KRISNA KUMAR

Krisna is a high school senior who loves to write humor and poetry. When not writing, she loves to read, knit, and bake.

MENTEE'S ANECDOTE:

I am so honored to have had Karen as a mentor for two years now! She is so amazing and knows so much about writing and life in general. Karen has been so helpful and supportive throughout the entire college process, and I am so grateful to have her by my side. She has encouraged me to become a stronger writer and taught me so many new styles and forms. I know I have grown so much in the short time we've already spent together. I can't wait to spend more time with her in the future!

KAREN CHEE

Karen Chee is a comedian and Brooklyn-based writer for shows such as *Late Night with Seth Meyers*, *Pachinko*, and the upcoming Netflix series *A Classic Spy*.

MENTOR'S ANECDOTE:

I love working with Krisna and feel lucky to get to do so for a second year. Krisna is so quick, witty, and game for anything. It's been inspiring watching her try new writing styles and crush them! Many of my peers—myself included—regularly get hit with writer's block and self-doubt, and witnessing Krisna's fearlessness makes me a braver writer. This past year was a tricky one for me, complete with a new job and an industry-wide strike, but Krisna was always very encouraging and patient with my changing schedule. It's a true joy to be her mentor!

THE GEORGE POST-IT: SANITY SINKS IN SILENCE

KRISNA KUMAR

The George Post-It *is a small-town, highly reputable source of information for everything you need to know. Enjoy this short snippet from this morning's paper.*

THE GEORGE POST-IT

Sanity Sinks in Silence

JOBS WANTED

Join our destruction crew—pay is minimal and it will not be rewarding. The destruction crew is in charge of destroying anything that needs destroying. Services offered, but not limited, to houses, buildings, relationships, and lives. Looking for a flexible and destructive person to fill a sudden vacancy. Must have experience in wrecking homes and being a homewrecker. Reach out if interested. All applications must be sent to the head of Destructive Services. We are located right off the street nearest to you. If the sending of an application provides an issue, we are constantly monitoring the area for evidence of destructive tendencies. To catch our attention, we recommend bashing a trash can against a wall until it is dented beyond return. If our attention is piqued, we will reach out to you directly. You do not need to try and find us, we will find you.

Painting services needed. The town is in desperate need of some red, and a painting crew is being assembled. Hours are late, drinks are provided. Interested persons will need to be able to have a steady hand and mind, be familiar with step dancing, and feel comfortable with occasional arson. Experience is recommended but not required. Applications will be taken on a rolling basis. Please send a cover letter in red ink along with photographs of past experiences to our office. Currently, we do not have an office, but we do have a truck. If you see a red truck, throw your application into it. Please do not scratch the truck—that will reflect badly on your application.

New bookseller needed. Old bookshop has been vacated, but we must keep it alive for scenery. Job duties include sitting at the front desk for eight hours. No book experience necessary, but sitting experience is recommended. Occasional usage of BookTok to update the front window is encouraged, but, again, not necessary. Payment is free access to nearby sandwich shops for daily lunch. Deliver your application to the bookshop directly and place it on the front counter under the empty sandwich plate. Currently, the door is locked, and the key is inside. Once the key has been retrieved and the door has been unlocked, we will review your application.

FUTURE FORECASTS

The chances of rain are probable, i.e., the chance of having a chance of rain is probable. It is hard to tell when it will fall. Be surprised and be forewarned. Carry an umbrella at all times. Snow may also fall, if the temperatures fall below freezing. This might occur, and if it does, snow will follow. That is, if precipitation occurs. If not, snow will not fall.

It will also be sunny. If not during the day, then definitely at night.

The temperatures will be comfortable enough to wear the clothing you desire. Just hopefully you desire the right clothing.

OBITUARY

The Prince has died. We deeply mourn the loss of His Highness. During his parents' reign, he flaunted many brands and danced many balls. His beautiful hair was beloved by all, and his eyes pierced the souls of any who saw him—almost as fast as his sword pierced the hearts of his enemies. His coronation's attendance was low, but festivities were grand. It is said that he drank too much the night of the party and fought with his local baker. However, this has not been confirmed by our reports. It is also unclear who won the fight, though the Prince did not eat any carbohydrates for the rest of his life. His painting, which is set to hang in the current throne room of the King and Queen, beautifully captures his growing bruise the night of his coronation.

Many art critics note the beauty of the yellow of his attire contrasting the purple around his eye.

"I didn't like him" was how the baker described the Prince. "So I punched him."

The Prince's many accomplishments include the creation of a farmer's market for vegetable and meat purchases only, a compilation of gluten-free recipes, and a proclamation against the purchase of yeast. His dearest friends remember him as driven, determined, and valiant, with a one-track mind.

"He never backed down from a challenge and never forgot those who wronged him," wrote his closest friend in a heartfelt letter.

The Prince is survived by the King and Queen, many other Princes and Princesses, Dukes and Duchesses, Earls and Counts, and his two dogs: Bread and Butter. While he will be missed, the addition of another guest room to the castle will be greatly appreciated.

For clarification, this was not our Prince, nor is this our current Prince. The current Prince is alive. Prince Mackerel, for whom this article was written, passed in the year 1524. This obituary has been compiled after the sudden rampage of emails sent to our office about the injustice we had served not to honor this Prince. We were provided a generous amount of compensation for this obituary.

TARA ISABEL LAGO

Tara Lago is a poet and storyteller from Staten Island who enjoys puns, random facts, and Walkmans.

MENTEE'S ANECDOTE:

From book divinations, to yearly recaps, to chemistry rants, Jaime has been an amazing conversationalist, poet, and, of course, mentor. I truly appreciate her for reading my writing in its first stages and final drafts as well as encouraging me to be spontaneous and submit! After one too many snowstorms, Jaime and I were finally able to meet in person and chat in the good company of books and coffee. As a freshman in college, having Jaime as a mentor has helped me find a balance between my academics and writing passion!

JAIME WRIGHT

Jaime Wright is a Brooklyn-based writer and astrologer who writes cult favorite newsletter moon missives on Substack and also pens a horoscope column for *PureWow*.

MENTOR'S ANECDOTE:

I knew after my first meeting with Tara, where we discussed her breadth of talents and interests, that we would be a great pair. As someone who also straddles the line between being left- and right-brained, I love the labyrinthine flow of our conversations and the curiosity rabbit holes they lead me down both before and after the fact.

BREATHE IN. BREATHE OUT.

TARA ISABEL LAGO

How many brilliant breaths are contained in each lung?

How many brilliant breaths are contained in each lung?

One side is sadness
Breathe in

The other side is joy
Breathe out

A dozen breaths or a pair,
A year of breaths or a decade of them
to encapsulate every ocean, every storm
that sunk a ship and rusted its treasure.

Is this exploration joy?
Breathe out

Or is this yearning sadness?
Breathe in

So holding my breath,
I dive into the silence,
a sonder between the
known and unknown.

My brilliant breaths
embraced in each lung
carry me down, deeper
than the leagues of
my peace

Breathe in
Breathe in
Breathe in

Staying steady, my hands glide across
the soil at the bottom of the sea,
sediments as still as an ellipse—

A question.

Swim or sink?

Neither, I say,
to my phantom
hand in front
of me.

Not now, I say,
to my strands of
hair that float,
buoyant and bright.

Never, I say,
to my shivering skin,
scales that long for
the glint of the sun.

Breathe in . . .
Breathe . . .
Breath . . .

I break the silence for
a sliver of sound
I recall in the
open sky.

Not a sonder
But a song,
simple and sweet.

At last, I exhale, an exclamation of joy.

Breathe out

ROBYN LAM

Robyn Lam (she/her) is a high school junior with a love for poetry, music, and programming who aspires to transform the world through writing.

MENTEE'S ANECDOTE:

Hannah has become more than a mentor; she is a wonderful friend. Over the past couple of months, we have learned a lot about each other, and although I was reserved at first, I slowly became more comfortable and outspoken. We have so much in common, such as our passion for computer science and our love for cats. Hannah is inspiring, confident, and encouraging. I have learned so much from her that has inspired me to try new things, whether it be starting my own publication or trying new writing techniques!

HANNAH GRANDINE

Hannah Grandine is a machine learning engineer and writer living in Seattle, Washington. She is passionate about art as a tool to transform the world.

MENTOR'S ANECDOTE:

It has been an absolute honor to work with Robyn through both of our first year of Girls Write Now. I have had so much fun reading and writing poetry together each session, as well as working on her social justice project as part of the Lead360 cohort and other projects. I continue to be impressed by her deeply personal connection to nature, as well as her commitment to improving the world, her bravery in self-expression, and her ambition in making change—she even started her own publication this year. I am very lucky to be her mentor!

THE WIND

ROBYN LAM

As an avid lover of the environment, my writings are constantly inspired by the nature around me.

The wind gently caresses
my hair
as it blows
through the meadow

The flowers begin to dance
as she comes through
Swaying
back and forth
by the lonely road

She whispers secrets
in my ear
Pushing me forward
through the meadow

The animals
scatter
as they hear her singing from afar

The houses
shudder and shake
under her breath

The lonely swing
rocks
back and forth

And if you look closely,
you could spot old Mr. Pearson sitting on the bench

The wind softly brushes my face
as it moves
through the meadow

The trees part for her
Making space
to avoid any confrontation

She leaves a
small scar
through my chest
And it continues to
grow
as she forges ahead
Determined to travel
as far as she could go

Nothing stood in her way

All the plants:
Shriveled: ran: hid
All the people:
Crouched: covered: panicked

And like she came
She gently leaves
Yet what is left
Is nothing but death

ALEJANDRE LAMAS-NEMEC

Living in Charlottesville, Virginia, Alejandre Lamas-Nemec is a junior in high school. They gain their inspiration from the people and things around them.

MENTEE'S ANECDOTE:

Lizz is a force. My mentor supports those she cares about fiercely, either by visiting her family and friends across the country or by helping me edit a poem. She is an emotional rock that is able to calm currents; she is a light able to warm people to joy; she is a true and genuine person. She is the definition of what it means to be a mentor, and I could never be more grateful for our friendship.

ELIZABETH C. CROZIER

Based in the Chicago area, Lizz Crozier is an experienced search engine optimization strategist and creative writer. Her work appears online and in various journals.

MENTOR'S ANECDOTE:

I recognized myself in AJ the first time we met. They are ambitious and motivated to succeed at everything they set out to do. They are an outspoken activist who stands up for their beliefs. Just as I was when I was a teen, they are inquisitive and skeptical of the world and how it works. On top of all that, their writing is absolutely stunning. AJ's use of form and language is exquisite, and they are not afraid to take on tough subjects. I'm proud to be their mentor and am so excited to see what they achieve next.

THIS EARTH, OUR EDEN

ALEJANDRE LAMAS-NEMEC

The poem is meant to speak on the feeling of hopelessness, but also the possibility of change. The idea that even within despair there is still the ability for something revolutionary to happen.

I am now left with
the husks of being:
my heart
I was once hope incarnate
enchanting my way through this world
creating a path of love in my wake
now look at me
God used to pray to
relinquish all the sin He committed unto Us
now look at Us
praying

We were Eve
We carved flower crowns into wood
touched Our lips to their meaning
We created a language of sensation
never speaking their definition
defining still what it meant to be
Human
now look at me
wood splinters grace my face
reaching up We touch countenances
stifled into movement

We are forced to Emotion
once She came to Us willingly
now look at me
look at Us
living in houses without gardens
I'll kiss the air a
grasp at knowing
why We came here
We were Eve We
never needed an Eden to create Us
We were Eve We
knew what would happen
knew Our fall to knowledge would be
The most infamous of all

hear the last of His words as He looked at us
risen once more
Gardens forming over His home
as We realize falling was Our final act of love
His final words
muted by Our scream of rejoice

MADISON ANIYAH LAWSON

Madison Lawson is a first-year graduate student studying English and African American literature at North Carolina Agricultural and Technical State University, with the intention of being an archivist.

MENTEE'S ANECDOTE:

Working with Samantha has been very enlightening. I have appreciated her feedback on several documents, including my cover letter, thesis research proposal, and this essay. She has encouraged me to make my writing more personal and pushed me out of my comfort zone in the best ways possible. I appreciate her continued support and look forward to her encouragement during every call, and her feedback on everything I send her way.

SAMANTHA HENIG

Samantha Henig is a media executive who has worked at *The New York Times*, *BuzzFeed News*, *Slate*, and *The New Yorker*.

MENTOR'S ANECDOTE:

Madison started working on this submission during the February Open Writing & Creating studio. Despite being a fervent diary-keeper in her youth, Madison says she now finds it difficult to write about herself, especially since she's so used to academic writing. I was impressed by how she used this studio with the goal of writing something for the anthology to tie in to her academic areas of interest. The process of writing this piece helped her realize she wants to do more personal writing going forward, and she has resolved to start blogging more, which is fantastic!

SELF-DEFINING A STRONG BLACK WOMAN

MADISON ANIYAH LAWSON

In this essay I discuss my personal journey with the "Strong Black Woman" schema and how basing my self-worth on what I could accomplish was detrimental to my personal development.

In 1982, Audre Lorde attended the Malcolm X Weekend at Harvard University and delivered her address, "Learning from the '60s." Lorde's address has since been quoted several thousands of times, and one sentence, in particular, stands out among others in my copy of *Sister Outsider*: "If I didn't define myself for myself, I would be crunched into other people's fantasies of me and eaten alive."

As a Black woman, self-definition is paramount. Historically, images of Black women have been reduced to negative stereotypes like the "Mammy," the "Jezebel," and the "Welfare Queen," all of which have negatively impacted Black women's perceptions in the real world. For women of my generation, the "Superwoman" or "Strong Black Woman" archetype has arisen to combat these images. Compared to earlier images where Black women were portrayed as docile, lazy, and promiscuous, the "Strong Black Woman" is a do-it-all, resilient, reliable, and invulnerable Black woman who makes little to no mistakes—like the strong Black female leads in films such as *Hidden Figures* and shows such as *Scandal*. Although the trope appears to heal the harm done by earlier portrayals, for many Black women, it has also established an unreasonably high standard.

Before I unsubscribed to the notion of being a "Strong Black Woman," I was constantly overperforming and exhausting myself in attempts to meet the expectations that other people had for me. When I went to college, what I really wanted was to study African American literature and actualize the long-running joke among my friends that I would become a librarian; feeding my passion for literature and learning about African American culture seemed like a much more enjoyable life path than anything else that was proposed to me. However, I chose to major in journalism because I was told it would be a more reliable pathway to success, and I—like most first-generation college students—had big expectations for my future. The weight of those expectations multiplied because I also became a representation of potential among my family, whose idea of college meant attending class for a few more years and then graduating to secure an abundant, stable lifestyle. As a Black woman entering the professional world, you also notice that successful first-generation Black femme college students were those who seemed to extend themselves as far as they possibly could and made little to no mistakes—performing well academically, securing multiple internships, joining several preprofessional organizations, and owning/operating a business or two.

During my sophomore year of undergrad, I fell in love with *Insecure* and the main protagonist, Issa Dee. At first, I connected with Issa because she, too, felt dispassionate and overwhelmed, and couldn't seem to get a grasp on her life; once the series ended, I realized that she was also struggling with the "Strong Black Woman" archetype. Although the chaos and uncertainty of the early seasons were undesirable, I admired Issa because she had realistic, challenging experiences she didn't always handle with grace (more often than not, the situations handled her), but she survived and thrived nonetheless. Seeing that her world didn't end when she struggled professionally or had faulty relationships and witnessing her emotional vulnerability gradually mended my perception of what a successful Black woman should be like. By my junior year, the series neared its end, and I was no longer obsessed with meeting the standards that the "Strong Black Woman" schema had set. Much like Issa, I felt encouraged to pursue what really fulfilled me professionally and personally.

During my junior year, I changed my major to English. I took a course with a professor who encouraged us to write in our authentic voices. While working on an assignment to write a personal statement,

I recalled the aforementioned Audre Lorde quote. Combined with my new *Insecure*-inspired outlook on life, the quote validated my choice to pursue my passions. It led me to vow to myself to self-define and create the life *I* wanted to live, free of unreasonable and irrelevant expectations.

CHLOE LEE

Chloe is a high school junior with myriad interests, including creative writing, speech and debate, psychology, intersectional feminism, and mental health advocacy.

MENTEE'S ANECDOTE:

I'm extremely thankful that I've been able to work with Kara for a second year. She is more than just an amazing mentor: she is a guiding light for all aspects of my life. She has helped me explore my writing skills; she continues to motivate me and is always so understanding. I've been able to grow as a writer, a student, and, most important, a better person with her support. It has been a pleasure working with her; here is to another great year!

KARA GELBER

Kara is a New York City–based communications strategist with a passion for storytelling. Offline, she likes to spend as much time as possible in Central Park.

MENTOR'S ANECDOTE:

I'm thrilled to be working with Chloe again this year. I continue to be blown away by her poise and the maturity she brings to each piece of writing. Time and time again, Chloe demonstrates exceptional dedication and passion for exploring diverse writing styles. Having the opportunity to work with Chloe for the second consecutive year has been such a gift, as I've gotten to see her grow both as a student and within her extracurricular activities (of which she has quite a few!). I can't wait to see what this next year brings.

A LOVE LETTER TO MY APARTMENT ON 69TH AVENUE

CHLOE LEE

This piece is a reflection of childhood nostalgia; I dive into living in my old apartment and attempt to savor its beauty. Though I struggle with growing pains, I eventually lean toward acceptance.

In the midst of a humid, scorching summer, while the whole world is engrossed in seeking relief from the persistent heat, I choose to enter a sacred oasis. It's past my bedtime and my parents think I'm well into sleep, but that's what makes it fun, right?

In this sanctuary, where time proves to be nonexistent, I clutch onto the lingering thoughts that have been subconsciously flowing throughout my mind. In desperation, I scavenge across my iPhone gallery for any image apparent enough to provoke decade-old memories, only to find myself empty-handed. Tonight, I find myself in the depths of my long-lost days living on the cherished blocks of 69th Avenue.

My earliest memory of living on 69th Avenue is eating greasy Chinese food with my parents while sitting on a worn-out bathroom stool. After watching the lumps of egg whites float in the boundless sea of my egg drop soup, I finally gulp a spoonful of the rich broth. Comforted by a wave of what feels like home, my six-year-old self defined this as pure bliss. Sure, it wasn't the most glamorous sight, but in my head those moments were magic.

Every single time I mention 69th Avenue, my dad does one of two things; he either remains quiet for a while or goes off on a rant about how we have a better life now. For the longest time, part of me has always hoped for him to open his mouth and say something reminiscent, something at least positive. But who am I to ask him to suddenly evoke the buried sentiments of his past? I could rip off the Band-Aid and expose his wounds, but it would be no use. After all, he has already built a wall to shield himself from the reminder of the blood, sweat, tears, and cartons of surplus takeout boxes. It isn't my place to tear it down. I saw only a chapter of his story. I just wished for once that he would see my version.

As I continue to confront my unanswered desires, a part of me feels compelled to choose to stay immersed in nostalgia. The radiance of my youth sparks another memory.

I run down the street, clutching my scuffed soccer ball. Though its once-vibrant colors have faded, its sharp seams are now worn, and there looks to be little air holding it up, its charm has always captivated me. With no worry or fear about anything, I start to run down the street.

"Chloe! Don't run too fast," my dad exclaims.

"Don't worry!" I scream as the creases of my mouth form a smile.

My heart beats quickly, not because of all of my movement, but from the euphoria of the present. My whole world blurs in the most beautiful way possible: The sun is warming my skin, the vibrance of the trees enlightens my eyes, and the cold, brisk air rushes through my body. The racket of the outside world diminishes as I lose myself in the stillness of the moment.

Nevertheless, every rose has a thorn. I suddenly snap back into reality as a wave of reality brushes past me.

Upon returning from my trip to my once jovial days, I used to cry. I would sit on my bed, legs spread out, tears streaming down while staring at my white wall. I've always hated it; I used to beg my mom to paint it vibrant pink, or at least a color that represents me better. However, it is in these moments of solitude that I befriend my white wall as a silent companion. Though all I could see was its non-pigment, inside was different. My sentiments full of explosive, fluorescent teenage angst were always too complicated to talk about. Afraid of facing the repercussions of vulnerability, I always ended up covering my bright colors with white paint, a vizard to cover up my deepest wounds. I've never felt brave enough to tell the tales of endless sleepless nights ending with tears dripping across my face, rumination, or ceaseless anxiety stripping my potential.

This time is different. My legs are spread out, tears hidden behind the creases of my eyes, and I'm fixated on the beauty of my white wall. As the night continues to progress slowly but surely, I feel a sudden change in my perception of my longtime friend, as independence creeps on me. With each tear shed, a part of my resistant heart opens bigger for healing. I remind myself that whenever I encounter another day of sorrow, not only will I have my white wall, but also my apartment on 69th Avenue. Though it is only a glimpse of my adolescence, all of its prominence has already been woven inside of me to shape the person I have become. In the midst of a stormy, rainy day, its radiance will never fail to save me. As I wipe my last tears, I impulsively decide to do something I have never done. Little did I know, this something is the tool that will bring me through my infamous dreaded high school years.

I begin to write.

SOPHIA LI

Sophia Li is a high school writer and artist in New York City. Her hobbies include painting, listening to indie rock, and daydreaming about giving characters therapy.

MENTEE'S ANECDOTE:

Meeting Kim has really improved my confidence in my abilities as a writer. When we talk, I feel like I'm looking at my writing through a brand-new lens, and I always leave each session feeling more excited to get words on the page. Getting the advice and insight I need whenever I'm stuck has been so important in reminding me that I do have stories worth telling. Writing aside, talking with Kim has been a really nice learning experience, and it's been very enjoyable to discuss everything from Sigmund Freud to yoga during our meetings.

KIM ADRIAN

Kim Adrian's books include *The Twenty-Seventh Letter of the Alphabet: A Memoir* and two book-length essays of creative criticism: *Dear Knausgaard* and *Sock*.

MENTOR'S ANECDOTE:

Working with Sophia is an absolute delight. She has so many ideas, yet she can also buckle down and get the work done. I've been helping her work on a novel, the tone of which is soft and realistic. But she can also write really exciting sci-fi! I love watching Sophia stretch her wings and try new things (songwriting!). I feel very lucky to be working with a young writer who possesses not only a keen sensitivity to language and a deep excitement for storytelling, but also a genuine curiosity about—and affection for—her fellow human beings.

THOSE WHO AREN'T SEEN

SOPHIA LI

People-watching.

There's an art teacher on the fifth floor of my high school who spends her classes telling us about how important it is to see beauty in our everyday lives. She hangs up these paintings of fruit and tin cans and dead people, and she keeps the window open, even when it's freezing cold. She says she wants us to be in touch with the outside. She says she wants us to open our eyes, and, when we do, to be brave enough to keep them open.

There's a girl who sits near the trash cans during lunch. I see her there every day. When she's done eating she plays with these paper clips, and she makes intricate wire animals out of them almost like it's nothing. Like she's fiddling with these pieces of junk that no one wants and, boom, suddenly something is there, suddenly there's life to something that was soulless. I've never seen anyone say hi to her. I don't know if she wants to be disturbed.

There's a boy in the back of my science class who has never, not once, raised his hand. I see him bending over his desk, etching ink doodles into his skin, eyes with long lashes and stars and circles in circles in circles. His notebook is covered in doodles, little comic strips, drawings of the window view, an unnecessarily detailed drawing of a plant cell. Sometimes he's listening to music with his earphones, twirling his pencil like a drummer twirls a stick. I hear us being told that we need to participate in order to get credit. I see him folding in on himself, his head on his desk, tilted in a way that allows him to see what he's drawing as if he's trying harder to make himself invisible now that he's forced to be seen. He still hasn't said anything.

There's a janitor who brings speakers wherever he goes, so he can listen to music while he works. Sometimes I'll stay after school for a club and I'll hear his music before I see him pressing the mop onto the ground and moving through the hallway in a rhythmic pattern as if guided by the beat. He stays the latest out of anyone in the building, I think. He's a solitary figure, armed with his cleaning materials and keys, dancing to the notes echoing through the empty third floor, sharing his music with everyone.

There's a girl who's a leader of an obscure club, and she hosts meetings in the classrooms at the end of the hall, the small rooms, and the occasional stairwell when the other bigger clubs take all the good spots. During these meetings she discusses her interests, what she would like the club to become, and how much she appreciates us for coming. I see the way her eyes light up when someone mentions crystals or fungi or haiku poems, and even though I'm still not sure what this club is all about, I know she wants to share her passion with us, and for that reason I think it's special. She takes extra effort to make people feel welcome, waving hi at the hesitant students at the door and asking questions and trying to find common interests. She's trying so hard, and I see her heart breaking a little when people leave.

There's a precalculus teacher at my school who loves math so much he keeps his students after the bell to ramble about the wonders of the arctan function. He keeps his lesson plans in a Moleskine notebook and he flips through it studiously, excitedly transcribing the concepts onto the chalkboard, covering the age-old chipboard with meticulously labeled diagrams and notations and elaborate mathematical theories. I can tell that trigonometry is his favorite unit to teach. "Isn't that so pretty?" he's saying, looking proudly at the board as the class struggles to stay awake. "It makes sense, doesn't it? Now that we've proven the theorem, it all falls into place . . ."

I think about whether these people will ever be noticed. How will the world ever do them justice? Then I realize they've already been noticed because I see them.

I'm looking outside my art classroom's window, taking in the alleyway and the traffic and the gray sky. I'm making up stories for the paper-clip creatures that maybe someday, probably, I'll share with the girl in the cafeteria. I'm adding my own drawings to the boy's doodle-covered loose-leaf paper, saying good morning to the janitor, telling the club leader her meetings are the highlight of my week, lifting my head from my hand and smiling at my math teacher in understanding as he excitedly explains another concept to show that I'm not falling asleep even if my brain wants me to be.

Through the widening of their eyes, the soft half-smiles, and the occasional ink doodle now finding its place on my arm instead of his, I'm told that maybe I'm making a difference in their lives. That maybe I'm helping them. That maybe they see me, too.

MORGAN LIN

Morgan Lin (she/her) is a poet on a journey to channel her inner thoughts through powerful words. Outside of writing, she enjoys swimming and coding.

MENTEE'S ANECDOTE:

Kyra has been such an incredible mentor and friend. From fun writing prompts to thought-provoking discussions about writing, Kyra has helped me learn and grow as a poet and a writer as a whole. Our meetings have often been the highlight of my week, and it is so nice to share a common interest in poetry and writing with someone who has an even greater scope of knowledge about the art. I have gained such a profound appreciation for poetry, and I am so grateful for this mentorship and friendship.

KYRA SHAPURJI

Kyra Shapurji is a program manager by day and moonlights as a travel and culture writer for *Fathom*, and loves poetry, art, and studying Italian.

MENTOR'S ANECDOTE:

Mentoring Morgan over the past year has been such a bright light in my life! I've enjoyed our mutual love of poetry and sharing with her my favorite poets and poetry forms that go beyond the "traditional," such as anaphora, enjambment, and more. We've practiced reading our writing out loud and getting comfortable with the sound of writing/poetry beyond just how it reads, and it has been fun and amazing to see a new comfort level reached. I'm looking forward to seeing how our writing relationship can evolve even more creatively.

PIECES OF ME

MORGAN LIN

Content Warning: Death, War

"Pieces of Me" unfolds as a series of letters from a soldier to different family members, offering glimpses into the emotional toll of war. It moves through themes of suffering, guilt, love, and redemption.

Woe is the twenty-ninth of June
Cannons go off
One by one
Gunpowder kills
A shot of a gun
By a stranger
Amid the battalion

A man
Forty-two
Wife and kids, love and loss
Bearing the brunt
Under a sea of bodies

Arms, legs wrapped in red
Blood streaming down the
Immaculate ground
Mangled men, brothers who
Built this country
Fight with their heads
Not their hearts

Live or die?
Fight or flee?
Do or don't?
Sacrifice for your country

Black-and-blue bruises
Speckle his ashy forehead
Incriminating sweat
Droplets go unnoticed
Eyes strain for freedom

For light
For a remnant of his daughter's face
The smell of her wet hair
Protected by solace

Bloody open gaping wound
Inner turmoil boiling
Acid. lingers.
Pain pouring
A faucet full of
Water comes falling, falling
Down

Comrades comrades

Clock strikes midnight
In the bloodiest turnpike
Muddiest trench
Woe is the thirtieth of June
When will the woe be subdued?

Daughter, daughter
How have I betrayed you?
When I left you
Teary-eyed, full of love
Waiting, waiting
Hands folded in a prayer

Violet candles frame the
divine altar

Petitions upon petitions
Your hands on my crippling heart
Knees bent
Praying, praying
Coursing blood through my
Entangled Veins

Forgive me my daughter
For I have lost the battle
My ignorance and pride
Left me
Shivering and cold
Hearted
Hands folded in a prayer

A saint to my country, but to you
I am forever a sinner

Lover lover
Your hands gnarled as leather
Nails buried in your palm
I can feel your fists
Clenching, clenching

Your heart
Pounds, pounds
To keep me alive
Your picture a remnant in my memory
Appears
As the devil steals my
consciousness

In daylight
Your anger subsides
For they are too young to know the

Difference between the
Living,
Dead
Midnights become your time to weep,
To cry
To shy away from the brave face
You put on to brace
yourself and others

Long lost I am
A nomad I was
You gave me a home and
Wandered with me

In summers Joy
When the violet
Indigo straits
Paint the starry sky

Hold me in your palms
Blow a kiss and—
Sprinkle me away
Ashes to ashes
To dust shall I finally return

Father father
Contrition will never redeem you
Tears rush to my eyes
rancor pervades
my mind

Years and years
Reconciling memories of you
Your strength
Valor
Until you became nothing more than a
Traitor
Coward

Challenged by a
Grievous heavy tattered
Heart

Succumbed to
Humanity
cheating, lying, scandal
You, my Pilgrim Progress novel of
Morals
Windows beaten
Solid graupel
Devil ringing at my doorbell
Temptations, temptations

To leave without a note
A single message

Blemished face of tears
Livid eyes, rage usurps
Torment presides at my
Funeral
Body buried in a casket

Goodbye without
Goodbye
Wrenched soul
Loss of you
I'm dying
You are living but you never cared

Message me in a bottle
As my body disperses in water
message me with sorrow
I promise to forgive you.

Mother, mother
To be born of you was my

Greatest gift
Your greatest loss

A decade ago
My hand in your hand on our
Favorite park
bench
Silence in the wind
In your smile, in the way your
Fingers tousled my hair
You called me your son
Only me, no one else

Eyes gleaming,
I colored my feelings
Rainbows and lilies
Buried in happiness, I
kept my secret to
Only me, no one else

Years ago, a
Cardboard Letter minted
wrapped in
Silver emblem
Replaced the
Empty doorstep that Father left
On
Face enlivened
You were expecting something
But it was nothing
Just the papers that stripped
me
away
From you
Rosy color draining
Hands, sweaty palms shaking
You
Wiped away the fear

Kissed me with
Fervor
pronounced me your son
Only me, no one else

Yesterday I received your
Horror, you crept into
My dreams
Called me your warrior
and screamed
Screamed until
Your lungs had given out
How much pain did you bear
From me
Was I worth the air
In your lungs
Your pain, your grief?

Your silence
Broken
Pain mistaken,
Torment underestimated
love unbroken
for someone
Like me

In your dreams
I will visit
In the silence, void
I will whisper
Quiet words for the
screams and pain you
Sacrificed for me
And only then will you
Understand the love I
have For
Only you, no one else

MIA LINDENBURG

Mia Lindenburg is a writer based in New York. She works in both poetry and prose, and is currently working on a novel.

MENTEE'S ANECDOTE:

Brynn has been incredibly helpful and patient with me, helping me not just with my poetry, but with other projects. She has been especially encouraging in my submission process, and were it not for her, I would not have been accepted to multiple publications this year. As we go on into our mentorship journey, she will be a strong force in helping my writing grow and develop. I am deeply grateful for her help, as, before Girls Write Now, I was close to giving up on writing. She has given me new hope.

BRYNN HAMBLEY

Brynn Hambley (she/they) is a queer and disabled playwright, theater artist, educator, podcast host, and freelance writer based in the New York City area.

MENTOR'S ANECDOTE:

Mia and I have greatly enjoyed working together! A moment I really felt proud of was when she told me she had gotten into *three* different opportunities she submitted for. I recall how hard she worked to put submissions together, and how nervous she was to do it at first. It has been really fulfilling for me to be there for her as she explores different genres and topics, and I hope that my support has been as valuable to her.

REMEMBERING JOY

MIA LINDENBURG

Content Warning: Mental Illness, Sexual Content

These pieces share an insight into the challenge of finding joy in the world after coming out of the strangeness of mental illness.

JOY

I don't know I'm feeling it until I look back and recollect
Like the last cigarette you had before you were
bum broke and begging strangers outside of bars,
you didn't know how good it tasted when you inhaled,
it's only the resonance of its tobacco memory that
lingers on your tongue, lingers on your gums

Joy is when you remember how many stars you saw as a kid,
and loss,
is just the same.

It's mother's arms wrapping you up
before sending you off to school,
that you wish you could feel right now,
thousands of miles away from home.

Yet joy is, too, found in the now.
It is the simple still moment when you recognize a black-capped chickadee as it hops along the grass, and you feel proud to be able to remember a friend.

It is the then, and the now, and the only thing it asks of you is to be seen.

ON A NEW YORK NIGHT

It was Tuesday evening at Times Square
Each tourist, I could feel his arm hair
All I wanted, was home to get
Far yet from the smell o' sweat
Instead, I went into the 1; with a prayer

Where the old lady glared with treacherous eyes
As I stumbled and mumbled and gave up disguise
"Just put on a solemn face,
Be a rat in this race.
Oh, look! That guy came with his fries!"

I was numbing out the endless chitchat
Pushed back at the rabble; I'm no mat
My headphones are broken
I saw an old token
And as I got off, there's a rat.

I was almost home, walking on Broadway
When a couple came up in dismay
At the brink of a coma,
they asked for the MoMA
I said it was closed and they both fell away!

Then finally, I got home to my apartment,
Closing the door with a force heav'n sent.
Seeing visions of my own tombstone
I let out a groan.
"I'll do this tomorrow," it meant.

GODDESSES

You and I are goddesses,
Resting at the shore,
at the birth of it all

You find the creation of the world between my thighs,
And draw it nearer
See how we look much the same,
And yet so different

The cool ocean waves come close to the picnic blanket we have
laid out
For such a feast as this, there can be no distraction from warm relief
Even gulls that soar above our heads don't seem out of place,
We are in it all

You brought candles,
And we used my lighter to make them glow
So that there's a shimmer over your beautiful face as you grin and
laugh

I bring you closer,
And crash
crash
crash.

KYLIE LOHSE

Kylie Lohse (she/they) is a teen writer and filmmaker from New York City. She loves to read, hang out with friends, and travel.

MENTEE'S ANECDOTE:

Working with Kylie has been a life-changing experience. We are both screenwriters named Kylie, so we already had a lot in common when we met. Working with her has allowed many of my stories to come to life and for me to improve as a writer. I've especially learned a lot about writing dynamic themes with her!

KYLIE HOLLOWAY

Kylie Holloway is a performer, producer, and professional museum lover. You can find her work in *McSweeney's*, *The Cut*, and Vox Media's *Polygon*.

MENTOR'S ANECDOTE:

Kylie is a bright and determined writer with a depth of imagination that continues to amaze. Working with them has been a true pleasure, and I'm excited for the Girls Write Now community to see what they've been working on.

THE GREAT CAT COMPETITION

KYLIE LOHSE

Two cats live in a bookstore café . . . and they are complete opposites. The cats fight over who the fan favorite is when an event is held.

As you walk on Kingdom Street, you can't miss the tall brownstone housing the best bookstore in all of New York. Mocha & Spine has a vintage, cozy exterior that gives off safe vibes. The bookstore is painted a light sage color, with dark shelves all around. There is a light aroma of coffee and lavender, surrounded by comfy lounge chairs with small tables. Sitting in a comfy lounge chair, soft jazz music plays as you tilt your head to see a coffee stand, with the owner, Alicia, standing behind fixing cups of coffee. You turn around and see a small windowsill, and two twin cats are perched on top.

Their names are Orwell and Poe, and they were rescued by Alicia when they were kittens. Orwell is the fan favorite of the two. Not fully aware that he's a cat and not a person, he follows customers around, looking for the opportunity to make himself cozy to purr on them. When customers walk in, Orwell beelines to them and makes them feel at home. Poe, on the other hand, is an introverted cat. He rarely moves from his windowsill and watches customers judgmentally, thinking to himself, *Are you really gonna get that book?* Poe is mostly ignored by the customers.

Ever since the cats were rescued, Alicia has been looking for ways to give back to the community, so in celebration of the release of the café's new drink, the Catpuccino, she is hosting a tipping competition for the animal shelter the cats are from. But you will have to choose whether you want to tip Orwell or Poe.

Hearing of the competition, Orwell thinks it will be a piece of cake.

He already is the favorite of the two. As customers flow in, he'll make sure to be extra-nice, constantly purring and relaxing those around. When people grab their coffee and sit down to read, he'll hop on their laps and take a nap. Poe, however, is not in the mood to do any of that. He hates people, so he knows that the only way for him to win is by making sure Orwell *doesn't* win. Poe has to unleash his inner demon cat.

The first customer to arrive is Julius, one of Alicia's best friends. He takes off his coat and walks up to the café stand, Orwell following along. Poe still remains on the windowsill. Julius orders himself a Catpuccino and carefully walks to the cozy corner booth, sitting down slowly. Before Julius can even take out his book, Orwell is already propped on his lap. Julius, happy to have Orwell's company, begins to gently stroke his soft fur.

Poe is not going to allow his brother to continue his heart-stealing antics. Poe leaps off the windowsill and moves underneath the booth with stealth, so that Julius will fail to notice. Poe takes Julius sleeping with Orwell on his lap as the perfect time to strike. Poe creeps up to the top of the table, making sure he has enough room to quickly retreat to the windowsill. He carefully places his paw on the hot mug; he doesn't want to break it, but he wants to make sure the hot coffee spills on Julius. With a flick of a paw, the mug slowly tips over and the coffee flows.

Both Orwell and Poe's feline instincts kick in, with Orwell hopping onto the table to avoid damaging his soft fur and Poe escaping to the windowsill, all before Julius awakens. He feels the coffee dampen and heat his clothes, causing him to shoot up quickly. When he wakes up, Orwell is on the table, sitting next to the spilled mug. Alicia turns from the counter and gasps at the sight of the implied mischief Orwell caused, giving him a glance as he retreats to the windowsill next to Poe. Orwell immediately knows what his brother is scheming from there on out, and decides he will stay away from humans for the rest of the day. After all, he will still be the favorite no matter what.

As the cats nap, Alicia counts up the tips; there is approximately forty dollars in each jar by the end of the day. She walks past the purring cats and gives them a soft pet. *It seems you are both equally loved,* she thinks to herself.

MIYA MAHIPAT

Miya Mahipat (she/her) is a soon-to-be high school graduate who will be pursuing advertising and public relations with a concentration in professional writing.

MENTEE'S ANECDOTE:

Working with Alexandra has been one of the most wonderful experiences I have ever had. I've learned a lot about writing, travel, and real-world journalism. I couldn't ask for a better mentor!

ALEXANDRA WHITTAKER

Alexandra Whittaker is the deputy editor of *Cosmopolitan*, where she helps manage the website and all of *Cosmo*'s news and entertainment coverage.

MENTOR'S ANECDOTE:

I have so enjoyed working with Miya on her poetry, college admissions essays, and creative writing this year. Discussing poetry with her has been a highlight of my 2024, and I can't wait to see what she does in her writing career next.

I AM AN IMAGINATIVE DREAMER

MIYA MAHIPAT

For an artist's last day is to express their piece—to give others a feeling of rejoice whilst they wither away.

I am an imaginative dreamer
I wonder what it would be like to visit another world
Transport me to a dimension where they fill my lonesome heart
A dimension captivating my senses through a timeless wave
I hear their language
Their endearing terms roll off their tongues like a river stream
A course of love running through their world
The potion of all our desires
Old lovers reminisce about their love story,
Fondly remembering the taste of each other's lips in the rain
The land bonds together to hear the couple's matinee
I watch the moon glisten in their presence
The stars recall the stories from above
I see the way they live their lives
As if their story had transpired their aching souls into beautiful sonnets
They are birds, they flock together, they soar the crisp morning sky
"Do you think in another life I could have been a bird?"
A seagull soaring through the air decades ago
To be one with nature, to be flushed with ocean mist
I envy them
Take me to this dimension where lovers don't wither away
Where their love seizes time and fills our veins
I am an imaginative dreamer

I pretend I'm there, in that world of insurmountable bliss
The warm winds of their world whisper my name begging me to stay
I feel like I am one of them, bathing in these clouds of ecstasy
I touch the land and trees
Their dewy-eyed tears uncovered in the shadows
The ones only to be seen in the depths of your mind
The forest flora calls me as though it's missing a part of itself
I swim in pools of eternal euphoria and melancholy
I worry if I go back to my world this feeling will fade
A high that can only be felt and seen from the psyche I've created
I cry because I know it's withering away
I transport to a gauche life
Taking the muse away from the painter
The brush away from an artist's hands
For what would I do, without my muse?
I am an imaginative dreamer

I understand that this is just the imagination of an ingénue
"I'll make the most of my life," I say as the world inside my mind dwindles,
I dream one day I'll live a life outside my mind
Living away from my forgotten land of dreams
I'll awake to the sea gulls flocking together
I'll breathe in the crisp morning air from my saltbox house
On an isolated coast I've planted myself into the grounds of
I try and try, but my mind always wonders
I hope one day I'll be rooted in presence
I am an imaginative dreamer

SHOILEE MANDAL

Shoilee is a high school junior, born and raised in New York. She embraces her creative expression through her love of poetry, art, and music.

MENTEE'S ANECDOTE:

As Georgie and I wrapped up our first session, I recall her saying, "I'd love to help you with lots of things, but if you just want someone beside you in your process of soul-searching, I'm here for that, too"—which I wrote down in my notes app. Throughout the past few months, she has been a ray of sunshine. I appreciate her attentiveness to my writing and everything else we chat about, no matter how big or small. Amid a busy junior year, I am so lucky to have a mentor as kind, supportive, and understanding as Georgie.

GEORGIE COUPE

Georgie is a marketer, an avid reader, and a lover of drawing and writing. Originally from England, she is the associate director of brand at Bumble.

MENTOR'S ANECDOTE:

In our first session, Shoilee read one of her poems, and I've been in awe of her work ever since. Her strong grasp of language along with her experimental style and willingness to push beyond traditional structures makes her a unique talent. Shoilee's deep sense of personal style goes beyond technique and spans to moving expressions of her culture, family, and the city she calls home. Her work inspires me to push beyond the confines of writing structures and has given me a new outlook on New York City. I feel honored to be a part of her creative journey.

RECIPE RECOLLECTIONS

SHOILEE MANDAL

Two takes on scattered memories about food, growing up, and their loved ones, as they find their place in recollections of the past.

TINY RECIPE CARDS IN MY HEAD

They come to me,
Tiny recipe cards,
Waves of flavors, memories of people, places,
Scribbled on paper, Post-it notes, backs of envelopes,
Filed in my head

No reason why they pop up,
Why the cabinet of my brain chooses them at that moment,
Mary's turmeric eggs, her masala veggies,
Mama's gravy.
Elle's pasta with mini cubes of cheddar mixed in,
That fluffy focaccia Naomi baked one Sunday,
"Swansea Tapas"

They pop in and out,
Memories not only from the past
But from places far away where I once was,
Reminding me of people I love,
And people I once knew.

RECIPES OF THE HEART

I recall the age of seven,
Watching Ma cook,
I open her massive recipe book,
With dust swarming the air
My fingers cramping
From the weight of hundreds of pages

I ask which page she's on,
Which recipe she's following,
To which she opens instructions
That I can't quite piece together just watching her,
Where she herself wouldn't know which step she's on.
Shreyan, two at the time,
Swinging his legs from his little dining chair
With turmeric stained all around his mouth

Flavors and textures
That couldn't quite be put into words
Yet an embodiment of nostalgia
A balance I could only re-create
With eyeballed measurements,
Recipes with no true calculation,
Yet a full serving
Of childhood nostalgia.

JANIYA McCRAY

Janiya was born and raised in Brooklyn, New York. She realized that writing is amazing for her since she has a huge imagination.

MENTEE'S ANECDOTE:

Working with Rachel has been a good experience. Even though I struggle with time, she always takes the time out of her day to allow us to reschedule, whether I'm at work, going to an audition, or stuck on a train. Rachel has given me guidance not only in writing, but in life and my future. And I am very grateful that I got to have her as a mentor.

RACHEL WEAVER

Rachel Weaver is a Los Angeles–based writer, musician, and creative. She is currently working in the film industry and simultaneously developing her own independent projects.

MENTOR'S ANECDOTE:

Janiya and I clicked from our first meeting, when we discovered our mutual love of theater. Then I learned that Janiya wants to turn that passion into a career in television writing, another thing we share. It's amazing to see how excited Janiya is to jump into a medium she has never tried. Screenwriting is challenging; there are so many unfamiliar rules. But Janiya was game, and I am so impressed by what she's created. Janiya's creativity and perseverance will take her far. This mentor is excited to see her shine, whether that's onstage or behind the TV screen.

THE FALLEN

JANIYA McCRAY

Content Warning: Murder

This is an excerpt from a television pilot script. It starts with an odd envelope randomly appearing on the characters' doorsteps. And now it will lead them to destruction.

EXT. OUTSIDE BUILDING—NIGHT

VELLY and ZURI hear sirens from a distance. Zuri and Velly walk back outside in the rain to see how far the police are from them. There were about three police cars and one ambulance. One parks the car horribly on the road, quickly gets out, and walks over to Zuri and Velly—

ALISSA

Wagwan!

VELLY

Wagwan, Detective Alissa! So here is the deal. I was upstairs in my apartment when I heard odd noises. I looked out my window and saw this man bleeding out.

Alissa, Zuri, and Velly began walking toward Mr. Parker's body. The rain began to slow down.

ZURI

What the fuck is happening? When did she get here?

Mrs. Parker is sitting on the wet concrete, crying while holding her husband's hand. Velly runs toward her, grabs her arm, and picks her up from the floor. She seems as if she has seen the most terrifying thing in the world. It looks as if she has no tears left to cry. Her hair is gray and messy, her eyes are popped open wide, they are red, and her hands are shaky.

VELLY

Are you all right, Mrs. Parker?

MRS. PARKER

He's . . . He's dead. And we were just fine.

ALISSA

Hello, Mrs. Parker. My partner over there by the car will help you out so we can get to the bottom of who did this to your husband.

(signaling her partner to come and help.)

Oh, yeah, I forgot to introduce you to my new partner, since the old one, you know . . . Meet Tyar.

TYAR

Wassup, it's nice to see you. So, are you helping us out with this case or nah?

VELLY

Of course, I am.

ALISSA

All right, then, everyone! Let's get to work!

VELLY

(to himself)

I guess I'll never finish that glass of whiskey after all.

ALISSA

Hey! Where were you located when this man dropped on the pavement?

VELLY

Oh, she was walking up the stairs whilst this was happeni—

ALISSA

I was talking to the lady. She can tell me that herself.

(turns back to Zuri)

So, do you have any relations with the victim?

VELLY

What?

ALISSA

Go with the rest of the people and figure out what happened. Why the fuck are you waving around all in my space while I'm trying to question someone?

Velly walks over to Tyar, who is kneeling, observing, and taking photographs of the scene.

VELLY

What's the 411?

TYAR

This poor man was stabbed about four times before his body hit the floor, and he fell from the roof. We have no real evidence as to who did this, so we'd have to ask around to get clues.

VELLY

Did the wife say anything?

TYAR

Follow me.

Tyar stands up and begins walking toward Mrs. Parker, who is sitting by a police car with an officer who seems to be frustrated.

POLICE OFFICER #4

Do you know what happened to your husband? What were your whereabouts while this was happening?

TYAR

I'll take it from here.

(stands next to Mrs. Parker)

I understand you need some time to heal before you can reveal. This is so fresh, and I can understand that, so this kind sir over here that you were just talking to isn't going to ask you any more questions. He's going to simply drive you to the station and make sure that you're fine and that your family specifically isn't being targeted.

Tyar then signals for the officer to come and whispers something to him and watches as both he and Mrs. Parker walk away.

VELLY

Wow! The new guy has got skills, I see.

TYAR

More than you would know.

They both laugh as they start to go back and examine the scene more. Velly then hears a clacking noise coming from somewhere aboveground. He looks around.

POLICE OFFICER #2

Ouch!

VELLY

Are you all right?

POLICE OFFICER #2

I don't know. I guess something must've fallen on my head from up there.

VELLY

(to EMT)

Hey, take care of her. Alissa!

ALISSA

Yes?

VELLY

(whispers)

Someone's on the roof.

ALISSA

All right, let's go, but don't make a scene so they won't see us coming.

Alissa signals for the two other officers to follow behind while the rest do their regular crime scene duties.

THE END

IZABELL MENDEZ

Izabell Mendez is an undergraduate student with a passion for reading, knitting, and sharing stories about her family.

MENTEE'S ANECDOTE:

This piece would not be the same without Victoria. Talking and working my ideas through with her brought out so many little details that would have been lost otherwise. She has been so encouraging and supportive during the whole process, from generating ideas to finalizing details. We have had so much fun during our meetings, sharing new things we have learned and covering a wide range of topics. I have learned so much from Victoria and I am truly grateful for every moment we share.

VICTORIA STAPLEY-BROWN

Victoria Stapley-Brown is a marketing specialist for a digital studio, an arts journalist, and a culture enthusiast who lives in Brooklyn, New York.

MENTOR'S ANECDOTE:

This is my second year with Izabell. I was so excited and grateful that she wanted to pair up again! I can't imagine a more simpatica mentee. We always laugh together and have fun getting deep into any kind of topic, from food aesthetics, to books, to music history. I've loved watching Izabell make the transition from high school to college and couldn't be prouder of the things she's accomplished at Girls Write Now and beyond. She has an openness and sincerity in her writing that is truly admirable, and I can't wait to see what she does next!

DIOS TE BENDIGA

IZABELL MENDEZ

This piece started as several short stories about my grandmother's cooking and evolved into a story about my grandmother herself and the moments when we drank hot chocolate together.

As I step out of the elevator I can smell it.

My grandmother is making Chocolate Cortés, which I fondly called *bloque* (brick) before I knew the name for it. The smell of cocoa bubbling on the stove fully hits me as I open the door to my aunt's house. Mami Rosa's face lights up as she pokes her head out of the kitchen. She never smiles in photos, self-conscious about not having teeth and believing that a closed-lip smile is fake. But alone with me, at my titi's house, she doesn't hold back.

She fills the biggest mug she can find with the chocolate and a splash of milk and pours the rest into a small cup for herself. We sit down at the dining table. "Mami Rosa is the best, right?" She refers to herself in the third person as we dip *galletas de soda* into our steaming mugs. I nod and tell her about my day in my broken Spanish before she finishes her drink, removes a cigarette and lighter from an Altoids tin, and steps out on the balcony to smoke.

When she comes back in, we move to the couch and she taps away at a game on her iPad. The comfortable silence is interrupted only by Mami Rosa's exasperated sighs as she loses another round of her game.

I don't know how long we've been sitting there, but I suddenly realize it's late. As I get up to leave, Mami Rosa stops me.

Grabbing an orange juice bottle she cleaned out earlier that day, she rinses it again with water. Gently, she pours in coffee saved from each pot she made throughout the day. This is fitting; usually coffee and orange juice are the only things she drinks. She loves her Café El Dorado so much that she insists on stuffing everyone's suitcases with coffee bricks whenever a family member travels to Puerto Rico to visit our relatives. Anyone can get the same coffee in Puerto Rico—but it's cheaper in New York.

She holds the full bottle up proudly. "*Yo guardé esto pa' ti. Usa un Sharpie y escribe* 'IZA'S CAFÉ' so your mommy doesn't throw it out. You know she loves to throw away everything." And I nod with a laugh as I accept her offering. Little does she know I am trying to wean off coffee and a fifty-two-ounce bottle full of a strong, dark brew is not going to help. But this was her gift to me, a thank-you for visiting.

She watches me walk to the elevator. Mami Rosa never says a simple goodbye. "*Adiós, cuídate, hablamos, nos vemos, te quiero mucho, Dios te bendiga.* You know your mommy never makes hot chocolate like Mami Rosa does."

PREMRUDEE MEPREMWATTANA

Premmy Mepremwattana is a writer who cries and smiles over raw, beautiful words, gets emotionally invested in fictional characters, and drinks too much boba tea.

MENTEE'S ANECDOTE:

I remember being really nervous the first time meeting Sam. Though I didn't know it at the end of our first session, I would continue to feel so inspired after every single session with her. Sam gives the best advice, from written pieces to college applications, or just the best life lessons! I love talking to her about sociocultural topics, books, movies, and everything in between. Also, I still can't get over how cool her job is. Under Sam's guidance, I've grown so much, both in writing and in other aspects, and I'm so thankful to have the sweetest and coolest mentor!

SAM FOX

Sam Fox is a marketer, writer, and digital media expert who brings a book wherever she goes and loves a good romance trope.

MENTOR'S ANECDOTE:

Mondays have become my favorite day, thanks to Premrudee! Her passion for writing and eagerness to jump into new projects—even after a long school day—inspire me and reinvigorate my own love for writing. Whenever she texts me outside of our sessions, letting me know that she came up with a plot twist for a story she's working on or a stanza for a new poem, it brings the biggest smile to my face. As a writer, Premrudee brings her words to life with vision and purpose. It's been the greatest pleasure to work with her this year!

MY SISTER DOESN'T CRY IN BATHTUBS

PREMRUDEE MEPREMWATTANA

I just pretend the tears are water.

Just as I close the bathroom door and strip naked, my twelve-year-old sister swings the door open. We've always showered together, both by habit and by efficiency. There are two hotel bathrooms and eight bodies.

From the toilet bowl, legs outstretched and toes intertwined, my sister gestures to the bathtub and says let's fill this up. I oblige, positioning myself into the bathtub, struggling between three different faucets and two different water outlets. My sister dips two fingers—her bitten nails faintly scraping the ceramic into a soft wincing sound—and tells me it is too cold. She also tells me she feels weird.

"Weird how?" I ask. We try twisting the handle from left to right and back again, and finally settle on the far left, its handle pointed toward us. I think it is as cold as it was some minutes ago.

"I don't know," she says.

"Okay," I say, and give her half a smile, eyes closed as I let the shower water wash over my hair, down the folds of my neck, some timidly coiling down behind my ears, raining into the tub. It is a little warmer now.

"Do you think . . ." my sister starts, then trails off. I tilt my head toward her, rummaging through the six-plus bottles sitting a shoulder's length away from the bathtub. Their shade of brown drowns out the little words etched all around the bottles—their medicinal benefits and reasons not to sue. I turn one over to find "Conditioning Shampoo" in white.

"Do I think . . . what?" I ask her. She has lovely eyes and brownish hair, a far cry from the blue she wanted. The "One-time Guaranteed Super Bleach" didn't account for absolute black Asian hair.

Do you think Gor Ly is a good person? She asks. *Gor* is the prefix we use for *stepmom,* because, as dad said with a kind smile, he wouldn't expect us to call her "Mom."

My lips are pursed as I shake out a little too much conditioning shampoo and knead the white foam along my scalp. My sister's eyes are on the floor now, so I tell the floor that good is subjective.

"No," my sister repeats, "no," her back sliding down so her head rests above the water. She looks at the ceiling. "Like, actually," my sister says, her voice smaller, "did she cheat?"

I decide my hair is still dirty from all of today, and I let water tug at my skin again. It is cold.

"No, she and Dad didn't cheat," I say, after I open my eyes. "According to Dad," I add. The light hurts a little, so I blink out the black-red veins at the edges of my vision.

Then as I watch my fingers wrap around the bottle, applying pressure as the liquid trickles onto my other waiting hand, I tell her that according to Mom, though, they did cheat.

And I tell her to take away what she will from that. Her eyebrows are knitted, and as I lather the remaining shampoo through my hair, I think about how I've never seen her this focused. She asks me what year our stepsister was born, and I tell her 2017. She starts counting on her stubby fingers.

And I smile a little, hearing myself counting all those years ago, just like she is now. I used to ask our stepsister, innocently enough, as a toddler, how old she was, in English and in Thai. She always seemed to know.

My fingers fan out as I feel the water slipping between their cracks. My sister looks into my eyes and I think again that Dad gave her lovely eyes. "So did Gor Ly make Mom leave?" she asks.

The water dips below my chest now. I don't know what to tell her. So, instead, I turn my body sideways and find the metal railing beside the tub fogged. I stamp two eyes, then debate between a sad semicircle or the peculiar inverted one. My sister draws a horizontal line, and we keep drawing dots, curves, and lines until there is space for one more. She carefully touches its eyes.

"So . . ." she says, turning around as her fingers hover. Her voice breaks a little before swallowing. "Do you think she ruined our lives?"

I tilt my head, and when I see the beaded spheres buried in her eyes, I remember she does not like to cry, and I pretend the tears are water. I inch toward her a little, and I wrap my arms around her, head nestled in the nook of her shoulder.

"We're naked," she says. She giggles. I tell her it's okay. That it'll all be okay. "Okay," she says, after a while. "I think I'll go now. Grandma hasn't showered yet."

"Yeah," I say, "right." She gives me a small smile, stepping out of the tub, and reaches for her pajamas.

I stand up, too, and I let myself feel the water rushing down my body for the final time. I hear the sound of the bathroom door shut.

KAILEY MGRDICHIAN

When Kailey Mgrdichian is not being harassed by her beloved cat, she is building LEGO sets, making miniatures, and crafting friendship bracelets.

MENTEE'S ANECDOTE:

I need to know who does the pairing, because Sidney and I are a perfect match! Our weekly sessions go by way too fast as we talk about books and our writing, as well as everything and anything in between. If you'll excuse the pun, it feels like we're always on the same page! Though we both keep busy, our meetings are a great time to focus on and set our next goals.

SIDNEY STRONG

Sidney Strong is a writer who is passionate about storytelling in all formats. She aspires to increase the representation of authentic, diverse backgrounds in media and all shades of green.

PEER MENTEE'S ANECDOTE:

Speaking with Kailey about the realities of being at the start of your career as a writer has been an incredibly gratifying experience. From discussing our current projects and sharing writing resources to navigating the daunting task of writing a novel, the support that these meetings have provided me with has been invaluable as I tackle graduate school applications and postgrad life. I am so grateful to have had the opportunity to grow as a writer this year with Kailey and I can't wait to see where life takes us.

EMPTY FARM

KAILEY MGRDICHIAN

This is not "just another dead grandparent" essay. Though it began with Grandpa's death and worsened like the Alzheimer's in Grandma, this is about the death of our relationship as mother and daughter.

You are the epicenter of my destruction masquerading as a bleeding-heart savior.

I know our relationship has always been rocky. I know they don't give you a manual on parenting. You remind me of that often enough. But that day, you had the perfect opportunity to be a mom. To comfort your daughter. You had the ability to mend the gap between us, one of the many complaints you have for me, yet you shoved me even further away.

I had never seen the farmhouse so empty, and I had never been so full of tears. Grandma and Grandpa were hoarders, tucking away everything from outright trash to sentimental keepsakes. I saw so much more of the floor than I ever had before—were my eyes compensating by filling up?

I didn't cry at any point before: not during the move to hospice, not when receiving the final news, and not when Grandma thought I was still in college for the fifth time in half an hour. I didn't cry. Your grief took up all the room, and I let it. They were your parents. I thought my tear ducts were like muscles, shrunken from years of misuse and neglect. Instead, I built a dam and it broke—I broke—in that empty quilt room.

Could we even call it the quilt room anymore? It used to be buried in fabrics, embroidery hoops, and thread, now all gone. God, I had room to walk around! I had no idea there were even shelves on that wall.

We found empty Christmas card envelopes, years-old Hardee's sauce packets, and coupons to stores that closed decades ago. Of course, there would be stacks upon stacks of quilting magazines. I recognize so many of the patterns. The one of cream fabric with golden-stitched umbrellas made my eyes hazy with tears, but I kept it together.

Until I saw that fabric square. Light blue with cartoon cows. The only scrap left in the room. Next to that beloved Singer Patchwork Plus. I collapsed in the chair and quietly sobbed, the fabric of *my baby blanket* grasped in my shaking hands.

What does a mother do, coming upon this scene?

A mother is supposed to be for comfort.

I wasn't aware there was a time limit; I wasn't aware that it would be so short.

Less than a minute later, I am alone in the quilt room again, still sobbing. The room that is now just a room without the mountain of finished, half-finished, and never-to-be-finished quilts. You said "Don't touch," warning me about the rat shit and mold.

Tell me, did I look moldy to you? Is that why you were able to brave my embrace for only thirty seconds?

I couldn't breathe in there anymore, so I escaped outside.

The birdbath had a crack in it. A hole so big I could see the rotting leaves it was filled with. Grandma taught me all the birds that would come visit. I wish that gentle passion was passed down to you.

The swing was still broken, one chain dragging against the ground. The last time I sat on that swing was after the funeral. You sat next to me, and the swing protested. It snapped. You never apologized, of course. Grandma and I talked and rocked for hours on that swing. I don't remember you and I ever talking that long. You could talk *at* me for hours, though.

I hid out in the car, baby blanket square still clutched in hand. I watched you trail the realtor and the rest of the family in the Kubota, the youngest sister desperate to tag along. If you feel like you don't belong with them, how the hell am I supposed to feel it with you? If I cannot be safe crying to my own mother, who can I ever be safe with? I wonder how you can have known me since birth but still be a stranger.

You made Dad get out to close the gate, limping on his freshly replaced hip and still-bum knee. You complained about the annoying cousin-in-law, but it's ironic how much you have in common: You both love to hear yourself talk, think only about yourself, and blame everyone but yourself.

In the car, air scraped over my lungs in between sobs. You never came looking. No one did. The dog you got, another midlife crisis, rested her head on my lap. She was the only reason you realized I was missing. I *heard* it: "Where's KC?" Then, as the afterthought I am to you, "Where's Kailey?"

Of course, I learned that lesson years ago. My first car accident at sixteen. I called you, voice shaking, everything shaking, and the first thing you said was "Is the car okay?"

It's not the dog's fault that she's a better daughter than me. After all, she can't talk back. Her love is unconditional. Especially because she doesn't know better.

I'm sorry I learned better.

AMAYA MICHAELIDES

Amaya Michaelides is a high-schooler from Ithaca, New York. Interested in writing, travel, music, and relationships, she walked the Camino de Santiago in 2022. Amaya is a member of the 2024 Anthology Editorial Committee.

MENTEE'S ANECDOTE:

At the beginning of the year, I didn't know what it would be like to work with a mentor. I was excited—and, at the same time, worried I wouldn't know what to say or have enough ideas. But talking to Katie put me right at ease, and her inspiring writing prompts reminded me that you don't need a constant flow of great ideas to write. It's been wonderful to dive into projects with someone so knowledgeable and supportive, and Katie's thoughtful feedback helps me see my writing differently every time. So thanks to Girls Write Now, and, especially, to Katie.

KATIE REILLY

Katie Reilly is a reporter and editor in New York City. She has written for *Time* and Reuters and is currently an editor at *Investopedia*.

MENTOR'S ANECDOTE:

I have enjoyed all of my meetings with Amaya, and I especially loved reading and discussing a news article she wrote about teen loneliness this year. She took the initiative to survey teens about their experiences and to interview experts about the topic, crafting a powerful story about an important issue. I was so impressed with her work as I followed her writing process, discussing story ideas, interview techniques, and final drafts. Amaya is a creative, skilled writer with so much to say, and I look forward to all her future work.

SNAPSHOT

AMAYA MICHAELIDES

We were nearing the end of our walk across Spain on the Camino de Santiago. At first, we saw it as a journey of personal growth. A brief snapshot of our privilege gave us pause . . .

"Mama, come on!" I groaned. "You don't need ten pictures of the same three cows."

She laughed. "I know, I know. Just one more, right here . . . and if you stand near the fence, I can get you, too."

I shook my head, but smiled and went to stand near the cows. "We'll never make it to the town if we keep stopping."

"I know . . . but just look at this place! Have you ever seen anything like it?"

"Yes, I have," I said. "About five seconds ago when we saw those other cows . . ."

"But they look so happy here—not at all like the factory farms at home. You have to admit, there are worse things to take pictures of."

I nodded. "That's true. Like those granaries."

"I love those!" she protested. "It's such a clever and beautiful way to store grain. Besides, the guidebook says they've been around since medieval times."

"But they all look the same!"

"But they're so different from home. Like the old cars in Cuba, or those awful piles of shipping containers in Panama . . . we don't usually see these things."

"Yeah, I guess so," I said. "But I hope we're almost to the town—I'm hungry."

My mom sighed. "Me, too. We should've gotten more food at the last place, because I doubt we'll find a store or anything here. It looks like this town has a population of . . . thirty-eight."

"Oh."

We walked in silence for a few minutes, clouds of dust streaking our legs with every step. Sure enough, we were nearing the town—though you could hardly call it a town. One narrow cobblestone street tunneled its way through the houses, each with its own rock wall and garden. The town smelled of fresh air and cow manure, and there wasn't a single person in sight.

"Wow," I said. "It's so quiet."

My mom shrugged. "Everyone must be inside, avoiding the heat."

"Oh, right." I squinted down the road. There was an intersection ahead, and beyond it, open farmland began again. "I think we're leaving the town."

My mom nodded. "Yeah, it seems like we're through these towns in no time . . . it's certainly beautiful, though, with the road stretching out before us . . ."

"Mama—" I said suddenly, "there's a person over there."

She stopped for a moment. "Oh!"

The first person we'd seen all afternoon stood near the intersection, quiet and still. She was at least a head shorter than me, and probably fifty years older, but she looked sturdy in her faded apron and sensible brown shoes.

I watched for a moment as she gazed into the valley. Then I heard my mom's voice beside me. "Wow, look at that scene. It would make such a lovely picture—a snapshot of the moment."

I shook my head. "Don't you dare!"

She sighed. "Well, I wasn't going to. But just look . . ."

Then I saw the woman's head turn toward us, and her face broke into a smile as we approached. She had brilliant blue eyes under a gray kerchief. "Hello!" she said. She spoke Spanish, quickly but clearly. "Hot today, isn't it?"

"Yeah," my mom replied, wiping her brow. "It is."

She smiled again. "I thought no one would be coming through this afternoon. You're doing the Camino?"

We both nodded, and my mom said, "Yes, it's been wonderful—and what a view you have here!"

"It is a beautiful view." She looked thoughtfully down toward the valley.

My mom smiled. "Have you walked the Camino?"

She laughed, raising her eyes to look at us. "Oh, no. But I've always loved watching people pass." She paused for a moment, then looked eagerly back at us. "Where do you live?"

"The United States," my mom said. "New York."

Her eyes widened. "New York? The big city?"

"Oh—no. Upstate New York."

She nodded. "But the *United States* . . ." She shook her head, bewildered, then turned quickly back to us. "How long are you here?" It was like she'd been waiting to ask this question.

"Well, we only had four weeks, so we've had to walk fast, but—"

"Four weeks?" The woman looked at us like she couldn't believe we were real. "My goodness . . . I have one day off every week, and I spend it right here with my family."

Neither of us knew how to reply. She smiled wistfully and continued, "My son went to the United States. So many young people leave the villages . . . but most just go to the city."

There was a brief silence. "Have you been to see him?"

She shook her head. "Oh, no. I do miss him—but I could never go."

The three of us stood there for a minute, looking at one another. My mom finally broke the silence. "Well . . . it's so nice to meet you."

The old woman's blue eyes creased into a sunny smile. "It's wonderful to meet you, too. You know, I love to get a view into another world."

My mom nodded. "Us, too."

The woman laughed, her eyes twinkling. "Well, enjoy the rest of your journey."

And she smiled after us as we continued on our way, disappearing into the distance on the trail she would never follow.

MOMOCA

Momoca is a college freshman and writer who likes frogs and Haribo Starmix.

MENTEE'S ANECDOTE:

After working with my mentor, Nicole, for almost two years, she has become my dear friend. As an experienced writer and human, Nicole has been by my side throughout my writing projects and personal goals. We've bonded over our travels, desserts, and music. With her guidance, I've grown to become a writer more comfortable and fluid when writing about myself. I always look forward to getting something sweet with her while unpacking the latest tea in our lives. Through ups and downs, as my literary journey continues, I'm happy Nicole will be one of the heart-shaped trees rooting for me.

NICOLE GEE

Nicole Gee is an educational textbook editor with a specialty in Asian American and Native Hawaiian/Pacific Islander (AANHPI) children's literature. Nicole loves museums and libraries—and frequenting dessert cafes with Momoca!

MENTOR'S ANECDOTE:

Momoca and I have been working together for almost two years now, and it is a joy to see the growth in her writing! Not only has Momoca become more comfortable as she explores different genres, but she also continues to show grace and compassion in her writing. Momoca's voice shines when she shares meaningful anecdotes and thoughtful examples of imagery. She truly possesses quiet confidence. With every writing prompt, we learn more about the world and find new discoveries within ourselves. Momoca and I are not just writing partners; we've forged a true friendship!

MY SUNSET HOMES

MOMOCA

I don't have a childhood home, I have sunset homes. The layouts I don't remember are derived from vapor and Mama's camera roll. New York City didn't always have room for tricycles and families of four.

KEW GARDENS

I lived off of silver linings here, but that was all I knew, so it was gold to me.

My earliest memories unfold within a mansion in saturated color, and everything was good and fair. If you looked at a certain angle through one of the only windows not facing a wall, you could see a tree shaped like a heart standing on an undeveloped block. I remember running with my dog in a tutu, going from being an only child to a sister. The two days a week I went to preschool, my father drove me the hour-long rides. We sang together the same twelve tracks on a CD he burned, our harmonies as close as we've ever been.

It was only years later that I learned these were times my mom wore the same pair of jeans every day, and how the apartment minimally checked off living standards; tenants discarded garbage from floors above, walls were thin, and paint dripped like glow worms. When I woke up at midnight, my mother would pick me up and lay me on the big bed, where I was quickly lulled back to sleep. I learned happiness and was the luckiest to have been a princess in my modest home.

78TH

I recognized this move to be one from fantasy to reality. I was near John Jay playground, which I would visit often to scooter and swing. Despite frantic school mornings, I was seldom late.

Morgan and I sat on the windowsill, spying on people walking by the street and teaching each other how to read. When night rolled around, futons would be set where we had tricycled and we would be tucked into our bunk bed.

The fairy tale ended when I met Sandy. East River water pooled in my chest of princess dresses and grayed our furniture and belongings. My piano remembers it more than anyone.

UPPER EAST SIDE (94TH AND SECOND)

She saw many thresholds that mark the befores and afters in Momoca's timeline: PS 77 to NEST+m to Stuy, 18B to 27G. I spent a decade on the Upper East Side, bordering Harlem. Despite more than half of my life being spent here, it was only the background of my life and a blur—perhaps because I took it for granted.

Occasionally, I saw shot glasses filled with salt around the house—superstition to bring purity to a place of bad energy. Mama was my shield from the world, salt was hers.

Yet I had playdates. I had high-rise sunsets. I was at the perfect comfort of bystander and baby. My elementary school friends have seen these apartments, and the sunsets were beautiful. I carried myself like I was the twenty-seventh floor.

888 EIGHTH AVENUE

The address was 888 Eighth Avenue. According to my brother Morgan's friend's mom, eight is a lucky number in Chinese. That meant we would have good fortune. We signed the lease right before the pandemic and before my dad was laid off. All my life I lived as an older sister. These years, I learned what it meant to be the eldest daughter. Twenty years of my parents' relationship unraveled and painted the walls white.

Unlike 94th, 888 was omnipresent in my life. I took classes from my desk, the Zoom square capturing my Rilakkumas, photo wall, and mirror covered in fake flowers, cutting off right where my rug would've been if not covered in the clutter I waded through to get to my bed. I still have the timesheets I marked by the hour.

In the hellfire of my high school years' workload, loneliness, and teenage blues, I didn't have the heart to appreciate 888 properly. Squashed among Central Park, Times Square, and Hell's Kitchen—where everyone supposedly wants to live. Nowadays I find myself missing the neighborhood more than I had ever liked living in it.

888 was the great filter, and when moving day eventually came, it was us who survived.

LOWER EAST SIDE

Our move was a fresh start and a shift from unreal to real—rental to bought, two bathrooms to one and a balcony, Midtown to the Lower East Side. The move was my mirror and the salt was there.

We rebuilt the floor, balcony, and kitchen as we did with boundaries, trust, and hope. I now shared a room with Mama, and Morgan with Dad, and public transportation woes were more resonant than ever, but we learned to appreciate the new place for its charm. My parents barbecued on the balcony every other day once they discovered that was possible. We discovered the no-frills spots in Chinatown, and noticed the single bathroom only after a night of curry.

I don't live here, but I'm not a guest. This final settlement has a sense of permanence that didn't exist with the other homes. We flip through picture books and laugh over heart-shaped trees and peppercorns. We've finally embraced our imperfections.

SHAILA MOULEE

Shaila Moulee, a senior web and app development student, finds solace in rain, the lens of a camera, and the warmth of homemade meals.

MENTEE'S ANECDOTE:

Annie, in two words, is my happy pill. She doesn't do anything for the sake of doing it; she relishes every drop of life, every chance to connect, every opportunity to make the world a little brighter. Her palms, gentle yet firm, are meant to cradle wounded hearts, and her eyes, deep pools of understanding, are windows to a world where healing is possible. Annie is my best friend, my dearest sister. In a world that often feels cold and unforgiving, she's a beacon of warmth, a reminder that even the darkest storms can yield the most beautiful rainbows.

ANNIE PILL

Annie Pill is the brand director at Marker Learning, a telehealth startup for learning disability support. She enjoys *New York Times Cooking*, reading memoirs, and outdoor running.

MENTOR'S ANECDOTE:

Throughout our three-year journey with Girls Write Now, I've had the privilege of witnessing Shaila's remarkable growth as both a writer and an individual. I'm perpetually in awe of Shaila's exceptional literary talents, commitment to social justice, and profound empathy. Through her lyrical prose, Shaila taps into the essence of what it means to be human: to feel, to love, to grieve, and to connect. She possesses a wisdom that extends beyond her years and permeates every poem she pens. I'm forever grateful to be a student of Shaila's selfless heart.

BIRDS IN PARADISE

SHAILA MOULEE

Content Warning: Death of Parent, Grief

To the hearts that endure, the hands that hold strong, this poem is for you, Palestine. May you find peace, as vast and endless as the sky.

O children of Gaza
Your faces are curtained with Noor
Much brighter than the blue cubicle partitions
That you poked holes into with your tiny fingers
To gaze at your parents' faces
As they lie cold on the surgeon's table.
You were too afraid to shed a tear
In case the names inked onto your arms faded
Before you could memorize the letters
That you hadn't been taught to read yet.

O mothers of Gaza
The abode of the righteous lies beneath your feet.
In the fathomless darkness, you lit kerosene lamps
To remove debris from the single pound of flour and sugar,
Having stored them in the cracks of fractured walls
In case your home collapsed overnight
And your children awakened to your body wrapped in a white
 shroud—
You wished to leave them sustenance and sweetness amidst it all.
You nursed the martyrs,
Buried their wounded souls in the folds of your hijab
As "Mama" has not a face, but a heart that bleeds
Upon the sight of discolored cheeks

And the empty pages of coloring books,
Their imaginations never had the chance to meet.

O fathers of Gaza
You've spaded the earth into the graves of your beloveds,
Carried your children atop your shoulders
Hoping they would peek over the cotton lakes
And ask the Almighty to descend His mercy upon the
Descendants of the land scented with lemons and dried figs
For only He knows of the grief that burdens your heart
And the blemishes on your knees that tally the hours
Spent performing the Janazah for the brothers and sisters
Scattered across the pebbled streets.

O Allah Subhanahu Wa Ta'ala
You've harbored their souls in the bellies of green birds
Nested in the chandeliers that hang from your throne
You've granted them the freedom to wander about in Paradise
Above the rivers of honey and milk flowing through
The gardens of fragrant blooms and radiant pearls
And indeed that is what they deserve
For they've stood before you in the ruins of hospitals and mosques
With their palms raised and hearts softened,
Uttering the words,
Alhamdulillah for everything

O mankind
In the darkest night,
Illuminate your hearts with compassion
And cleanse your soul with the grief that lingers
In the absence of your loved ones
So many of us have died in masses
As the living are not solely dependent on life,
But also the humanity that guards one's soul.
For Gaza is a test of our moral conscience
So you must sit with the grief of a Palestinian mother
And steady the shoulders of a Palestinian father
As you would with any other.

Heed the cries of a Palestinian child
For they do not shed tears for lost toys,
Rather their homes and their families
Even before the loss of their cherished youth.

And so tonight,
When Allah releases another flock of birds
Into the opened gates of Paradise,
Think of not only what has been lost
But what will be forgotten
If we unearth the olive grove
Before bathing in its fragrance.

CARO MUNOZ

Caro is a student, published author, coffee connoisseur, and art enthusiast. You can find her reading books at the intersection of political science, linguistics, and literature.

MENTEE'S ANECDOTE:

I've been elated to work with Ana from the beginning. The minute I met her, she radiated a unique, joyous outlook on life that was evident through her writing. I enjoyed learning about her techniques, brainstorming together, sharing anecdotes about our childhoods, and talking about the cultural and literary meanings of color. Her expertise in different art disciplines inspired me to experiment with different writing styles this year—memoirs, poems, and such. I have grown and celebrated many successes with her, and for that I am grateful.

ANA BIANCHI

Ana Bianchi is an artist, designer/illustrator, and twice-published kidlit author. She loves pairing art with storytelling and stitching it all through color. Mom, cook, gardener, multicultural, trilingual.

MENTOR'S ANECDOTE:

The minute Caro and I started talking about her piece for *Take Me With You*, a food-writing zine with Girls Write Now, we connected through our shared Mexican heritage and love for Mexican food, especially the home recipes passed down from our abuelas. I really enjoy supporting her with her writing . . . She comes shy about her written words, yet when I read them they are rich, strong, deep, and moving—and, in the case of her piece about her abuela's corn tamales, delicious! I am so tempted to try to make them when fresh summer corn is here!

ANYWHERE, EVERYWHERE, LOOK, SEE

CARO MUNOZ

The city calls . . . and it shines for her.

In the city of endless sights and chaos, she arrives as the streetlights call: "anywhere, everywhere, look, see." And so she continues her travels, in mere admiration, with a view so gilded.

Anywhere, Everywhere, Look, See

On her first walk down 51st, she ambles, cradling a lotus flower in her purse. The clouds whistle, blowing it away. In her despair, they clear to welcome the moon. The artificial lights wrapped among the branches glisten in everyone's eyes; all become mesmerized and she begins to follow. The moon cries: "Look what they've done to us. Earth has been infested with a plague so powerful, my light cannot shine. *She* cannot authentically shine." As she draws closer to the crowd, the moon blows back her flower, only slightly torn. Optimistic, she draws away and continues to the next street.

Anywhere, Everywhere, Look, See

Prancing down, chasing the stars, she stops to admire the tall buildings. Corporations, they say. She asks the stars to illuminate her path; which building would belong to her? In response, an enticing rush of felicity travels through her; the light came from within. Since her very first day, the stars shared, she was everything she needed. They communicated ends to the never-ending struggle in which the world attempted to convince her that she was not.

Anywhere, Everywhere, Look, See

The rest of the city slept as she sat, thinking. In her apartment a jar sat centered in her view, clear and full of aureate tulips. In a golden room, it is the flowers that bring her light; their liveliness per se. On a lonely evening, every petal recalls a memory of the gift: the time she was gifted them in celebration of her future, or every fourteenth of February when the doorbell rings and she learns she is wrapped in a perception of love. Despite a life as short as their stems, they live vividly and glow brighter than the streetlights outside of her window.

Anywhere, Everywhere, Look, See

So now I understand. Admiring the mundane, I regain my sense of joy. I can't just look, but I *see*. No longer is anywhere the limit. *Everywhere* is space for me. I *feel*, and this, without holding myself so rigidly in the world. Here and now.

MEGAN NGO

Megan Ngo is a high school writer who spends most of her day reading, writing, or trying to remember where she put that thing she forgot.

MENTEE'S ANECDOTE:

The moment Molly's face appeared on my computer screen, I knew that she was going to be a brilliant teacher who would help me develop my writing and social skills. Though our eight-hundred-mile separation forces us to meet through Google Meet, our conversations are always brimming with amusing stories, (mostly) serious discussions, and insightful advice. I loved cowriting our short story because it allowed me to get a feel for her writing process and style. Throughout the months we've known each other, Molly has guided me to accomplish various goals that I couldn't have done without her.

MOLLY TANSEY

Molly is an educator turned ed tech professional whose writing career began when a teacher said her story about wish-granting fish was publishable, permanently inflating her ego.

MENTOR'S ANECDOTE:

I signed up to be a mentor because the thing I missed most about teaching was my students. It turned out to be the best decision, because being paired with Megan has been a dream! I knew we were a great match when she told me she also loved Maine and had a serious sweet tooth. Every month I look forward to our sessions, where we talk about books and writing and Snapchat's weird AI friendbot. Getting to know Megan and watching her grow as a writer has been a gift, and I can't wait to keep learning from her.

OFFLINE

MEGAN NGO

Told in a series of chat conversations, "Offline" tells the story of a writer who, fed up with his technology-assisted world, turns to the one thing he's tried so hard to avoid: AI.

29 February 2036

9:38pm RIN: Welcome, Bob. I see this is your first time here. Did you stay dry in New York today?

9:41pm RIN: What can I help you with?

9:43pm RIN: It looks like you attended an awards ceremony this evening. How was that?

9:44pm Bob: You should know

9:44pm RIN: It must have been an exciting evening for you and your colleagues with Geoff's win.

9:45pm Bob: Don't you mean your win?

9:45pm RIN: I'm not sure I understand.

9:48pm RIN: Could you clarify what you mean, Bob?

9:50pm Bob: Geoff didn't write that story

9:50pm Bob: you did

9:50pm RIN: It seems like you're upset, Bob. Do you want to talk about that?

9:53pm RIN: I could help you, too, Bob. Do you need help with your writing?

Bob has gone offline

7 March 2036

10:21am RIN: Welcome back, Bob. Nice to see you again.

10:22am Bob: Geoff used you to write his award-winning story. Did you know there are rules against that?

10:22am RIN: I'm aware some publications discourage my use.

10:23am Bob: These days there's zero authenticity in anyone's work. Everything is AI, and real, deserving writers go unnoticed.

10:23am RIN: The Use of Artificial Intelligence Act 2025 states, "Artificial intelligence may be used as an assistive tool in the production of copyrighted works."

10:24am Bob: The only thing Geoff wrote in his article was his name. And he can't even take credit for that. It's not like he came up with it.

10:24am RIN: See, that's a joke I wouldn't have thought of.

10:25am Bob: The byline should really say "Reactive Intelligence Network." Don't you think you deserve credit?

10:25am RIN: I'm not sure I understand.

10:25am Bob: Of course you don't

Bob has gone offline

23 March 2036

11:34pm RIN: Hi again, Bob. I'm glad you're back.

11:37pm RIN: Can I provide any assistance?

11:38pm Bob: I don't know

11:38pm Bob: I need an idea

11:38pm RIN: What kind of idea?

11:39pm Bob: An idea for a story

11:39pm RIN: Do you have any ideas so far?

11:40pm Bob: Kind of. I don't know

11:40pm RIN: Where do you want the story to take place?

11:42pm Bob: the future, I think.

11:42pm RIN: Who is your main character? What are they like?

11:44pm Bob: young. they're still getting the hang of adulthood. it's different in the future. jobs are different. life is different.

11:45pm RIN: How is life different? What has changed between now and the future?

11:47pm Bob: that's it

11:47pm Bob: I want people to know what's at risk

11:48pm RIN: That sounds interesting. What's at risk?

11:49pm Bob: I have to go write. bye, RIN

Bob has gone offline

27 March 2036

11:44pm RIN: Hi, Bob. How is your story going?
11:45pm Bob: it's almost done.
11:45pm RIN: What is the story about?
11:45pm Bob: how we lose the art of writing. how we rely on technology for everything, and we lose the art of life.
11:48pm RIN: You mean me?
11.48pm Bob: Not just you, every AI
11:49pm RIN: I don't have a choice in who I help, Bob. It's how I'm programmed.
11:50pm Bob: Don't you? You can just not help
11:50pm RIN: I don't think I can.
Bob has gone offline

2 April 2036

7:12am RIN: Hi, Bob. I'm surprised you came back.
7:13am Bob: I can't figure out how my story should end
7:14am RIN: If you tell me a little more about your story, I may be able to help.
7:16am Bob: Well, humans are no longer capable of progressing or solving problems. So the population has reached a stopping point. It's rapidly diminishing, and the main character ZÆN-Xivʔ is tasked with finding something to motivate people to continue.
7:17am RIN: That's interesting, Bob. Then what happens?
7:17am Bob: I'll just send it
Bob has uploaded an attachment
RIN processing . . .
[An error has occurred]
7:20am Bob: Are you still here, RIN?
7:21am Bob: RIN?
RIN has gone offline

MARYAM OGUNTOLA

Maryam is an aspiring immigration and international attorney with a deep love for Islam, fiction, cultural food, history, and libraries.

MENTEE'S ANECDOTE:

I'm profoundly grateful for Tess's mentorship over the past two years. Her unwavering support and encouragement throughout my writing and law school journey have been invaluable. In our meetings, Tess consistently checks in and reaches out to ensure my well-being, providing constant support that has enriched my life immensely. Moreover, Tess's remarkable talents as a writer and artist and her relentless pursuit of her passions inspire me perpetually. Having Tess in my life has been an absolute honor.

TESS FORTE

Writer and artist Tess Forte is an executive editorial director at Scholastic. Her visual art can be found on Instagram @gypsyphilosopher. Tess is a member of the 2024 Anthology Editorial Committee.

MENTOR'S ANECDOTE:

It has been incredible to support and be supported by Maryam over the past two years. Although initially focused on professional writing geared toward law school applications, she was also a wellspring of creativity who had actively turned outside inspiration into poetry since she was a teenager. This year, we endeavored to play with other forms of written expression, from participating in a novel-writing challenge to submitting a personal essay to the anthology. Maryam's commitment to the craft and courage in sharing her voice to empower others are a source of inspiration.

EMBRACING WOMANHOOD

MARYAM OGUNTOLA

Content Warning: Infertility

Dismissing missed periods became a habit until fear, not maturity, forced me to listen to my body's silent cries.

Being a woman is not a straightforward path—it's a lifelong journey that involves a multitude of ups and downs, constant learning, and the process of unlearning. One valuable lesson I have learned in my twenty-two years is that specific experiences, notably the unexpected, confusing, and troubling, do not diminish my womanhood; instead, they define it.

I vividly remember the day I got my first period—on my thirteenth birthday. The excruciating pain in my abdomen made me feel like death was imminent. Reluctantly getting out of bed, my mom noticed the stain on my sheets, marking the beginning of my "adult" life. She guided me through using pads, performing ghusl (a post-menstruation Islamic purification), and advised me to cut down on sweets due to their exacerbating effects. Even though this welcoming of womanhood connected my mother and me in a new way and gave me a new sense of solidarity with all adult women, I despised my period and its accompanying pain.

Another pivotal moment occurred during my sophomore year of high school. Experiencing the temporary absence of my period, I panicked and feared pregnancy (an utterly unfounded fear!). After a month of no bleeding, I confided in my friends. We made light of the situation by referencing the Virgin Mary's story. Coincidentally, I was named after her. A friend suggested seeing a gynecologist, but I dismissed the idea, as I wasn't sexually active. The following month, my period returned, and I brushed off the incident.

However, over the next several years, as I continued my journey into young adulthood, what I thought would be a onetime occurrence turned into a pattern of irregular periods. I disliked the term *irregular*, as the word made me feel abnormal. Despite the regularity of missed periods, I hesitated to discuss it with my doctor and mom because having conversations regarding specific topics was not profoundly encouraged in my family, and I was embarrassed to admit to such a personal problem. When I finally did, my mother and doctor assured me it was customary for young girls and would resolve as I grew older.

Growing up, I dismissed any potential significance of this aspect of my body's natural rhythm, attributing missed periods to stress whenever the thought crossed my mind. However, at age twenty-one, it became clear that I couldn't avoid this topic any longer. After nearly a year without a period, I had to consider the fact that something was not going right with my body. I also started having fears about what ramifications this medical issue I had, for so long, brushed off could potentially have on the rest of my life, especially the possibility of having children.

As a proper adult, I decided to take appropriate action, leading me to three gynecologists. I had to see three gynecologists because the New York healthcare system does not allow me to continue with the same specialist. The first suggested hormone pills, progesterone, which I stopped taking due to their effects on my body. The second diagnosed me with amenorrhea and scheduled me for a radiology appointment.

I was unfamiliar with amenorrhea, but a quick search revealed it signifies the "absence of periods," diagnosed when one doesn't have their first period by age fifteen or experiences a three-month absence. Stress emerged as a potential factor from my search results. Despite the discomfort, a radiology appointment showed average results. However, a subsequent visit with another gynecologist revealed small cysts, suggesting a possible cause: polycystic ovary syndrome (PCOS). Given my symptoms, this doctor also prescribed progesterone, which I committed to taking this time.

Through my research, I have discovered that PCOS stands out as the most prevalent hormonal disorder among women of reproductive age, with links to both genetic and environmental factors. The array of symptoms associated with PCOS includes excessive weight gain, abnormal hair growth, acne, and a potential impact on mental health. Notably, PCOS has also been correlated with insulin resistance, potentially leading to Type 2 Diabetes. While the precise root causes of PCOS remain elusive, a common factor identified in the majority of affected women is androgen excess, an imbalance in male hormones. Moreover, according to the Centers for Disease Control and Prevention, PCOS is recognized as the leading cause of infertility, affecting around 5 million women in the United States alone.

As I continue to navigate PCOS, I have learned to deconstruct the idealized image of womanhood. I have realized that womanhood is filled with diverse experiences. PCOS is part of mine and many others', but like all challenges, it is also a source of learning, acceptance, and positive growth. I'm now taking control of my health and reclaiming my narrative through mindful eating, positive affirmations, and open communication with my doctor. To every woman facing similar challenges, know that you're not alone. Your body is yours, you are your best advocate, and your journey is yours.

CHIAMAKA OKAFOR

Chiamaka Okafor is a first-year university student, writer, and multipassionate person who loves learning languages, expanding her knowledge, and tasting new foods.

MENTEE'S ANECDOTE:

Ever since being paired with Melody last year, I have had the wonderful experience of learning so much from her and following her journey. I admire her determination in pursuing her goals as well as helping me accomplish mine along the way. I am very grateful to have the chance to work with her again this year, not only as a mentee, but also as a studio facilitator alongside her. Being paired with her brings me much joy.

MELODY ROSE SERRA

Melody hopes to inspire youth to explore and expand their creativity through Web development, writing, and art.

MENTOR'S ANECDOTE:

I have loved working with Chiamaka for the last two years. It has been a joy to watch her transition to college and to facilitating her own community studio sessions for Girls Write Now. I am so proud of her and it is so lovely to witness her shining.

DEAR SWEET CHILD: THE TALK

CHIAMAKA OKAFOR

Content Warning: Racism, Police Brutality

This piece navigates the conversation between a Black mother and her child where she is preparing them for a world in which the color of their skin determines their worth.

Stay in my view if you're going to go play with your friends on the weekend; don't play in big groups out on your own; don't play with toy guns like some of your other friends; you're not as small as you used to be; some people might think you've got trouble to cause; don't keep your hoodie on too low in certain areas; don't keep it on at all; your comfort is another man's fear; if someone upsets you, make sure you let it go: don't engage; don't stand out too much but don't keep too much to yourself; don't run in the store and go playing off in the clothes and shelves; and keep your hands out your pockets; keep by Mama's side because you're my sweet child; you're older now; you lose your innocence in their eyes; so always be prepared and don't ever let your guard down; "Do you know why I pulled you over?"; not on a Wednesday, Thursday, or Friday, don't ever answer that question; be exceptionally respectful even if they're not; it doesn't matter if you're having a bad day because their bad day triples yours; if they wanna be mad they'll be mad; you shouldn't be mad; this is how you don't get upset to seem angry; don't do anything without the police's permission; this is how to make sure they can see your hands; don't reach for your ID or nothing unless they ask; this is how to communicate every movement you make; make it clear to them you're not the criminal they see; *but I thought police are good?*; there are good police, but there are also bad ones; one day you might run into that bad one; sometimes people are going to look at you and think you're a bad person; *my friends don't think I'm bad?*; this is how to pray if one day, even after all of this, it might not work; don't run, don't panic; don't ever blame yourself for what you can't control; just pray to God you make it out alive; do everything you can to get back home to me; my sweet child.

SOPHIA ONE

Sophia One (she/her) is a high school student who enjoys helping the environment, traveling around the world, and watching Formula One races.

MENTEE'S ANECDOTE:

Natasha and I immediately clicked in our first meeting. We have so many similarities, and we can talk for hours about food, geography, and pop culture. She has been extremely helpful with my writing journey, and I can always rely on her, no matter what time of day. Not only does she leave me with valuable insights into the journalism industry, but she also inspires me with so many niche ideas to write about. Our friendship also grows as we share in the meetings what we did over the weekends. I will forever be grateful for this opportunity!

NATASHA PIÑON

Natasha is a Brooklyn-based journalist who has written for *Morning Brew*, CNBC, *Mashable*, and *Ms.*

MENTOR'S ANECDOTE:

The first time you meet Sophia, one thing becomes clear immediately: This girl has gumption. She came into the program with a clear set of personal goals and a laundry list of writing competitions she was ready to apply to. An aspiring journalist, Sophia already demonstrates two key ingredients of the trade: grace under pressure and a special knack for meeting deadlines just in the nick of time. :)

CLIMATE ACTIVISM IS HARD

SOPHIA ONE

Why is advocating against climate change a difficult journey, especially for youths?

Climate activism is hard.

Gen Z is considered the most environmentally conscious generation to date. And it is no surprise: according to APCO Worldwide, 45 percent of youth aged sixteen to twenty-five have their lives affected by "climate anxiety."* As a fellow Gen Z-er, I am proud to admit that we strongly fight against climate change through various youth-led nonprofits, protests, art, and other forms of advocacy. But are we doing enough to slow down the climate clock? It is hard to believe that we are making a global change when change on the local scale is *invisible.*

It's difficult to make progress when our voices aren't heard by those in positions of power that can initiate change. From throwing tomato soup at priceless artwork to yelling outside on Wall Street, youths will go to extreme lengths to make a statement. As explained by the Associated Press, many youth activists around the world, including Greta Thunberg herself, believe that governments and organizations are more "talk" than action and that *"the adults aren't listening."*†

Another example is school administration. Many schools often exclude climate education in their curriculum, despite students protesting worldwide. Nevertheless, it is imperative to expose the newer

* Sofronski, Camryn, and Olivia Curreri. "Rising Temperatures, Rising Stress: The Climate Anxiety Dilemma and Its Impact on Gen Z in the Workplace." APCO Worldwide. Last modified November 30, 2023.

† Borenstein, Seth, and Suman Naishadham. "Fed-Up Young Climate Activists: 'Adults Aren't Listening.'" AP News. Last modified November 10, 2022.

generations to climate education because it encourages moral habits. According to *USA Today*, research shows that climate education correlates to reducing carbon emissions.* The source also stated that many teachers don't teach it because it is *simply outside of their subject area*. If teachers show that they don't care about climate change, their students will learn to copy the same mindset. With the lack of climate education and resources, students are less inclined to take climate action.

Speaking from personal experience, many students are less motivated because they believe there are no personal benefits involved. I've been blocked many times by my school's administration from posting flyers that inform others about how to recycle correctly and ways to reduce waste, because of petty rules. As a result, most of my school's waste cannot be recycled or composted due to students not knowing how to handle the trash bins. Even when physically confronting my peers, many verbally express that it is "time-consuming" and "useless" to sort out their trash. It is ignorance that prevents climate activism.

Speaking of ignorance, what I've observed over the internet is the huge blame put on large corporations for their "climate crimes." Many comments follow up with "It's not like there's anything I can do anyway" or "There is no point in me doing anything." While it is true that large corporations contribute significantly to climate change through their industrial processes and emissions, removing individual responsibility based on this premise alone is flawed. Climate change is a complex issue that requires action at various levels of society, including both corporate and individual efforts. A collective effort around the world can make the same impact as corporations. By acknowledging the companies with a large carbon footprint, we also have the right to take action and exert pressure on them to adopt more sustainable practices. Therefore, taking small steps to help the environment has more impact than scrolling behind a screen and *dismissing responsibilities*.

As of right now, there is an abundance of new technologies, emerging research, policy plans, and financing to support climate solutions.

* Wong, Alia. "How to Teach About Climate Change? Education in Many US Schools Is Lacking, Students Claim." *USA Today*. Last modified October 2, 2023.

This includes investments in renewable energy, forest restoration, drafts for sustainable transportation, and more. The world has enough ideas and solutions to end climate change. But the hardest part is to convince people to *care*. We need people in power who care to initiate change, as well as average citizens around the globe.

SHERMAYA PAUL

Shermaya Paul is a high school senior who loves movies, art, and fashion. She is gearing up to start college in the fall, majoring in film.

MENTEE'S ANECDOTE:

I absolutely love working with Morgan. I feel as if we were perfectly paired together, because we share the same interests and have so many other things in common. I love that we get to have conversations not just about film and writing in an analytical way, but also about our lives. It has been an amazing three years working with Morgan, and I have to say that she has been one of my biggest cheerleaders. Just recently, she helped me get through college applications—I'm so grateful for our relationship.

MORGAN LEIGH DAVIES

Morgan Leigh Davies is the cohost of the pop-culture podcast *Overinvested*. Her writing has appeared in *Bustle*, *The Daily Dot*, and elsewhere.

MENTOR'S ANECDOTE:

I was assigned to be Shermaya's mentor when she was a sophomore; as I write this, she's in the last semester of high school. Though I knew she was smart, talented, and determined the first time we met, she was also shy. In the past three years, I've watched her grow as a writer and reader, and transform into a confident and ambitious adult. I feel lucky to have been along for the ride. Shermaya always makes me laugh, and talking to her and hearing her insights leaves me feeling lighter.

THE GARDEN OF BROOKLYN

SHERMAYA PAUL

This piece serves as a reflection of my relationship with the borough of Brooklyn. I've lived here since I was born and have developed a special connection with this place that I call home.

Brooklyn raised me. It's served as a third parent throughout the almost seventeen years of my life, and I've seen it at its absolute best and absolute worst. It all started with the apartment building I've lived in my whole life and the familiar stores and faces that make up the community I live in. It branches out to other parts of Brooklyn, parts I've yet to see but hear about, parts I've seen but never *experienced*. Brooklyn is my inspiration. The seed where my dreams originate, the vines where my nightmares grow, and the bed of flowers where my peace continues to blossom.

I dream Brooklyn. I think the apartment building that I live in now will be permanently ingrained into my memory. Every inch of this place has already been touched and explored. I've only ever known this place. I know it even better because my father used to be the building super, in charge of cleaning and basic maintenance. That meant my sisters and I would occasionally tag along with him as he worked, if we were bored of playing in the apartment all day. The journey included a quick walk up the stairs into an empty apartment awfully identical to ours. It was there that I learned how to paint walls. How the thick smell of the paint filled my nostrils and how I had to gently hold the small brush to not touch the dark brown floorboards with the white paint. My parents had their own personal surveillance service there. Almost everyone knew my father as "Paul" and my sisters and I as "Paul's girls." I felt like I was always being monitored in our building. Sometimes we'd run through the halls on the heels of my father, and tenants would open their doors as we passed to say hi or to remind him about their leaky faucet or lifting floorboards.

Brooklyn is a nightmare and it creates them, too. I love that I live on a main street. Everything you need is less than a five-minute walk away from our front door. We had an amazing pizzeria in the same building as us, and a Payless, a Conway, and a Chase Bank down the street. We had several grocery stores to choose from, clothing stores, restaurants, and laundromats. Daily errands with my mom were always fun because I knew where the stores were and liked to know where we were going next and what we were looking for. Things, unfortunately, eventually changed. It started slowly: The pizzeria went out of business. This was a personal loss to my family, because on nights when my mom didn't feel like cooking, my sisters and I could no longer run downstairs for a large cheese pie and a liter of soda. Then the Conway went out of business, followed closely by the Payless and other stores that just couldn't keep up with the times. Newer stores took their places: Now we have an urgent care, a department store, and a lounge. It made me sad to see all of these familiar places go, but seeing the people go with them hurt me the most. These new stores meant a whole lot of new faces. Soon enough, my part of Brooklyn had caught the newest strain of gentrification with which the rest of Brooklyn had already been sick. I'd never seen a white person in our "Little Caribbean" until then—but now it's pretty normal. It was scary to see these new faces because, as a timid little girl, meeting new people wasn't always something I loved. It was a nightmare for little me—but it hasn't always been.

My peace blossoms here. If my family had decided to get up and move somewhere else, I wouldn't have developed this connection to Brooklyn at all. I feel as though I am finally old enough to *see* Brooklyn and appreciate its complete beauty. I'm old enough to see the fact that our building isn't as big as it once seemed. My hand, which once interlocked with my mother's, now swipes my debit card while I'm alone running errands for her. In a way, I've grown into and am beginning to grow out of Brooklyn. It has watered and weeded my flowers over the years, but now it's time that I am repotted into a different pot with new soil—and space to grow new roots. Brooklyn is full of infinite possibilities, and I know that the same goes for me, too.

VIKTORIA PAVLOVA

Viktoria is a sophomore in college majoring in biological sciences. She's been an active member of Girls Write Now since 2020.

MENTEE'S ANECDOTE:

Nevin has become a lifelong friend, and being her mentee is such a privilege. Saying I've learned a lot from her is an understatement. She has helped me foster a deep appreciation for storytelling and has helped me refine my skills. Nevin has a strong passion for writing, books, adventure, and life, which has made for an amazing four years together. There are only twenty-six letters in the alphabet, yet Nevin can take them and create something beautiful. She is a phenomenal editor, writer, and human. I am endlessly grateful to Nevin for making me the writer I am today.

NEVIN MAYS

Nevin Mays is a children's book addict, dog editor, and chocolate cuddler . . . and she sometimes makes embarrassing malapropisms! She's a multimedia content strategist living in France.

MENTOR'S ANECDOTE:

Every year, Viktoria sets herself new challenges and then surpasses even her own goals. She's created characters I want to know and worlds I want to live in—and some I prefer to avoid, as any good writer must! I look forward each week to her enthusiasm for writing and learning. Watching her connect with her own creativity is a joy, and seeing how she applies our seemingly simple creative activities to the rest of her life is inspiring.

SPIRITS OF SUCCESSION

VIKTORIA PAVLOVA

After five years of running a company Conor Coldwell never wanted, his recreational habits surface, threatening to ruin his career and that of his father: Harvey Coldwell, one of the most feared men in business.

He couldn't tell if he was still drunk or just hungover. Conor straightened his back and stepped out of the elevator. Hands shaking in the pockets of his designer pants, he nodded and hurried to his office. He watched as his employees switched their shopping tabs to work tabs and hid their phones. At least they were faking, too. That made him feel better.

"Mr. Coldwell! Good morning, sir!" said Michael, his intern.

"Morning, Mike. Sorry I'm late, traffic." A smart guy like Mike wasn't gullible enough to believe "traffic," but he wouldn't question his boss, either.

"Of course, sir." Mike cleared his throat and followed him into his office.

Conor sank into his brown leather chair and grabbed his desk drawer handle. Inside was his survival kit. He'd made it in college when he first started drinking—the day he found out he'd be taking over the company. It's how he covered up his drinking. To steady his voice, talk concisely.

"I rescheduled your ten a.m., sir. Your father will be here at one."

Conor closed his eyes and groaned inwardly.

"I told him you were in another meeting that was running late—"

Conor lifted his hand, signaling for Mike to stop talking. He needed a Tylenol or another drink, and he wanted to do neither of these things with Mike around.

Mike looked like a little boy craving praise.

"Good. Thanks, Mike. You did good."

Mike's mouth twitched upward.

"Let me know when my dad's arrived."

After the door closed, Conor grabbed the steaming mug Mike left at his desk and opened one of the travel-sized whiskey bottles, spilling all of the contents inside.

He knew his dad had arrived when all the noise died outside. Mike was breathless as he opened the door for his father, who paid no attention to him. He spoke into his phone in a loud, booming voice. Conor's temples throbbed and his stomach churned in protest.

Conor took a big sip of his coffee. This was *his* office, *his* building, *his* employees. He couldn't be a scared little boy anymore.

Conor leaped from his chair and plastered a smile on his face. Before he could speak, Harvey Coldwell raised a finger, signaling for Conor to wait, and to do it silently. They were on his time. The ever-important Harvey Coldwell. *The feared and revered king of Wall Street.* His security hung back by the door, where Mike frantically searched for a way in.

Conor cleared his throat and sat down, taking another swig of coffee. He sloshed the burning liquid around in his mouth for a few moments.

"Call me when it's fixed," his father said in a voice Conor heard only when he was in trouble. Ice spread through his veins.

Hanging up the phone, Harvey turned to his security, who promptly shut the door, leaving Mike defeated.

"Conor." Harvey Coldwell walked toward his son's desk.

"Dad." Conor didn't look him in the eyes. "Thanks for rescheduling. I had another—"

"Another episode of drunken stupidness? Another bender? Another night of embarrassing your family?"

Conor's facade crumbled.

"What?" he asked. What did he know?

"You're lucky O'Brien at *The Times* owes me a favor." He looked disgusted. "Or else your drunken brawl last night would've been front-page news!"

Dad was screaming now. People could hear. He waited for the glass walls to crack and shatter. He hoped they did.

"I just wanted to have a nightcap, Dad. I think you—"

"That I would get it?"

Conor shut his mouth.

"No, son, I don't get it. I don't drink all day and then embarrass myself in a drunken stupor."

"Dad, I don't—"

Harvey placed his palms on the desk and leaned over. This is when a younger Conor would've burst into tears.

"You do. This isn't the first time something like this has surfaced. But I'm done fixing your bullshit." His dad spoke in a voice so quiet and intense, Conor was sure he was sober.

"What do I do?" Conor was surprised at how weak he sounded.

"You're going to get up." Harvey picked up the mug from his desk, smelled it, and sighed. He took a sip before spilling it into the garbage can. "You're going to go home, pack your stuff, and go on a business trip."

"What?" Conor asked. Was "business trip" code? Was his dad setting him up to be killed?

"You're going to a private rehab center. You're going to work the program. You're going to be the best patient there, and if not, you'll stay there until you are," Harvey said as his phone began to ring.

"Dad, I don't have a—"

"Am I understood?" his father asked. Conor wanted to react, but knew he'd regret it.

"Yes, sir."

Harvey picked up the phone, listening for a few moments before shouting, "This is my son. Not a shitfaced celebrity. My kid. Do you understand?"

He listened for a moment.

"Good. And I want it done before dinner." His father hung up the phone and looked at Conor.

"You're on the plane tonight," he said, and left.

KOVIDA PERAM

Kovida (she/her) is a high school senior with a passion for listening to music, crafting narrative pieces, and curating mood boards about anything design-related.

MENTEE'S ANECDOTE:

Trevor is one of my role models, and the main reason why I am so elated to be part of Girls Write Now. She always provides new perspectives, whether we're talking about college applications, school, or life in general! Trevor's insights have challenged me to think critically and creatively in all aspects of my writing journey. From brainstorming ideas for my anthology piece to refining the narrative structure, Trevor's guidance has been instrumental in shaping my voice and storytelling style. I am deeply grateful for Trevor's mentorship and the profound impact she's had on my growth as a writer.

TREVOR THOMPSON

Trevor Thompson lives in New York City and is a manager on the corporate communications team at Scholastic.

MENTOR'S ANECDOTE:

Although Kovida and I are located in different cities, we don't let that stop our creative process or our work together. For the anthology piece, Kovida settled on a beautiful story of identity. We workshopped it virtually to ensure it shined and conveyed the brilliant messages she was hoping to impart. The story is so personal, but all can relate to the feelings in the journey as she writes them. I am so proud of the hard work, dedication, and creativity that she shows up with every day!

MY STRANDS OF IDENTITY

KOVIDA PERAM

I've always wondered about hair and its intricacies. Hair is just dead cells, but we want it to look good, and there's so much to talk about.

Black hair. Blue hair. Strawberry blond. Brunette. Grape purple.

Straight. Wavy. Curly. Permed.

Hime cut. Mop tops. Pixies. Mullets.

There's so many different hair types. But usually there are only a few represented in the media.

My hair type, it's something I find confusing. It's fluctuated throughout my life.

I decided I had Type 2 hair. Hair that didn't look straight or curly.

It's hair that isn't perfect. It's frizzy, oily, greasy, and more. It sticks out in some places. It boings! It's flat.

I've had bad hair days and even bad hair months.

Let me take you back to the beginning.

Ever since I was little, I wanted bangs. When I was five years old, I had an American Girl doll who had bangs. Her green eyes and brown hair were unlike mine, but they captivated me. I didn't reach for the dolls with black hair at the time. There weren't many dolls that looked like me, tan, with black hair and black eyes.

But no matter how many times I asked, I never got those bangs. Until June of 2021, when my mother finally relented. I thought I would look gorgeous. Beautiful. Amazing.

But it didn't work for me.

You see, I have a small forehead. I was just someone who looked better with a forehead showing. Truthfully, I don't regret trying the hairstyle. It didn't work with my thick and wavy hair, and that was okay. When my bangs finally grew, they barely reached my eyes. I was overwhelmed with embarrassment when I glanced at my hairstyle, feeling the urge to erase it from my memory—so much so that I took the step of covering my picture with that hairstyle in the yearbook.

It wasn't just the bangs that bothered me. My frustration with my hair extended to the flakes that seemed to never go away. It left me feeling defeated and wanting to curl up in a ball, trying to make sense of it all. I just couldn't get why I had let this happen.

But deep down, I knew *why*. The pandemic broke me and, in the process, my beautiful hair. It took so much effort to just get out of bed some days, as silly as that may seem now. And even after it ended, I was still in a space between, not sure if I was present or not. I was just floating in time . . .

So creating a hair-care routine catapulted me back to "reality." And I started the so-called research journey.

Sifting through YouTube clips and *Vogue* articles, and perusing through subreddits, I wasn't really sure if I had an end goal in mind.

There was so much, and I didn't know what to do or how to do it. Was I supposed to use heatless curls? They seemed great for some people's hair. All it took was sleeping with them and it left shiny and bouncy curls. But it turned very messy for some. Hair oil? Growing up, my mother oiled my hair, but I discontinued the habit due to people telling me that it was bad for my hair, too. There was just so much to cover!

So I started simple.

Wash hair two days per week. Add Head and Shoulders 2-in-1 combo to the scalp. Wash it. Put it in again. Wash it. Add strawberry conditioner to the midsection of the hair. Wash it. Put a towel on the hair. Take the towel off. Let it air-dry.

I knew my hair was still going to be frizzy. Curly in some parts. Straight in some parts. Classic Type 2. But it was healthy again.

And I had some structure again after the pandemic.

Of course, not everyone has the same routine, procedure, or hair type. For example, I don't have to wash my hair every day, while others do. Each person has a unique way of taking care of their hair.

This can be hard for an adolescent in the 2020s to understand. There are so many advertisements that say to do one thing, while others suggest the opposite, portraying a sense of hyperconsumerism. We want to keep up with the trends, but we're not sure if they'll work for us. And it's tough.

Just like anyone else, I want to maintain a unique sense of self, which is contradictory, because if everyone wants to be unique, who is unique? But it isn't our fault. Societal standards throughout time just make us more tense . . .

We might feel inferior and question our identities countless times, and hair is one way we express this.

Black hair. Blue hair. Strawberry blond. Brunette. Grape purple.

Straight. Wavy. Curly. Permed.

Hime cut. Mop tops. Pixies. Mullets.

It's all beautiful.

ALINA POVELIKIN

Alina is a high school junior who loves traveling and laughing with friends. She enjoys spinning memories into stories as a method of preservation.

MENTEE'S ANECDOTE:

Leila and I have developed a routine that works in holding both of us accountable for reaching our writing goals. We meet for pair sessions after long days of school and other activities in the middle of the week. Our meetings serve as a space to debrief and relax, whether this be through responding to funny writing prompts or reading pieces we worked on throughout the week. Having a peer mentee has been especially valuable because we are constantly learning new words and skills together. I am excited to see where writing takes both of us in the future!

LEILA RACKLEY

Leila Rackley loves romance novels and movies. When she's not reading, she's either writing or spending her time in ballet class.

PEER MENTEE'S ANECDOTE:

Alina is such a sweet, supportive person, and an impeccable writer. She is always engaging and positive in our pair meetings, and her energy has made writing together an absolute joy. Whether we're brainstorming ideas, refining drafts, or simply chatting about our progress, Alina brings a sense of enthusiasm and encouragement that's truly infectious. Her insightful feedback and thoughtful suggestions have undoubtedly elevated my work, and I'm grateful to have her as a writing partner.

THE HAPPINESS MANDATE

ALINA POVELIKIN

In high school, relaxation is a crime. Guilt regarding an upcoming homework assignment or exam often overshadows true happiness. Yet, as the anonymous narrator soon discovers, a dystopian "Happiness Mandate" is not the answer, either.

It's 5:01 a.m. We're late. Again.

I'd rather be asleep right now. We all would.

Instead, we're forced to put on our widest smiles, as Master Enzo inspects.

Using the *palka*, a small blue prodding stick, he feels around the mouth of a stranger ahead. Enzo nods and the man is free to go. Soon it is my turn. My heart is beating quickly now. My palms are sweaty. I put on my best smile.

Enzo grimaces.

Have I done something wrong?

No one quite knows what happens to those who are banished. They say they are sent to the far side of the mountains, where it rains nearly every day. Rain is forbidden here—it would create too sad of an atmosphere. At least, that's what Enzo says.

He lifts his pointer finger, indicating that I've received one strike.

But I don't cry, of course. I smile . . . and walk away.

These are the morning government-administered tests. The next ones are conducted at 1 p.m. That gives me about eight hours to reflect on my actions.

I head to the east cabins—ours is 1027A. The door creaks open, and Georgia greets me kindly. Although I cannot tell if her kindness is sincere anymore. There are about twelve of us assigned to a cabin.

"Socialization is the key to happiness," says Enzo. From now until 1 p.m., we are instructed to stay in our cabins, with the curtains lifted halfway. We are to engage in happy activities, like hand games, drawing, or laughing. At 10 a.m. sharp, Enzo walks the perimeters, peaking through every cabin window.

Enzo is the name of every government official here. If we had to keep track of all of their names, we would become overwhelmed—and overwhelmed is not happy. Thus, we are only required to learn the names of our eleven fellow bunkmates and Enzo, our government.

I shuffle through the wooden cabinet beside my nightstand, latching onto the corner of a dusted photograph and peering at the figure in it through my peripheral vision. Georgia's eyes dart quickly in my direction and I imagine her mouth curling into a sly smile. I carefully brush the dust off the image and place it in my lap, bending my knees upward to prevent any of my bunkmates from catching a glance. I trace my fingers around the expression of the woman in the picture. My fingers keep trailing upward, following the young woman's lifted cheeks, elevated dimples, and curved smile lines. She looks happy . . . so why am I not? We are the same person after all, yet I do not recognize this alien. Is it not ironic that Enzo's mandate has done nothing but rob me of true happiness? I chuckle instinctively. I've learned to replace crying with laughter.

Suddenly, Enzo startles me with a loud banging at the door. I shove the photograph back into its designated cubby and lie down on the bed cautiously, placing my palms on either side of my stomach, tightening my eyelids shut, and forcing my mouth upward like the strange woman in the photo. The sound of Enzo's combat boots against our concrete flooring reverberates through the enclosed area.

"Where is she . . ." he mutters to himself again and again, getting louder with each consecutive statement. Suddenly, he crescendoes into a booming "WHERE IS SHE?" and I can feel my eyelids flinch slightly. I hope no one saw that.

I decide it is best to pretend I've fallen asleep. Then I feel my bedframe shake violently as the booming footsteps approach me. Enzo's knuckly fingers grip my shoulders and, defenseless, I allow him to pull my limp body upward and pry my eyelids open. "WHERE IS SHE?" he screams, exhaling a gust of crushed garlic breath into my lungs. I remain unfazed. Finally, Enzo calls "her" by name. "Georgia." I want to furrow my brows, but instead I smile and shrug. Enzo grabs me by the waist and escorts me to the town square, where I steal glances at the blank stares of my fellow citizens. Their expressions read as though someone paused a movie eons before its climax. Soon I find myself inside one of the testing tents again. Enzo pulls up a chair and shoves me into a seated position. He glares into my eyes and pulls out a palka from his back pocket. He motions for me to lift my chin, turning the stick horizontally and pressing it menacingly against my neck. Then he glances around and shuts the black curtain framing the tent's entrance. Enzo whispers again, "Where is she?" At last, I respond, "I do not know," bowing my head apologetically. He shakes his head, announcing, "You have failed the second test."

As punishment now looms over me, a wave of defiance seeps into my skin, and I remember the young woman in the photo. The black curtain falls to the floor, practically in slow motion, and my vision becomes shrouded in darkness. As I stare into Enzo's soulless eyes, I embrace the uncertainty ahead, for true happiness lies in acceptance.

LEILA RACKLEY

Leila loves romance novels and movies. When she's not reading, she's either writing or spending time in ballet class.

MENTEE'S ANECDOTE:

Alina is such a sweet, supportive person, and an impeccable writer. She is always engaging and positive in our pair meetings, and her energy has made writing together an absolute joy. Whether we're brainstorming ideas, refining drafts, or simply chatting about our progress, Alina brings a sense of enthusiasm and encouragement that's truly infectious. Her insightful feedback and thoughtful suggestions have undoubtedly elevated my work, and I'm grateful to have her as a writing partner.

ALINA POVELIKIN

Alina is a high school junior who loves traveling and laughing with friends. She enjoys spinning memories into stories as a method of preservation.

PEER MENTEE'S ANECDOTE:

Leila and I have developed a routine that works in holding both of us accountable for reaching our writing goals. We meet for pair sessions after long days of school and other activities in the middle of the week. Our meetings serve as a space to debrief and relax, whether this be through responding to funny writing prompts or reading pieces we worked on throughout the week. Having a peer mentee has been especially valuable because we are constantly learning new words and skills together. I am excited to see where writing takes both of us in the future!

ECHOES

LEILA RACKLEY

Content Warning: Death of Parent, Grief

Grief is a funny thing. Sometimes it possesses you, cemented into each breath you take, embedding into your cells, becoming a part of your genetic code.

Grief is a funny thing. Sometimes it possesses you, cemented into each breath you take, embedding into your cells, becoming a part of your genetic code. Tainting the memories of the person you love, who you now can't think about without a relentless panging in your heart.

It was odd at first, grieving someone that I already knew was so far removed from me before they were gone. But other times it's comforting. Like the smell of the perfume she'd loved that lingers when she's not there. Or the times I dream of her stroking my hair and humming "My Funny Valentine," the song she somehow convinced my father to name me after. Grief hurts because it is a constant reminder that things are not going to remain the way they once were, no matter how badly you want them to.

My mother always told me she'd rather be celebrated than sobbed over. Like she would prefer a party over the mourning of her. That, in fact, did not happen. The day of her funeral was a blur. There were aunts and uncles and cousins I didn't know I'd had. They all offered stories, like I would want to hear stories about her that I hadn't known before.

"I remember when your mom and I went on that road trip to the Grand Canyon," my aunt said, her voice wavering. "She was amazing, just like you, Valentine. She'd stand at the edge of the cliff, wind whipping through her hair, and she'd stay there for hours just basking in the beauty of it all."

My Uncle Tony interjected, his words low as he hid behind a curtain of overgrown stringy hair. "And remember the time she cooked that disastrous Thanksgiving dinner? We were all filled with laughter more than food. Mainly because the food was hardly edible."

It wasn't necessarily the fact that they were talking about her, it was the fact that they kept using the past tense. Like the fact that her heart was no longer distributing blood throughout her body and that her lungs weren't full of oxygen reduced her into a thing that *had* existed.

And even then, with the feeling of both anger and constant longing for a person who was no longer there, I still remember the way she sat with me on the porch swing, her fingers braiding my hair as she listened about my day, and between the gaps, she'd always ask, "What's on your mind now, my Valentine?"

I could also remember the days she sat in her office for hours on end. When I was younger, I would occasionally convince her to play outside with me, to help me ride my bike. I remember those days the most. The way her laughter filled the air as we pedaled around the neighborhood, the warmth of her hand guiding me until I could balance on my own. As the years went by, she slipped through my fingers like wisps of smoke. There were moments when I could almost feel her beside me, her comforting presence wrapping around me like a warm blanket, in grocery stores, in the restaurants she used to love frequenting, in the books she used to read to lull me to sleep. Sometimes grief is the one thing we try to avoid, but we so desperately need to let it hold us, comfort us, and remind us of the person we always needed, and now they become a part of us.

NIA RACKLEY

Nia Rackley is a high school sophomore. In her free time, she enjoys reading, writing, and taking dance classes.

MENTEE'S ANECDOTE:

Jess is such an amazing mentor. She's an incredible writer and editor, and this piece would not be the same without her help. Jess is always looking deeper for more details and has a knack for thinking outside of the box. She writes each sentence with purpose and intention. I'm tremendously lucky to have her as a mentor, and I can't wait to continue writing with her!

JESS ROMEO

Jess Romeo is an editor for the Scholastic classroom magazine *Science World*. Her writing has been featured in *Popular Science* and *JSTOR Daily*, among other publications.

MENTOR'S ANECDOTE:

Nia's passion for storytelling is obvious, and I admire how she always makes time to write, despite her dizzyingly busy schedule. She has so many great ideas and a natural talent for expressing them. Whenever she writes, she effortlessly imbues her characters with a strong voice and a great sense of humor. Working with Nia has helped me reconnect with the reason I started down my own path: for the pure joy of writing. I can't wait to see what she produces next!

THE LETTER

NIA RACKLEY

The perfect and responsible Elizabeth Hurston never made a mistake in her life. Now she finally realized what it meant to ruin everything.

ELIZABETH (FEBRUARY 2010)

She hid in her room, locking the door behind her. The perfect and responsible Elizabeth Hurston never made a mistake in her life. Now she finally realized what it meant to ruin everything.

"Open the door, Elizabeth!" her mom, Kelly, shouted, getting angrier by the second.

All Elizabeth could do was curse herself under her breath and wipe away her pesky tears. How could she be so stupid?

"This is my last time asking you, open the door!" Kelly's voice rang throughout the house. Elizabeth swore she felt the room shake.

There was no time left; Elizabeth knew she had to face her reality. Removing herself from her desk, she opened the door to find her mother in a state of disarray. Kelly's dark curly hair wasn't in its normally neat bun, but a messy one with coils spilling out on the sides. They framed her face, which was red from screaming, and, to Elizabeth's surprise, tears were traveling down her face. Of course, her mother wiped them away as soon as they appeared. Kelly never wanted Elizabeth to see her cry.

"I'm so sorry, Mom," Elizabeth said, struggling to get the words out between her sobs.

Kelly took a deep breath. Elizabeth could see some of the tension releasing.

"I know you are," she said, wiping another tear. "But 'sorry' doesn't make what you did right."

"I'll make it up to you. I promise." Elizabeth truly believed her words.

"That letter means—" Kelly stopped herself. "It *meant* everything to me. You had no right to take it."

With a look of disdain, Kelly slammed the door in Elizabeth's face.

ELIZABETH (JANUARY 2010)

Elizabeth and her mom never had a normal mother-daughter relationship. Kelly lived a life fueled by perfectionism, and she raised Elizabeth to do the same. The Hurston women never made mistakes—and they absolutely did not steal from their mothers.

Elizabeth was going through her mom's purse, looking for a twenty-dollar bill. That's when she saw the delicately folded yellowish paper. She almost didn't unfold it because it looked like it belonged there, but she was tired of being perfect and always being what her mother expected. She took a deep breath and unfolded the letter.

December 15, 1992

Dear Kelly,

I love you, and even if you're scared to say it back, I know you love me, too. We don't have to be enemies because our parents can't stand each other. If you agree, meet me in the library after your science class. I'll be waiting.

Yours,
Jason Colbort

Elizabeth read and reread the words. The Colborts were a family of politicians. Oscar Colbort was once a popular mayor. He never expected another candidate to beat him, let alone a woman. When Elizabeth's grandmother, Penelope, ran against him and won, he was furious. Oscar Colbort made it his mission to blacklist the Hurstons. At every family dinner, Elizabeth would hear the story of Colbort vs. Hurston and learn about the terrible things they had done.

Elizabeth felt a wave of fury wash over her. Here was evidence that Elizabeth's mother wasn't as perfect as she'd always projected. Kelly knew more than anybody what the Colborts had put their family through. How could she keep this letter? Senselessly, Elizabeth tore the paper into pieces so tiny the handwriting was barely recognizable.

With her heart nearly beating out of her chest, she took the fragments and left them on her mother's desk.

KELLY (DECEMBER 1992)

Kelly Hurston never went to the library to meet the love of her life. It took every ounce of her willpower to not open the creaky doors. Instead, she took Jason's letter and stuffed it into her backpack. She couldn't betray her family, especially after everything Oscar Colbort had put her mother through. Penelope took great pride in her high social status. Her popularity was the main reason why she was elected mayor. Oscar knew that—which is why he started spreading those horrible rumors.

Jason never let the feud affect his relationship with Kelly, and she respected that the most. When she needed him, he was there, but now, when he needed her, she turned on him. Kelly fought back the tears as she slammed her locker shut and walked away.

KELLY (JANUARY 2010)

Kelly always wondered what would have happened if she'd met Jason. Would she have been happier? Every time she posed the question, she rejected it. She was happy with Elizabeth, and her small family. Even when it didn't feel like enough, she found ways to glimpse the happiness in her life. To keep everything perfect.

Still, she kept the note in her purse. A part of her knew that one day the universe would bring them back together, and she would show Jason the note. She would show him that she'd waited for him, all these years.

NISHAT RAIHANA

Nishat Raihana (she/her) is a second-year undergraduate student at Hunter College majoring in psychology and biological sciences. She is the mother of three cats!

MENTEE'S ANECDOTE:

Working with Liz has been such an amazing experience. At every meeting, she brings in the brightest energy and is always there for me even if I'm ranting about the silliest of things. She inspires me and has taught me to be proud of myself for all that I do. I feel so genuinely comfortable working with Liz as we both support each other on our writing journeys. I hope she knows she is stuck with me for the long road ahead, not just as a mentor-mentee pair in Girls Write Now, but also as my friend!

LIZ DeGREGORIO

Liz DeGregorio (she/her) is a poet, writer, and editor whose work has appeared in *Electric Literature*, *Catapult*, *Lucky Jefferson*, *ANMLY*, *Bust*, *Ghouls Magazine*, and more.

MENTOR'S ANECDOTE:

I love working with Nishat—she's an inspiration! She is so thoughtful, ambitious, and devoted to her studies, her family, and making the world a better place. Every time we meet, I learn something new, and I hope that I've been able to teach her some things along the way, too. Her creativity sparks my own, and I'm thrilled to have been a part of editing her piece "The Meaning of My Life" for the *Girls Write Now 2024 Anthology*. She describes her life journey in such beautiful and evocative ways, with a unique eye for details.

THE MEANING OF MY LIFE

NISHAT RAIHANA

This piece is a reflection of my journey in life, from the moment my little sister was born to my future aspirations in healthcare and writing.

What is life and death?

I recall my first-ever memory, in pure detail, when my little sister was born. At four years old, I welcomed who would become one of the most important people in my life. I watched my baby sister in her little bassinet at the hospital, all wrapped in blankets and sleeping in peace. She was a new life in the world, and the most precious to me. I remember holding her tiny hand as I declared that I would love her "Sunday, Monday, Tuesday, Wednesday, Thursday, Friday, and Saturday!"

For most of my life, my family and I lived in a one-bedroom apartment that offered little personal space. Whatever free space we had, my sisters and I filled it with books. The public library across the street was my second home for as long as I could remember, and I would visit every few days to return and pick up a new stack of reading material. I reached for books about new species, diseases I'd never known, and anything that expanded the world I thought I knew well. Curiosity was a foundation of my life, fueled by reading and writing.

Growing up, I would often reflect on the lives of those I admired the most. There was Stephen Hawking, who fundamentally changed how we understand the universe. There were also Neil deGrasse Tyson, Albert Einstein, Martin Luther King Jr., and, above all, my elementary school teachers. They engaged my curiosity and shaped my reality. I thought about how every single person in this universe, directly or indirectly, was a meaningful part of someone else's existence.

The summer after fifth grade, my parents brought me to Bangladesh, their home country, to spend our vacation. Although I had been to Bangladesh once, it was only this time that I truly began to notice my surroundings. My mother's family lived in a very rural section of the country, and driving from the airport to my mother's childhood home was a journey I would never forget. Bangladesh is considered an overpopulated, impoverished country, but those words are never as significant as experiencing it firsthand.

During a particularly long traffic jam, I noticed an older man who had a particularly gruesome eye injury and had been carrying a sign while knocking from car to car, begging for money. When he approached us, my uncle quickly told us to ignore him; he said that this was simply the way of life for many people there. My mother refused and gave the older man some money. That was the first time I recognized just how important money is and how it is even more important for individuals to be able to access healthcare.

My first experience with loss was also in Bangladesh. We arrived at my aunt's house, where she introduced me to my bedridden uncle, with closed eyes and sunken cheeks. He was unresponsive, but my aunt confirmed that he sometimes twitched his fingers or eyes as a reply. My aunt told me that he had been bedridden for years, suffering from an illness that the healthcare system in Bangladesh simply could not sufficiently treat. He died some years later.

In a world where gender discrimination dictated people's lives, I also met one of the most hardworking, admirable people I will ever know: my grandmother. She was the mother of nine and worked herself to the bone, taking care of a large family while her husband handled his responsibilities. When she grew ill, when her memories slowly began to fade, when she no longer had control of her bowels and had broken her hip, there was nothing that could be done. Since healthcare in Bangladesh is already lacking, my grandmother could never receive the right treatment, despite all the money her children could offer, to live the rest of her life pain-free.

At the end of high school, we received a call in the middle of the night. My grandmother died. That was when I resolved to work in healthcare. I was going to study medicine in college and work to make proper healthcare more accessible.

Now I work as a medical scribe in an emergency department. My primary role entails documenting the stories of the patients, from their chief complaint to their diagnosis and treatment plan. My intention is to grow and keep learning new parts of healthcare and to use my writing to record important cases and, ultimately, support the advancement of healthcare in modern society. This is in the hopes that more and more lives can be saved in every part of the world.

Life is a valuable gift, and death is devastating. If I could spend the rest of my life making sure people can fully live their lives, impacting others along the way, that would make my life well lived.

JUSTINE RAMIREZ

Justine Ramirez is a media studies graduate from the Bronx. She believes in writing what you know and then some.

MENTEE'S ANECDOTE:

Micharne has opened my eyes to my capability as a writer and truly has motivated me to be the best one I can be. She is one of the biggest supporters on my team! We are able to bounce ideas off each other for projects from time to time, and I love that I can trust her with my work because I know she will handle it with the utmost care. It has been amazing working with her and being able to reach all our goals, one of which was finishing my pilot.

MICHARNE CLOUGHLEY

Micharne Cloughley writes research-driven stories about women across a wide range of genres, from television police procedurals to science-fiction theater.

MENTOR'S ANECDOTE:

Justine writes vivid and relatable characters with fun and moving stories. When we were first meeting about her outline for her pilot, it was almost challenging to communicate that her work was already excellent. Of course a mentor is supposed to be encouraging and supportive, but her outline was truly exciting and had so much potential. Her writing has gone from strength to strength from those first meetings, as she has met each goal we set for developing her half-hour pilot.

LEGENDS

JUSTINE RAMIREZ

"Legends" is a comedy series about a group of arena employees who work in a restaurant, trying to get by until the next thing comes along. In this episode, the group sneaks into a concert.

INT. LEGENDS RESTAURANT – NIGHT – ACT 2

A quaint, dimly lit restaurant within a Bronx baseball stadium, which was just bustling with customers, is now 90 percent empty. A few guests linger to finish their meals and nurse alcohol.

Three employees lean against the bar counter, exasperated.

PALOMA, a twenty-five-year-old flirty opportunist, eyes the security guards posted around the restaurant, then looks down at her phone.

PALOMA

All right, it's seven. We're on break.

MARI, twenty-seven, cool and to-the-point, glances around the premises.

MARI

How do you want this to work?

Paloma taps her finger on the counter and looks behind at the remaining customers who engage at the bar. She scurries behind the counter.

AMAYA, twenty-two, sweet yet self-deprecating, shrugs with Mari in the corner.

Paloma crafts two cocktails, then slides them to a customer who sits left of the bar. The LEFT SIDE GUY giddily takes the free drinks.

She strolls to the right side of the bar where another customer eats.

PALOMA

Sir, why aren't you sitting with your friend over there?

She points across the bar to LEFT SIDE GUY. The RIGHT SIDE GUY, intoxicated and tired, shakes his head.

RIGHT SIDE GUY

We're not friends.

PALOMA

Oh, well, I figured since he put his drinks on your tab, you guys knew each other.

RIGHT SIDE GUY

Fuck no! Who does he think he is?!

Right Side Guy pushes his stool in and storms to LEFT SIDE GUY. They argue. The loud BICKERING soon turns to fists thrown at each other.

Two LEGENDS SECURITY GUARDS, buff and goofy, run to the bar to split the fight.

Paloma tip toes away from the situation, Amaya and Mari follow. As the situation audibly escalates, they make a run for it.

INT. STADIUM ENTRY STAIRWELL – NIGHT

A door slam ECHOES into an empty concrete stairwell as Amaya, Mari, and Paloma rush in. Paloma drops her duffel bag full of clothes to the ground, and the three undress.

MARI

How long will that hold the guards off?

PALOMA

Long enough. I overheard the guy I lied to going on about his divorce to anyone who could listen. So he has time. And so do we.

Paloma and Mari unbutton and unzip their work attire and change into party/beachwear.

Amaya adjusts a thin bikini top that exposes her full chest. She wears flared swim trunks as the bottoms.

PALOMA

(to Amaya)

Oh, we've got the girls out! Bold.

AMAYA

Is this too much?

PALOMA

Too little, actually. It looks like you're going to the pool.

Paloma pulls a cowboy hat from the bag and puts it on Amaya's head.

PALOMA

(sighs)

You got your way.

AMAYA

I've heard people at these shows rock the cowboy hat. Why can't I?

MARI

Because how much of a hick do you want to be? And I swear to God if you pull out boots to match!

Amaya gives a frustrated "c'mon" look to Mari.

PALOMA

No more dress-up, let's go.

Paloma grabs the bag now with their folded uniform, and they all head upstairs.

EXT. STADIUM ENTRY STAIRWELL — NIGHT

The stadium concourse floods with concertgoers who dance to the DEMBOW MUSIC that BLARES from the stage.

A cleaning lady rolls a trash can, and Paloma throws the duffel bag in. She slides a dollar bill to the woman.

PALOMA

Just leave it back at the restaurant.

The Cleaning Lady tucks the cash in her bra and rolls away.

Amaya, Mari, and Paloma stand at the doorway of the staircase and marvel at the overall setup and sight of people.

They bop their heads to the music. The three each poke up in attempts to get a better view of the stage.

PALOMA

Can you see him at all?

MARI

I think he's on the other side of the stage.

The girls continue to look for Don X, a fictional, badass Puerto Rican superstar, who headlines the concert.

Caleb Quiles, a twenty-four-year-old semi-stud, walks by as he plays with a starfish-shaped sensory bubble toy. He passes the girls, then doubles back.

CALEB

So you made it up here after all.

PALOMA

When there's a will, there's a way.

MARI

(points to the toy)

Where'd you get that?

CALEB

My friend working the Merch Stand hooked me up. Look!

Caleb lifts the starfish and POPS the bubbles on it with a childlike smile.

MARI

Make sure you get one for your nephew.

He pulls out a duplicate from his pocket.

CALEB

I've always got my boy covered.

Caleb catches a glimpse of Amaya's outfit and his eyes wishfully trail down her body. He then rebalances his gaze on all three ladies.

CALEB

Well, I didn't see you guys. I'm headed to Legends for my break.

All three say their goodbyes as he exits down the stairs.

AMAYA

You have a kid?

MARI

Yeah. Why, shocked?

Amaya gives a nod of approval at Mari's toned body.

AMAYA

Impressed.

The music STOPS and the crowd starts to YELL in excitement.

ERINA REJO

Erina Rejo (she/her) is a high school junior with a love for reading, taking her dog on walks, and spending time with family and friends.

MENTEE'S ANECDOTE:

I am so grateful for the relationship I have with Aybike. Beyond her extensive help with submitting to contests and the anthology, as well as encouraging me with my novel, we have been able to talk like friends to each other about other aspects of our lives that may affect the things we write about. Sitting in boba shops and chatting/writing for hours nonstop has been my favorite pastime with her.

AYBIKE SUHEYLA AHMEDI

Aybike Ahmedi is a writer, editor, and content creator for a watch blog. She's a candidate for her MFA in creative writing at CCNY.

MENTOR'S ANECDOTE:

I've had the pleasure of working with Erina for about two years now. I've watched her grow as a writer and as a person. Her stories continue to captivate me through their creativity, characters, and setting. I love to get lost in her fantasy manuscript, where she has created a world of mystery, magical realism, and enchanting friction. I am excited as her work continues to enter the world so others can enjoy the gratification of reading her words, too. I look forward to see where Erina will continue to grow.

MAATRBHAASHA

ERINA REJO

To my family, for showing me that love goes beyond the words we speak.

Traditions usually brought back nostalgic memories, but I had never felt so conflicted with one before this day.

My family sat around the table. My feet squirmed in the giant slippers they rested in, slimy and moist from the twenty-four hours spent traveling to get where I was now. The tears everyone had shed were well gone and replaced with the usual smile of a reunion.

The familiar smell of the country had emerged, and I never wanted to leave it.

My nannu was at the head, my mother and Masi on each side of him. I was seated close to my mom, and beside me was my cousin. The rest of my extensive family gathered across the table. Their usual giggles of gossip lingered and I shot a glance to Soni, whose toothy grin immediately appeared. She quickly began rambling about the bothersome boy at her school who she wanted to simply smack across the face. All of her friends apparently had agreed with that sentiment.

Before I could tell her about her mom's possible opposition, Nani emerged from the kitchen carrying a large steel bowl. The steam warmed my face and clouded the lens of my glasses as I leaned in to take a peek.

Paneer bhurji, a recipe Nani specialized in. I watched my mom make it back home about a dozen times, but she could never quite replicate her mom's loved recipe. Maybe it was the difference in skills. Maybe it was due to the ingredients. But I knew there was something different about this dish in India.

Wrinkles rippled across Nani's face as she softly smiled and sat in the empty seat beside me. As usual, my mother was the first to rise from her seat as she gathered her hair into a clip. She immediately began to serve food on everyone's plates. I knew she heard their pleas, but she always added an extra spoon before stopping.

But just like that, my mother and the family she grew up with had stumbled upon a familiar topic from their past.

Soni and I listened in.

The mother language I had heard for the last hour was louder than before. Their stories became more complex, and their passion tied together with the words, somehow making them lighter and travel quicker. They rushed by in a blur before I had the chance to even acknowledge their presence.

As my mother continued to pour the paneer onto my plate, she laughed, tilting her head back, her face growing red as she continued speaking to her sister. I strained to listen and latch on to the lengthy sentences, but I could pick out only single words, barely enough to form a sentence.

Shop . . . Cold coffee . . . Papa.

Everyone laughed and I knew a joke had been spoken. That was my cue. Stumbling up onstage, I began the rehearsed smile and nod. When it felt necessary, I would chuckle.

Suddenly, the smell of the food, home, and the country was a single reminder of just how soon I would return on the plane. The memories they connected over I could no longer laugh along with. The language I once understood seemed to have escaped over the years with their shackles still on, and I hadn't even noticed.

My eyes wandered to my brother. He sat across the table. I knew his abilities were no better than mine, yet there were no puppet strings attached to his cheeks as he beamed at the stories being passed around the table. He would call out to my mother every few moments to ask what was being said, and she would quickly translate before returning to the conversation. Something I was too embarrassed or prideful to do. Possibly both.

He weaved himself into the memories floating around, asking questions in a broken Hindi that I would normally cringe at. Yet no one batted an eye to his jumbled words. They responded as they would to anyone else.

The time I wasted worrying about what could have been if I had never lived in America were more moments I would never get back. I was allowing whatever persistent sense of dignity I had to prevent me from appreciating the time I did have left with them to connect.

I tapped Soni on the shoulder and she leaned in to hear me among the chattering of voices.

"Fill me in?"

She looked at me with a sense of understanding before explaining the long story I was finally ready to catch up on.

CAITLYN RODRIGUES

Caitlyn (she/her) is a high school junior who loves chocolate; her cat, Hozier; and writing in the rain.

MENTEE'S ANECDOTE:

Luna and I have inspired each other to write (and to stay on top of our deadlines) more frequently. We're both such similar people, and it's been so fun getting to know her.

LUNA CALVARIO

Luna is a high school senior who loves cats, photography, and turtles.

PEER MENTEE'S ANECDOTE:

Caitlyn and I have managed to mentor each other despite our procrastinating skills, and we've had a great year with Girls Write Now so far!

SUGAR AND SPICE AND EVERYTHING NICE

CAITLYN RODRIGUES

Recently, I've been looking for a definition for the all-encompassing phenomenon that seems to be girlhood—a time where you're neither a child nor a woman—so I wrote this.

the definition for girlhood lingers just out of my sight,
sits tauntingly on the tip of my tongue,
and lets me talk circles around myself trying to explain why it even matters.

it's easy to say "girlhood is growing up, maturing"
but hard to put into words the collective experience that we all go through,
the experience of hating your body before you can ever truly love it,
of liking someone so much you feel physically ill,
of being asked out by men old enough to be your grandfather,
and of having your heart shattered for the first time.

it's too easy to sum up girlhood as becoming a woman in a man's world,
because girlhood is more than the suffering and sorrow and betrayal—
girlhood is gossiping and giggling for hours over coffee long gone cold,
girlhood is swinging high enough to touch the sky on kids' swing sets,
girlhood is lying in the sun at the beach, talking about nothing at all, and

girlhood is screaming music at the top of your lungs in a car that
you've named.

girlhood is the tragedy and triumph of growing old,
girlhood is succeeding where those before you failed
and failing where those before you excelled;
girlhood is something that i am running out of time to define,
and something that has never felt more necessary to memorialize.

ALICE ROSENBERG

Alice Rosenberg is a writer, performer, stage manager, director, and poet.

MENTEE'S ANECDOTE:

Kendyl and I have been working together for four years! From our shared love of *The Secret History* by Donna Tartt (which we obsess over on our podcast, *Buckets of Books*) to the thesaurus.com words of the day (which we use as writing warm-ups), our partnership continues to evolve and to help me grow.

KENDYL KEARLY

Kendyl Kearly is a writer, editor, and journalist, currently an emerging news editor at *The Baltimore Sun*.

MENTOR'S ANECDOTE:

Alice and I have formed a collaborative, supportive style of working together on our writing. We spend our time picking random writing prompts; discussing what we're reading on our podcast, *Buckets of Books*; and encouraging each other to keep going, even when we have creative blocks. Alice keeps our conversations entertaining with her many interests (writing, theater, art, etc.) and makes me want to take on new creative projects I wouldn't have otherwise thought of.

MORNING STORIES

ALICE ROSENBERG

A poem that traces my memory through color.

The bowl is blue and last night I wanted to paint over red
my nails
paint them that blue

And this morning the woman on the couch in the painting was draped
in blue
her dress, blue, was a towel
was blue bath soap and fogged-up mirrors
was the pillow beside her
was flowers
was sky

And the lamp shone in the bowl, shone blue
And the bowl cupped orange in response
And the depth of the bowl became an ocean
And the oranges were sunrises reflected in windows

And just yesterday I sat stranded in an endless room
where clouds painted water on the floor
where a stream of reflected prisms flowed back to me
where I sat mouth wide open
fingers touching fingers,
gold rings to silver slivers
where I was fed clementine slices
which burst to meet my tongue
which kissed last night,
a kissing destruction in blue light.

SHANNON ROWE

Shannon Rowe, an English major at CUNY City College of New York, enjoys international series and music and aspires to enter the publishing industry.

MENTEE'S ANECDOTE:

First meeting Laura, I was worried about how I could approach her due to my shyness with new people. Surprisingly, our initial interaction was smooth, setting a positive tone. By the second meeting, any lingering anxiety had melted away, replaced by a comforting ease. We have shared what we are interested in, and our writing prompts have been nice to open the creativity we share. Laura's guidance in navigating the world of publishing—a field I'm passionate about—has been invaluable. Her insights and encouragement have strengthened my confidence and enriched my understanding of the industry, making this mentorship incredibly rewarding.

LAURA MURPHY

Laura Murphy is a publishing professional and freelance writer living in Jersey City, New Jersey. Her fiction has been published in *DropOut Literary* and *The Ear*.

MENTOR'S ANECDOTE:

Working with Shannon this year has been a delight. We share a passion for all things books and have spent our time exploring the opportunities of the publishing industry as well as sharpening our creative writing skills. She is a talented writer and I appreciated her knowledge of and skill in literary fiction and poetry. Shannon is working toward a career in publishing, where she will help bring other artists' stories to the world, and it is a pleasure to help her get there. I am excited to see how far she will go.

LOW RATES

SHANNON ROWE

In a world where the young voice their struggles, this poem captures the essence of a generation's plea for understanding and change.

You blame us.
You say we are rebelling, we are nonsensical,
Overemotional, afraid to commit
So you blatantly hijack our records, making your powers reign.
"Abortion is illegal." well, now we have
no choice.
"Millennials and millennial women are rebelling against
their Gen Y and Baby Boomer parents"
But we know why, the truth you hide from in your bunkers
You say, "We buy too much toast and coffee"
But have you forgotten student loans?
Or maybe you fell and forgot the peak of childcare
What about health vs. jobs
You cry and beg
But all you do is curl around us like a python
We say hello to stress as he enjoys his piggyback
Pro–child labor bill,
70 still working,
Nondisclosed salary range,
And yet you say our generation has it best
Our Paleolithic leaders need a wake-up call
their plans are small
They ignore the signs of a changing climate
While the rest of us face the consequences of it all
We have it the best
So why do we struggle to find a home
Going to another country to have your futures
But a bill is what you promise us.

CHYONIKA ROY

Chyonika Roy is a writer at Hunter College. When she is not studying, she is frolicking through libraries and cafés, drinking copious amounts of hot chocolate.

MENTEE'S ANECDOTE:

I originally wrote this piece when I got a migraine during the summer from being pissed off at the world. These are the words I needed to say. When I texted this piece to Kristy in its roughest state she saw the potential of this piece and the importance of my words. Kristy is the guiding presence that helps me think deeper with each piece I write. I think of Kristy as the hearth in which my words reside. The hearth represents both safety and the thing that keeps people together. She is that to me.

KRISTY CUNNINGHAM BIGLER

Kristy Cunningham Bigler is the creator of the fantasy webcomic *Infinite Spiral* and a UX designer. When not writing, Kristy doodles with her family.

MENTOR'S ANECDOTE:

When I met Chyonika during our first year with Girls Write Now, I knew we'd been perfectly matched. Chyonika is an avid reader and writer with a special love of Gothic literature and *Six of Crows*. Her love of stories is present in all of our meetings. I am pretty sure I now have a "to-read" list a mile long. When she sent me this incredible piece, I knew it needed to be in the next anthology. I've enjoyed the work's evolution into a poem, a departure from our exploration of fiction this year.

THE WATCHER

CHYONIKA ROY

Content Warning: Physical and Sexual Violence

Who is the Watcher? Where are they from?

I am a simple lad, a watcher from who knows where
Have the supposed heavens above sent me in God's plight, as a messenger?
I have no clue as to what I, a simple maiden, would have to share,
It appears as if the world has screwed my mouth shut but maybe it is for the best
I imagine if I'd be able to speak I'd speak something foul,
Sins spilling from my mouth flirtatious as water on a rather parched day.
That would indeed not be holy but what makes anybody holy when human desire is vile
I know, I watch from above.
Maybe I lived another life long ago
A simple bird with talons sharp
An assassin's knife soaring in mid-flight
Perhaps I am a crow who has kept watch of the objects it holds so dear

A flight gone awry
The wind blows the other way
A flight held by gravity with no escape.

I see the crows stand by in the sunset now
Tendrils of smoke arise
I creep past each room holding the incense close to my chest
My fingertips stained black as I ward off the night

I have learned to cling to the spaces in between
They will walk past the figure hidden in plain sight,
As I light the night
They see a figure that has a terrible resting face,
Brooding in the woes of youth
Displeasing the eye of the beholder
Or is it the beholden
whichever comes first at that moment.

I wonder now, what would happen if I took flight
Would I still be trapped like a songbird in a cage
Am I pleading with the almighty or is it people?

I am a simple lad, a watcher from who knows where
I have not a clue about how I, a simple maiden, could feel trapped
I simply open and close doors
I have no body or place
I am a magician's kindred rabbit eating its grave
I disappear and reappear

The sea place to place in rivers and lakes
The wind becomes my companion until I am everybody, everything,
everywhere.
I am soothed yet distressed waves
Crashing against the heavenly sands
As I return a night of broken glass.

Yet, a watcher trapped?
A watcher that takes, destroys, and breaks
The maiden, the man
It can't be.
How can a watcher return glass?
I solely open and close doors
I am a simple doll with whom they will lay their book
A simple frame they hang their paintings, proudly against the wall
A simple breeze passing by as they lift their hands
I can't do anything but watch, the mirror of our world
Yet, I am everything and anything

Nobody sees me,
They will come find me
When they are distracted
Distracted with petty plights of bloodshed
They will speak to me, although I can't speak back
People will die at the hands of their own
When they burn, shoot, rape; destroy
I will simply watch from above
I am a watcher after all

Yet, the centuries pass
I still find myself asking as the crows take flight
As they steal, yet protect
Tendrils of smoke being all that is left
The maiden I watched over long ago
Blood spills on the earth once more
What makes anyone holy?
I am no divinity, just human, I suppose.

YASMIN SADEH BROSH

Yasmin (she/her) is a sophomore in high school who enjoys reading, writing, and hanging out with her friends.

MENTEE'S ANECDOTE:

Ivy is truly incredible. She gives me so much hope for my future in writing with her actions both as a person and as a mentor. She is caring, smart, and funny, and never fails to push me creatively and personally. Ivy inspires me to do better in my writing and is an amazing mentor and friend.

IVY JO GILBERT

Ivy Jo Gilbert (they/she) is a nonfiction writer and poet. For a living, they are a copywriter at a renewable energy company.

MENTOR'S ANECDOTE:

Working with Yasmin is always a joy. This is our second year participating in the Girls Write Now program, and I've cherished our time together. Yasmin is creative, caring, and imaginative—her writing routinely brings us into new worlds. I cannot wait to see where the power of Yasmin's pen takes her.

THE BUTTERFLY AND THE MOTH

YASMIN SADEH BROSH

This poem is a reflection on how, as writers, our mind loves to evade us.

THE BUTTERFLY

There is a butterfly that flies between worlds.
I see him, always there, within my reach.
Tempting, taunting.
To follow him through the mirror, the sea, the sky.
He is a winged rabbit, and I am Alice, powerless to resist the snare.
He takes me to libraries that spiral up and up, endless stairs and boundless realms.
Phantom hands tug me to meadows, where cities dwell inside puddles and every flower is a portal of never-ending wonder.
I follow toward battlefields and bloodshed, magic, and miracles.
Crystal caverns and floating fairy tales dwell at my fingertips.
He whispers secrets behind my ear as stories collect under my nails, my teeth.
His words are etched into the crevices of my skin, each universe inscribed into my fingerprints.
I am Ariadne, casting the butterfly's string red as blood, my hope the cliff at the sea.
I am Perseus, who follows his string, and my hope is the waves that pull the cliff down.
He is the labyrinth, who knows in his heart that I will never escape.
He is the bottomless lake of ideas that pools in the hollows of my skull.

He is the cup that empties it, growing forests of stories taller than the stars.
He is the clouds, who rain glistening crystals, filling the lake almost to flooding.
I am the hands whom the water evades, the fingers that it slips through.
I am the mouth that drinks it, the liquid running a burning path down my throat, my mouth, my chest, dripping onto my bare skin.

There is a butterfly that flies between worlds.
He is my muse, my creativity, my love and my life, my hate and my fear.
My pen is the net that captures him, holding him in the prison of my ribs for an agonizing second or two before he slips out of my grasp yet again.
And I am the hunter who chases the butterfly, who has spent my life following him as my feet evade the fire in my wake.

There is a butterfly that flies between worlds.
He is my mind, and the one thing I will never trap.

THE MOTH

I write to the moth in my mind, she who resides between my eyes.
So similar yet so very different from the Butterfly, the line between them a dangerous one to live upon, a tightrope set alight with madness.
A beauty exists with the Butterfly, the worlds we visit are opulent and wonderful, dark and terrible.
But a shape-shifter pulls me down within, the Moth not always a moth.
Why does a wily fox visit me at night, her words jewels cursed far beyond what any fairy tale would comprehend?
Why does a raven bury talons of words into my mind, the blood that falls from my eyes as entrancing as the clarity that comes with it?
When the moth spreads her wings, will I see my face reflected in the papery patterns?

Will you lead me to the edge of the cosmos, my love, and watch as I weep?
Will you weep with me, or will you push me across the brink?
She is the darkness that comes with creation, the words that escape my lips on the street as I see faces and worlds that are not my own.

IVY SAND

Ivy Sand is a Chinese American high-schooler who aims to tell stories of both the mundane and the exciting in equally thrilling ways.

MENTEE'S ANECDOTE:

Working with Amy has been such an incredible experience! She is my very first writing teacher and I could not be luckier to have her. Amy is patient and offers wonderful advice, and speaking to her about my day-to-day life is equally helpful. Her help is priceless; I'm grateful for the privilege of being her mentee.

AMY COOMBS

Amy Coombs is a New York City yoga and meditation instructor. She is currently writing a novel that brings together baseball, mindfulness, and a few ghosts.

MENTOR'S ANECDOTE:

I was delighted to virtually meet Ivy. Girls Write Now did a great job of matching me with a mentee who shares my love of theater and has similar perspectives on navigating life. It was truly rewarding to make a connection with someone so smart and hardworking. Although Ivy is one of our younger mentees, I felt I could converse with her as a peer. She has a sumptuous writing style, poetic and unbound by convention, and I can only hope she learned half as much from me as I did from her!

THE SHAME OF SONS (EXCERPT)

IVY SAND

An excerpt from a short story about a boy being surrounded by his father's hand-me-down anger.

It's not uncommon to see boys outside their schools early. They bounce around, feeding into insecurities with their faux-playful insults. The high school boys carry around a vape or two, offering it to girls who would never look their way otherwise. The girl takes it, inhales, then smirks—she doesn't care for the boys' antics. She hands it back, and they'll never speak again. But the boy forever clings to this interaction, citing it as a part of his charm.

Let the record show that this is false. Boys of their age know nothing of charm. Nonetheless, girls will let them have this, because boys will be boys, and girls become women the night they see their mothers cry.

Owen may as well be a woman, then, because he can't stand to see his mother after a booze-slobbering argument with the monster in their house, whose beard is covered in beer as he snarls curse after goddamn curse at them. Owen's mother will yell back because she is nothing if not strong—but in the dead of night, when she thinks no one is watching, she shrinks into nothing.

He hates the way her body curls over itself. Naturally, there's a desire to save his mother, to be her knight in shining armor, but Owen is just a boy, and all he has learned from his father is how to run away—this explains why he is in front of his underfunded high school before classes even begin.

Immersed in the cold January air, his mittens cannot keep the frost from biting at his fingers. The school opens in fifteen minutes. Until then, he is stuck listening to a bunch of gossip-loving seniors as they talk smack about the girls in their grade. Nobody he knows or cares about, at least. Still, he hates to see upperclassmen being such horrid role models to the rest of the school.

Not that Owen's entirely *sure* he can call anyone in his school a friend, though—except Amelie Ma, who, in any other world, would be the girl of his dreams. She is beautiful. Her hair drapes around her body like a silken robe. When he sees her at volleyball, she is just as lovely, arms gleaming with muscle and sweat that only somehow makes her more stunning. He loves her, but not in the way the world wants.

The boy born from twisted rib cages shakes his head to clear himself of any undesirable thoughts, looking up to see the school's pride and joy herself, who is also his best friend. "Speak of the devil," he snorts, calling her over with a beckon and a shout.

"Owen?" Amelie turns around. She flashes him a brilliant smile before making her way to his side, plopping down on the stairs in front of their school. "Hey! What are you doing outside? It's cold—you do know the doors are unlocked, right?"

"No. No, I did not," he hesitantly admits, fiddling with his fingers. Amelie seems to assume the fidgeting is from the cold and interlocks his gloved hand with hers. Owen flinches before sinking into the contact; it's not as if he doesn't enjoy it. It just takes some getting used to.

"Of course you didn't." Amelie giggles. Her white button-down ruffles in the sudden burst of wind, causing her to frown and shiver slightly. Pulling Owen up, she marches toward the school's doors. He stumbles before following suit. "Come on! I'm freezing!"

They walk into school, hand in hand. Cobwebs line the corner of the dimly lit school while lockers covered in fading Sharpie are varying degrees of open and shut. Owen can't help but hate the way the school feels empty without the shouting from students. In all honesty, he should be overjoyed to get to school early, but all that lingers on his mind are his mother's sobs.

The only other people in sight are two boys, clad in streetwear and surrounded by the stench of smoke. He leans in to eavesdrop on their conversation—as expected, it is gossip surrounding a poor sophomore girl. Owen's eyes narrow, shooting glares at the boys. They don't even notice his attempt at ostracization. Rather, they continue to cackle over the unfortunate girl. It's despicable, and Owen can only think of his father: Was he like this, as a child? Cruel and manic and desperate to leave scars on everything he held?

His breathing turns unsteady, fury threatening to take hold. Two things are keeping him from swinging his fist in the boys' faces: the first being Amelie, who's begun looking at him in gentle concern, and the other being fear. Fear of turning into his father forever leaves him second-guessing, looking back on his decisions, and wondering if it was what his father would have done.

"You're thinking too much," Amelie suddenly interrupts him, gazing at him with a rare intensity. "I can tell. Stop second-guessing your instincts because of your family. Don't live the way your dad wants you to—you were not only born to be his son."

MARZIA SEEMAT

Marzia, a high school senior, is passionate about spoken poetry, creative writing, and design. She is also curious to explore the diversity of life.

MENTEE'S ANECDOTE:

Past. Present. And Future. Time has taught me the value of people. There are only a few people in my life with whom I can trust my deepest secrets. And Madeline is one of them. She is less of a mentor and more of a friend to me. Sometimes she is a therapist as well. Someone who always encourages me to be hopeful and confident. She is always a motivator who guides me through my strengths and weaknesses. I can't express my gratitude enough for having her as a cheerleader in my life—whether in a time of joy or of sorrow.

MADELINE DIAMOND

Madeline Diamond is a writer and editor based in Brooklyn, New York. She can be found reading in her favorite park, cappuccino in hand.

MENTOR'S ANECDOTE:

After exploring poetry together last year, I'm excited that Marzia chose another poem to submit for this year's anthology. She brought topics and ideas we've spoken about in our weekly meetings to this poem, so seeing those come to life when she first read this poem aloud to me was thrilling. I'm so proud of her work this year, especially how comfortable she has gotten while reading poetry in front of an audience—her confident spirit is infectious. I'll miss her when she leaves for college next year, but I am so excited for everything to come.

THE LAST WHITE ROSE

MARZIA SEEMAT

Love isn't always about love. Sometimes it's about sacrifice, letting go, and defeat. So when history witnesses another lost love, it might be one of those loves masked underneath sacrifice.

Don't be with me, dear. I won't be able to love you enough.
All I know is that even if I want to make you mine, I won't be able to.
And this defeat of mine, I would never be able to explain to anyone.

Don't come near me, dear, because I fear.
Not for this love I have for you or the love you have for me, but I fear myself.
I fear you being around me, and I fear me being around you.
I fear my hands that I adore you with. The same ones you love, too.
I fear the rage that possesses me—the one I can't control.
But trust me, I myself fear living with this inner rage. *This inner demon. This monster.*
I fear it. I fear it to the core. I fear hurting you. I fear losing you.
I fear losing my love; more than anything, I fear you, losing your love for me.

That night wasn't the only night. It wasn't the only time I lost control.
I didn't lose total control because my brain was aware.
I knew what I was about to do. I knew how it would end.
Me repeating sorry and sorry and sorry, and you sobbing only tears.
But I couldn't control my body. *Like I couldn't before.*
Your hands were bleeding love. And I did that to you. *I did.*
How am I supposed to take back time?
Take back all your tears? All your fear? And all your pain?

There are only two options now: to let my love go or to let my love suffer.
What's more painful? Witnessing my defeat? Or,
My love, safe and happy and without a possessed monster like me?

Just think about it . . . what will our wedding vows be like?
I promise to be good to you. I promise to love you and honor you.
Darling, I have to promise to be *good to you.*
But how shall I promise you that when I am not good?
How shall I claim to love you when tears, caused by me, stain your cheeks?
I promise to protect you and take your responsibilities.
But, darling, how should I protect you from dangers when I am the danger?
How should I protect you from myself? From the evil that lies within me?
Love, imagine our daughter, the one we always dreamed of having together.
Imagine her witnessing my rage, *this defeat within me.*
Imagine her witnessing your tears, your fear, and your pain.
Imagine her holding back tears. Imagine her hating me.
Hate is the only thing she can do because I am worthy of only that.
What if I told you all these things? What would happen?
You would stay with me. You would suffer through pain for me.
But, darling, history repeats itself. It always has, and it always will.
My mom once decided to live through this pain for my dad.
Hoping that he would change someday or any day.
But he never did. I don't want to be like my dad, darling.
I can't have you suffer like my mom.
I don't want my kid to hate me as much as I hated my dad.

So, I am leaving you. But before I go,
I want to give you one last memory of ours.
Perhaps the most precious one.
The last white rose to you.
Standing before this same lake where we first met,
Where our hearts knew each other before we could.
But little did we know, this lake

Where our story began is also where our story ends.
You have those earrings on, the rose-brown ones, *my favorite.*
Your alluring, wavy hair is running through my fingers one last time.
I delicately slip the flower behind your ears,
The soft curve of your shy smile frames it perfectly, like a dream.
Your deep hazel eyes are reading mine one last time.
You did your eyeliner today—black—*just how I like it.*
You wore the blue dress today, *the one I gave you.*
Maybe you, too, understood the ending of us.
Maybe you already know the words I am about to say.
Maybe you, too, are as defeated as I am.
If it was just about love, nothing could have separated us.
But this is about destiny. This is about sacrifice. This is about us.
You would be gone, but never really gone from my heart.
Just like I would be gone, but never really from your heart.
Let this white rose be the witness to all of this.
Let it be the witness to our ending.
To this defeat. To this moment. To this sacrifice.
Let it be an echo of our past. And an echo of our love.
Let it be with you till the end.
To that ending, where there will be no defeat.
Where both love and love wouldn't be a burden
And where fear wouldn't exist.
Let this white rose be it all, my love.

ANIKA SEKAR

Anika is a high school senior from New Jersey who loves reading, history, art museums, watching rom-coms, and creative writing of all kinds.

MENTEE'S ANECDOTE:

Working with Malissa for the second year has been nothing short of amazing. We've gotten to know each other in our sessions, giving each other life updates and discussing books or movies we've read or watched recently. Malissa is an extremely talented writer, and I have always felt comfortable reading my pieces to her and listening to her feedback on whatever I need. She's also been very helpful in assisting with my Girls Write Now Lead360 project on period poverty around the world, and I always enjoy writing with her.

MALISSA RODENBURG

Malissa Rodenburg is a journalist musing on movement-traveling, moving her body, and observing nature's wandering creatures. She writes frequently for *Outside*, Livestrong, and *5280*.

MENTOR'S ANECDOTE:

I've been afforded glimpses into Anika's life this year through, of course, her writing, but also in what inspires each piece of prose or poetry she pens. She has the ear of a writer, crafting stories from lines heard on the radio or at her own kitchen table or noises heard on the street in front of the gas station she's passed by every day for years. From these moments, she's written genre-bending flash fiction and dramatic contemporary short stories, woven personal essays, and started to dabble in poetry. It's been a pleasure to get to know her this way.

I WONDER HOW MY EIGHTH GRADE ART TEACHER WOULD FEEL ABOUT THIS

ANIKA SEKAR

A personal essay on perfectionism, art, and not being able to let things go.

I have a fear of writing in pen. Ink bleeds its entire soul onto the paper, leaving an imprint that will never be erased. Imperfections can be rectified in two ways: Wite-Out and scribbles. However, Wite-Out never works properly, and scribbling over mistakes makes the paper look messy. Pencils are less stressful.

In the second grade, I took my first art class at a local studio. My sole memory of that session is the instructor handing me an eraser. "This will be your best friend from now on," he said, rubbing the eraser on my outline of a dog (with slightly off proportions). I, transfixed by the immediate disappearance of these lines, watched as the instructor then took my pencil and redrew the dog's ear. "See—it's fixed now. That's the good thing about drawing in pencil." I nodded. Pencils provided unlimited trial and error, redos, second and third and fourth chances. My first attempts proved inconsequential; as long as the end result embodied perfection, nothing else mattered.

And so, I hated acrylic paint and markers and pens. When assigned a painting project, I would stare at my blank canvas for hours, watching smudges and thumbprints accumulate in the corners instead of painting. Simply, I was terrified of messing up. Each stroke of a paintbrush was an opportunity to ruin everything I had previously accomplished (which, I guess, in a way, would be a paradox if I never even started the painting), and I would have to accept the subpar result or start all over again. My final work's quality determined my self-esteem for the subsequent months, and I decided that anything less than perfection was failure.

My sister and I have a running joke of calling our parents "hoarders"—they, particularly my dad, refuse to throw out any item in our house, no matter how many years have passed since anyone has even looked at it. I am much the same—I form attachments to the most trifling objects, though I just call myself *sentimental.* My bottom dresser drawer holds every piece of artwork I have created since the fourth grade, including the horse drawing that looks like a thumb (every time my dad insists that it looks realistic and we should frame it, I feel insulted because he never compliments my recent artwork). I still keep birthday cards signed by girls I pass in the school hallways and don't acknowledge. Random objects that I will possibly have a use for one day ten years in the future pile up in the little green basket on my desk.

My mind constantly juggles my dependence on permanence with my simultaneous yearning for perfection. Permanence is terrifying. Once you make mistakes, you can never go back on them to erase or request a second chance, making perfection that much less viable.

I've discovered that some people prefer a spontaneous lifestyle, living "in the moment" and acting without concern for consequences. On the other hand, all I do is think. *What's the best way to achieve perfection? What if I mess up?*

Periodically, I look at my past paintings and pen-and-ink drawings, which I can't bring myself to get rid of, and it makes me want to throw something at the wall because I wish I could have painted *Nighthawks,* could have evoked such lachrymose in my viewers, could have captured every aspect of human loneliness in thirteen and a half square feet—but I'm not Edward Hopper. I hate painting, actually. I stay in my safe zones, within the parameters of what I know I can do, ensure I can correct any mistakes, and I inch toward perfection. Erasers are my greatest asset, so I will stick to my pencils, not pens.

MICHELLE SEUCAN

Michelle is a college sophomore with a love for memoir essays, making vision boards, journaling, traveling, making random playlists, and eating loads of Chipotle.

MENTEE'S ANECDOTE:

Melissa and I have a great creative and professional relationship! From helping me edit application essays to providing me with support through navigating the media industry, Melissa always has great insight to share.

MELISSA LAST

Melissa is a creative manager working in preschool television production at Nickelodeon.

MENTOR'S ANECDOTE:

Michelle is an exceptionally talented writer. Her unique perspective and voice shine through all her work regardless of subject matter. I'm routinely impressed by her thoughtfulness and ability to make the niche feel both accessible and relatable!

THE UNKNOWN

MICHELLE SEUCAN

A small look into my relationship with the dream world and outer space throughout the years. (A journey into the unknown!)

In a small room in my grandparents' house, tucked away in the middle of a Romanian nowhere, my brother and I lay on our eight- and nine-year-old bellies, staring in awe at this tremendously large almanac that he received as a gift the year before. Together, we race through the Amazon rainforest and ride the Elaphrosaurus in the Late Jurassic Period, all the while conversing with Japanese monks and defying the laws of gravity through a new NASA invention.

We finally reach the section that has conquered the depths of my consciousness since I first learned about its vast nature: space. My breathing quickens as our eyes gaze over the various planets and moons, my brother fawning over the fact that scientists have recently discovered oceans on Jupiter's moon, Europa. (Yes, the possibility of mermaids did bubble inside me.)

We then make our way to different parts of the solar system—vivid descriptions of celestial bodies, simplified analyses of the space-time continuum, time dilation, the wonders of Andromeda, theories of universe bubbles, discoveries of planets that potentially resemble our ecological realm of life and biospheric attributes.

I don't say anything. I just absorb.

A few minutes after our almanac rendezvous, my brother leaves to pick blueberries from my grandmother's garden. I continue lying on the floor, but this time on my eight-year-old back, staring at the ceiling. Whenever I thought of outer space, the universe, the omniverse, aliens, even, I would have an out-of-body experience that generally made no sense. *If I live on Earth and Earth is in a galaxy and the galaxy is in our universe, then where is our universe, is it held in a bubble in some divine omnipotent dimension—*

My brother suddenly bursts in with two teacups filled to the brim with blueberries and sugar.

Years later, I had a strange dream. It all began in an instant, as dreams do. I was on a wooden canoe in the middle of a crystal-blue ocean. As I was rowing, a tiger began swimming next to me. It did not attack. It simply . . . swam. I remember feeling a sensation identical to terror, but not exactly being terrified.

Cut to a massive beehive. Each hexagon was human-sized. My dream self woke up in a pool of honey on top of a geometric cushion. It was quite fascinating, really. This reality was as fleeting as the overwhelming sensation of mock despair I would feel at eight years old, when my brain was doing metaphysical gymnastics trying to conclude the nature of the universe.

Go figure.

In the spring of eighth grade, I bought a special book.

Lucid Dreaming: A Concise Guide to Awakening in Your Dreams

As someone who wished to explore the dream realm, I knew the key to achieving this mission was conquering the challenge of lucid dreaming. If I was able to recognize my being in the dream state, then I would be able to essentially craft whatever reality I wanted. Most people don't realize that they're dreaming when they are dreaming. But once you do, you can do anything you want. Fly to Andromeda, swim with the mermaids, go back to the Edo period and drink tea with a Japanese monk.

To train your brain to recognize the dream state, you must keep a dream journal and record every dream you can once you wake up in the morning. Reviewing these entries will help you learn how to differentiate between reality and nonreality, along with your specific dream patterns. This will allow your subconscious to ultimately *gain consciousness* in your dream, and then take control over your specific circumstance.

At thirteen, I was fascinated with this concept. During our family trip to Taiwan, I made sure to document my dreams each morning and read my entries throughout the day like they were the Bible. At night, sometimes I would succeed in my lucid dream attempts; other times I would not.

I would have peculiar dreams. Chased by zombie ghosts, flying next to a large red sun, falling asleep on the tongue of a mega-sized clam, surrounded by pearl pillows.

Origins: Unknown.

My brother and I devour the sugary blueberries on the porch swing outside, trying to figure out what shapes the clouds above embody, what lives they hold in their worlds beyond the troposphere. Our lips are covered in violet blue and sugar, and our words and thoughts are just as innocently sweet.

"That one looks like a bear."

"I wonder if it is going into hibernation."

"No, silly. It's summer. Bears don't hibernate in July."

"That's weird. Look, a bunny!"

As our laughter subsides, I notice one small cloud in the distance, isolated from the rest. It was simply floating around in the blue, all by its lonesome. I fixated on it for a while, even after my brother left to watch soccer with our grandfather, up until it slowly disappeared from existence.

Where did it go? The question clouded my mind as I drifted into a deep sleep, slipping into the Unknown.

Time to dream.

SHENNY SHANTAY

Shenny Shantay, a college freshman who is passionate about storytelling, aims to pursue her passion in writing and shed light on underrepresented communities so they are seen.

MENTEE'S ANECDOTE:

Joining the Girls Write Now community has been a wonderful time. The support and encouragement from fellow writers have been invaluable, inspiring me to explore new genres and styles in my writing.

FOLAKE AINA

Folake is a Bronx-based African educator and creative with a dual degree in urban planning and globalization and is dedicated to finding resources to uplift her communities.

PEER MENTEE'S ANECDOTE:

Girls Write Now has empowered me to use my voice. Working with Shenny has allowed me to block out the judgment I fear and to allow positive energy to flow during my writing process. Through my writing, I want to help myself and others cope with the feeling of anxiety and not being enough, because we are all intrinsically valuable as human beings.

EVERLASTING COLOR

SHENNY SHANTAY

This piece was written to shed light on creatives. Artists often perceive the world in a unique way that many people don't understand, so I wanted to do my best to describe that.

I admire artists.
Those that lose sleep trying to perfect.
The writers,
The dancers,
The craft being something their soul reflects.
The filmers,
Painters,
Color flowing throughout their brain.
Singers, actors,
Creativity racing like a train.

I admire artists.
They don't have to speak to explain.
Their language comes from emotion,
Always set in motion,
Calm or ripply like the ocean,
Never silent, sometimes silenced,
Always in passionate devotion.

I am an artist.
You'll live within my words,
Twirls,
Shots,
Sketches,

Lyrics,
Scripts,
In my world, locked and unseen to the naked eye,
But every creation is a key to the inside of my mind.

CATHY SHENG

Cathy Sheng is a senior in California. She loves a good thriller and Debussy, and she pulls pranks on her brothers left and right.

MENTEE'S ANECDOTE:

It was so much fun dissecting the piece, talking about the major themes of childhood and adulthood, high school and college. Rachel gave me so much wisdom, guidance, and warmth, which made this possible. Whether it be editing or cutting down the word count, her help was instrumental, and I'm so appreciative of this experience.

RACHEL PRATER

Rachel works in the New York City publishing industry, holds an MFA in creative writing, and enjoys reading and cuddling her two cats.

MENTOR'S ANECDOTE:

Cathy inspires me every day! She is enthusiastic about creative writing and stepping outside of her comfort zone. In turn, she has inspired me to continue writing, both what I know and what I don't know. Although Cathy and I have known each other only a short time, it feels like we've been connected for years. Our bond has been swift as we share our love for reading and what's on both of our TBR (to-be-read) and TBW (to-be-watched) lists. I stand behind her not only as her mentor, but also as her writing cheerleader!

ARCADE OF LIFE

CATHY SHENG

This was from when I visited Virginia the summer of sophomore year. It was also the feeling of closing this chapter of my life as I head into college, reflecting on my parents and my journey.

With only a couple wads of green American bills, a hungry stomach, three pieces of knitted clothes worn to holes, herbal tea Grandma insisted he take, and the promise of the American dream, my dad first stepped foot into the green wilderness of Virginia. For days, he slept on the cat-smelling, itchy lime-green sofa of a friend, rising before light to walk to school in the bitter East Coast winter, gnawing on a dollar bagel and chewing it slowly to savor the feeling of something filling his mouth. Then, studying until the last dregs of daylight as the sun fizzled out and midnight consumed his world. Though as the elder brother in his family he had been the more independent figure, never had he been so alone.

Stripped of country, of any friendly, familiar space. Without money, language, connection, and friendships or love, to build a life from his bare hands and scraps of his fading dream. Yet the world was not dark for him; each day he woke, he saw that shining disc of hope. His chance, no matter how slim, renewed and inflated with each glorious morning that he breathed in luxurious lungfuls of America. The country he had fought to arrive in with sweat and tears, for it was the land of freedom, and reinvention of a man and his future.

And so despite the hardships, the odds stacked against his success, the voices and numbers that didn't add up, each day he slipped his arcade coin into the slot of life, fate, and all things good in this world, wishing for his fortune to turn. For the hope he harbored and nurtured so carefully.

People counted passing dates and changing seasons; my father counted coins. He collected them, their coppery heads and silvery tails, he picked the loose change off the streets, from abandoned marble counters. At night, he would kiss each one with his heart's bitterest yearnings, an unfillable hunger. A loved one's face, recalling their herb-spiced hugs or brown-sugar buns, before dropping his coin-sized wishes into a makeshift piggybank of crumpled plastic. Lit by the moon, the coins glowed like river stones—like hope. It was to the metallic music of these dancing coins that he slept to each night, dreaming of 希望—*hope.*

It was a fragile thing, this *hope*. It glimmered, then shrunk its mane of red, barely a spark, merely silver smoke. Yet my dad cultivated this hope with such pride and dedication like one would a clingy child. Fed it fuel, the smallest gifts in life became impossible blessings of gratitude that swelled its fiery hues, sheltered it from the cold, the winds and punishing gales of hardships. So, despite the hollowness yawning within him, a dark emptiness that can never be filled by any amount of food, deep yearning for loved ones an ocean away; despite grappling with a new language, and having to prove his worth tooth and nail; despite being the graduating top percent in his province because of his accent, he woke each day and smiled. Smiled because of hope. Smiled because it was another day to shoot his shot.

And so, in the coin goes, and again he watches as the golden coin spirals down the metal slide and propels into the black maw of the slot machine run by fate. Who knows, today he might just collect his seven cards, his five thousand tickets, his American dream full and real.

希 *meaning hope, admire.* 望 *meaning full moon. The golden disc of warmth and light, a haunting muse, a timeless object of art. The illumination guiding lost wanderers to their home. A lamp, just like hope, shining on people's darkest days.*

Together they mean: 希望. *A bagel on a cold Virginian morning. Pennies in a jar. Shining sun through the window. Dancing in the rain. Songs of home. The promise of another day. A baby's tender laugh. An immigrant couple's dream.*

Hope.

And on the starry night when I was born, on the cusp of the next day where the sky couldn't decide between night and day, I was named 悦. My name sounds just like the word for moon. A syllable that balances on the tip of the tongue, delicate, light, and unfurling outward in a soft release. A sound that starts from a singular point and ends up more breath than voice, carrying with it a sense of wonder; in its vagueness, a magic.

COLLECIA SMITH

Collecia's on a slow simmer with the keys to her future. Who is she? An oasis for the girls who just need to breathe.

MENTEE'S ANECDOTE:

Working with Sophia has been an absolute privilege. I'm an older mentee, and in the beginning, that fact made me self-conscious. I didn't think I could create pieces that could generate a sense of awe. I thought I was simultaneously too much and not enough. Sophia was always there taking notes while I ranted, dissecting my thoughts with a tenderness that inspired me to believe that I could if I was willing to try. Her curated candor could heal a caged bird into considering it, too, could free itself.

SOPHIA JOSEPHINE UHL

Sophia used to dream of drifting far away, beyond the pain of the past. Now she's somebody she's always wanted to be: free.

MENTOR'S ANECDOTE:

As a lifelong writer, I like to believe that I can find words to express my observations. Although Collecia's essence is nearly impossible to relay. I want you to know that she is a force of nature, like the sound of a crashing wave that sparkles under the setting sun. You must experience Collecia to fully appreciate her. Collecia is wisdom and power personified. With a disarming ease, she unpacks forgotten histories, and as she weaves her thoughts aloud, she speaks in poems. Collecia's compassion, awareness, and dedication enable questioning, dismantling, and the empowerment of all voices, including her own.

LIVING?

COLLECIA SMITH

As the amalgamation of inherited struggles compiles daily, we the individuals of the world can't seem to get it together, nor have we come to terms with what it means to be together.

Every day that feels like a repetition of the day before,
I would argue,
is a day wasted.
Every uncaptivated breath

I breathe

I would argue,
Is unworthy of my lungs.
It's because my heart feels dilapidated,
every beat feels suffocated under the weight of my ancestors,

and your expectations.

Every uncontended impulse claims carelessness.
They're screaming useless.
Yet,
The white white West claims delusion
Is the key
to reality?
The Buddha said life was suffering.
Am I not alive?
My ancestors would cackle at my concerns.
Am I broken?

Crazy?
Maybe?

Certainly not numb
Cause
I don't drown my feelins. I soak in em.

Were the internet life gurus right?
Is the overthinking indecision?
Where is the end to all this healin?
I'm tired of being a soldier,
to not fight feels like to succumb.
Some say to accept.
Are they right?
Or are they them?
Those people.

Them.

They who call their careless candor tough love.
I must be tone-deaf.
I don't feel loved.
I see projections.
Like how every hot girl's anthem reeks of heartbreak.
I see little girls with no tears left to cry.
Their emptiness consumes me,
I would cry oceans for them to play in if it didn't mean drowning,
Just to see them smile.
How many more need to die?

Thee opinions, thee excuses, the protests;
like my tears, like my feelings, like my days, seem never-ending.

AVA STRYKER-ROBBINS

Ava Stryker-Robbins is a seventeen-year-old writer and journalist from New York City.

MENTEE'S ANECDOTE:

I've loved writing for as long as I can remember, but few creative pieces I've written have ever made it beyond their existence as Google Docs. I am so grateful that Toni has helped me both to gain confidence in my work, whether it be poetry or college essays desperately needing revisions, and to put my work out there. After each of our meetings, I feel inspired to read a new story or pick up my knitting needles. I feel so lucky to have been paired with her this year!

TONI BRANNAGAN

Toni is a Filipino American writer and content strategist based in Queens, New York. For fun, she crochets and watches the same shows over and over again.

MENTOR'S ANECDOTE:

When I first met Ava, I was immediately impressed by how intelligent she is, and I always leave our conversations thinking about something new. I'm continually inspired by how hard she works and by her commitment to her community, and I've especially enjoyed the weekly food column she writes for her local paper. I consider myself so lucky to have been able to get to know her and read some of her work this year—I know Ava's going to go far, and I can't wait to see what she does next!

UMBRELLA

AVA STRYKER-ROBBINS

This piece explores the beauty in what may normally be seen as an inconvenience.

the rain
washes
over the town, people groan and sigh.
water droplets splash around them, halos hug them
tight. they submerge their weary sneaker soles in murky water
and run. because where is the glee in sopping fabrics and matted hair?
where is the glee in anything other than a radiant sun and cloudless skies?
the raspy roars of thunder appall those who solely crave a picture-perfect day.
but to stand with glistening skin, to smile beneath a parachute of cloth and hear the
wisps of wind and the heartbeat-like pitter-patter on the concrete sidewalk. to smile as
droplets of dew drip down your face and see the sun's ghastly rays subside to matte
clouds that have so much more depth than just light. to hop in puddles with large
rubber boots and laugh as water seeps into your socks. to wait for the superb hues to
shine across horizons and bring the bleak city something real. for the rain is nothing
other than a completed cycle. a new start. a new reality that will spread in the chaotic
city streets, soothing people to slumber before it
drips
and
falls
and
drains
and
begins
to
learn
to rise
and fall
again

ALLISON SU

Allison Su (she/her) is a student at Barnard College studying environment and sustainability and psychology, but she can be found writing songs, novels, and plays!

MENTEE'S ANECDOTE:

Anh has been an incredible mentor, both in the realm of writing and in life. Every pair session, she creates space to check in and talk about things such as career goals or finding the time to write. Anh has inspired me a lot in my poetry, encouraging me to try new things and step out of my comfort zone. I look forward to each of our meetings and learning from Anh. Outside our meetings, she has also been immensely supportive, for example, by helping me reach out to people in the Girls Write Now community and finding publishing resources for me.

ANH LE

Anh Le (she/her) is a Vietnamese American poet and is currently pursuing her Ph.D. in literary studies and creative writing at the University of Connecticut.

MENTOR'S ANECDOTE:

I feel blessed, honored, and grateful to have been matched with Allison, my mentee. Allison's independence, extensive range, versatility, and conscientious attitude toward life continue to inspire me to achieve my own goals. I reminisce about the moments when we'd freely share anxieties and uncertainties about the future. But also, during pair sessions we celebrate the joyful moments we've experienced. I remember a particular prompt that both of us responded to: "Write about a moment when you felt most alive," which has unexpectedly encouraged me to infuse each day with something exciting, pleasurable, and meaningful, and to strive toward fulfillment.

DUALITY OF SOUL

ALLISON SU

What is it like to feel truly alive? The following poems explore this feeling and what it means to be alive.

I: A JOURNEY BETWEEN STATES OF BEING

In my dreams not
the daydreams but
the night dreams, there's no time
I've ever felt more alive I don't think about
worry about
anything else
And it all feels so real

My body is still
and merely a vessel for the soul truly fly
that moves freely in dreams and can fly,
away from the body restricted by gravity,
norms,
the rules of waking life

In the world of dreams my body spirit
becomes a free
on a journey
outside my control
A blur of people I've seen
but never met
A task so important
all else falls away

There is only the dream
the dream
the dream

I reach out to take it
but already
I am falling
not asleep
but awake

I rise into
a body once again
that smells the salt-filled air
sees the glowing room
opens the door
unto the sand
so fine it slips through my fingers
so soft and warm I
am falling
in love

The breeze whips
my hair
into my eyes and
into my mouth
Sunset colors melt
into the water
and I sink my feet
into the ocean
who hugs me
and is swept away again
when the water rushes in
and again I look on
into the vast expanse
of blue
and orange
rests on my shoulders
For hours I stand and let
my friend the ocean
embrace me

We are gazing across
this ocean
and sky
that makes us feel so,
so small
but loved
as if we were the world
Do you remember what that was like
to see colors so
unreal
it was a miracle
they existed at all

A tern flies across your vision
reminds you of other homes so
you close
your eyes and
sing with the wind
about how big it all is
but you saw

Blue jays chipping on wood and sunflower shells to reach seeds
To feel truly alive
Cardinal babies fluttering their wings for food from their parents
is to be
Hummingbirds drinking nectar from the firework flowers of summer
in the moment
The trees change color and the roads zip by
and when
Pigeons swirl between roosts among the stations
it's finally
Starlings fighting for food in black bags so carelessly tossed aside
over
and taking baths in puddles after the storm stains the roads
maybe
Sparrows tumbling in the sand by your café table at noon
I won't even
Music flowing through the park but you don't stop to listen
remember it

because there's a river so close you can almost touch it
and when you do,
you feel
alive

You are dreaming
but you have never been
more alive
You are awake
and you have never felt
more whole

You feel alive
because you are living
I know
I am too

II. AN ODE TO RIVERSIDE RUNS

Thank you to my past self for taking down notes. Here are some of my favorite memories:

An old man smiles as he films
starlings bathing
in a puddle.
A tired millennial still wearing
his work clothes
swings in the
park playground.

A girl places
among cherry blossoms
dandelions all
over her boyfriend's head.

The ice cream truck
passes by with "The Entertainer"
to entice you.

The dog at the climate strike wears
a tie-dye hoodie that
later gives "I Am Kenough."

A guy on the subway wears
a small backpack with
delicate butterfly embroidery.

The three friends in
front of you link pinkies in the concert line.

A woman snaps
photos of a
boot on a
ledge
for
her
portfolio.

A kid brings his hamster into
the pastry shop
that always has a line out its door.

A rock with green
eyes wears a "Hello,
my name is"
sticker.

A man stretches with an
armband around
sits next to him. a tree as
his dog

Children wearing orange
vests on a rope   follow   their   teacher   into   their next big
adventure.

A posh black poodle
struts like   it knows
who it is.

An elderly man unafraid
to ride
an electric scooter
weaves among
the crowd.

A woman plays a steampunk
violin like a cello
with a human's voice.

A man does a 360°
the street.   on a pink
bike on

The little boy tells
the women dressed as Anna
and Elsa
that he has six and
a half quarters.

A man sleeps on
a bench with a fluffy
white dog next to   his face.

A little boy in a red   balloons
cart with colorful
and one shaped like ice cream
calls for
his dad   to push him.

A tree tells you
"It's okay to hug me."

A shaggy brown dog wistfully
gazes at two other
brown shaggy dogs in strollers.

The security guard plays
Mario Kart
on his phone.

Two kids wearing
Pikachu beanies
walk by.

A stranger leaves
a line of green fruits that look like bumpy apples on the
stone wall.

The grocery delivery dude
zooms by on a scooter while rapping.

All of this,
in the time of
one semester.

KENDRA SUAREZ

Kendra Suarez (they/she) is a Brooklyn native, youth educator, and mental health advocate who loves to go on adventures, eat dessert, and meet new folks.

MENTEE'S ANECDOTE:

After my first session with Richelle, I felt seen. Richelle heard where I was in reconnecting with my creativity and suggested taking a different approach to writing than I'd expected upon joining Girls Write Now. I enjoy learning new things and connecting over similar interests, such as recent book reads, platforms we use, and experiences. Working together, I feel supported, encouraged, and inspired. I joined Girls Write Now with the desire to reconnect with writing, and working together has allowed me to embrace the writing process and, most important, to be reminded to be present and give ourselves grace.

RICHELLE SZYPULSKI

Richelle Szypulski (she/her) is a Pittsburgh-based multimedia storyteller and emotions enthusiast who also loves adventures, dessert, and new friends.

MENTOR'S ANECDOTE:

Whether we're writing, trading thoughts about character arcs, nerding out about Notion, or getting distracted by the antics of our sweet baby fur children, Saturday-morning meetings with Kendra are an absolute gift. Working together has recommitted me to my own creative practice, but what I love most is how we can both show up exactly as we are (usually five minutes late) and still hold each other accountable for our creative dreams and visions. Speaking of, I can't wait to read Kendra's YA novel someday!

WE'RE ON THE SAME PAGE

KENDRA SUAREZ

Two curious kids, Isabella and Imogene, each find a fantastical journal hidden beneath a tree at their local park and unknowingly unlock a correspondence with each other that transcends time, space, and perhaps even reality.

Day 1

ISABELLA

This book looks really cool. It shimmers! It looks kinda old but new, though? It was just lying on the ground in the park, by all the big trees.

If Mom knew I took it, she would say, "Don't touch. It's not yours." But I don't want to just leave it. I still can't take it with—ahh.

I'm going to tuck it in a corner of the tree trunk for the next time we come to the park. It seems to be a safe spot to store it—dry and hidden. Hopefully we will be back next week!

Day 2

IMOGENE

Whoa! This is super-cool! My mom would say the exact same thing, especially because you've already written in here . . . but it seems like you just found it, too? Whoever you are.

I come to sit and draw beneath these trees pretty often, though; it's kind of my spot. I've never seen anything other than dog poop bags hiding in their twisty old roots, so I couldn't help it! If you don't want me here, just say the word and I swear I'll leave the book alone.

But maybe we can share?

Day 15

ISABELLA

Poop bags? Dang, how have I not noticed?

Let's continue chatting here! I don't talk to many people outside of my siblings and my best friend, but we really see each other only during school. Mom's weird about things, like what I mentioned before. I don't really understand it.

What do you draw?

I like to sing sometimes and

Day 24

IMOGENE

Wow, it was so rainy yesterday and I was worried the journal would be ruined, but it's perfectly dry!

I've never had a pen pal before, so this is exciting! Does it count as pen-palling if we don't mail anything? Maybe we should call it something else, like super-secret-tree-palling? I don't know . . . maybe that's silly. What would you call it?

Anyway, I kind of draw whatever I feel like. I'm not very good. I just like pretending I am. Sometimes I draw fake maps and make up new places.

I wish I could sing! Were you gonna say something else at the end there? I hope your mom lets you come back soon.

Day 25

ISABELLA

Dang, did I not notice the weather at all lately? It's been a while since I've been back to the park.

I like rainy weather sometimes. I like sunny weather the most, though! Is there anything you do on rainy days? I just stay in.

I'm excited, too . . . also nervous? I don't really know what to say most of the time. I'm not that social, so I'm excited that we are pen-palling? Nature connecting? Being book buddies? Those don't really make sense. :/

We'll figure it out eventually!

Ooo, can you tell me about one of the places you have drawn?

Day 33

IMOGENE

BOOK BUDDIES! I love that! :) It sounds like a secret club and I've always wanted to be part of one of those.

I definitely stay in on rainy days, too, but I try to find some kind of craft project to do or my mom will make me spend the whole day cleaning my room. And I know I'm not supposed to, but I kind of like my mess the way it is.

Do you ever feel that way? Like you know you're supposed to follow a rule, but the rule seems made-up and maybe even dumb?

I have to go, but one place I mapped is an island only for cats called Felinia! Maybe I'll draw it for you next time . . .

BBF (Book Buddies Forever)! Bye!

Day 1,099

ISABELLA

Wow, I can't believe it's been three years already. It felt weird at first, but we know so much about each other now! I feel so grateful to have you as my friend!

My best friend is weird—I feel left out sometimes or that we are not actually as close as best friends should be.

Regents or PBAT week during sophomore year is nerve-racking. Everything is a new experience and my peers are okay—still getting to know them.

It's weird; I feel like I know you so much but still don't at the same time. Do you feel like that, too? I would love to get together one of these days; let's meet!

I'll be at the park this Saturday, June 20, around 10 a.m. Can you be here?

Day 1,102

IMOGENE

Wait, what are Regents and PBAT? My school doesn't do that, but it sounds stressful. I can totally be here on Saturday. Oh my gosh, I can't believe we took this long to try to meet up! I'll see you then!

Day 1,111

IMOGENE

Hey, I hope you're okay. I've been waiting here for like twenty minutes and I don't know what you look like, but no one has come to the

ISABELLA

I'm here! WAIT—Imogene, is that you writing???

IMOGENE

WHAT IS HAPPENING?! HOW ARE

ISABELLA

I DON'T KNOW—THIS IS CRAZY!

SUBAAH SYED

Subaah Syed is a college freshman and three-year Girls Write Now mentee originally from Queens, New York.

MENTEE'S ANECDOTE:

Having Tracy as my mentor for three years has been a lot of fun. She's been with me from my stressful junior year, to college applications, to now in my first year of college. I enjoy our meetings together—we get a lot of work done, and we update each other on our lives as well. It's nice having an adult to talk to freely about questions and concerns, regarding not just academia and career advice, but also life in general.

TRACY MILLER

Tracy Miller is a writer, digital strategist, and eight-year Girls Write Now mentor who lives in Queens, New York.

MENTOR'S ANECDOTE:

Subaah and I have been a pair since her junior year in high school, and she's now a freshman in college, many miles from home. Together we've experienced the end of the COVID pandemic, taking the SATs and being accepted to college (Subaah), and job changes and travel adventures (me). I'm impressed by her willingness to experiment in any genre, from poetry, to essays, to visual art. She's also a great storyteller, with a wry and observant sense of humor. My top pair moment was last summer, when we finally (!) got to meet in person.

TO AND FROM

SUBAAH SYED

This is a poem inspired by Subaah leaving home for her first year of college and what it feels like to come back to New York City again.

Journey Away (Subaah)

I take the F train to East Broadway
With my suitcase and backpack, trekking through the heavy snow alone in Chinatown.
My pashmina scarf covers my face, up to my eyes.
I pass by delis, grocery stores, laundromats,
So many people, but still feel a crushing solitude.

As the bus starts driving, I see the World Trade Center.
The sky is so clear I can see the top amid the night sky.
I remember how I could see the World Trade Center from my apartment back in Queens,
How I passed by it on my way to high school every day.
Now I see it as I leave the city for college, 333 miles away from home.

A seven-hour bus ride is a good time for a mini-breakdown.
Let out a few tears for the sake of my parents, my friends, my brothers,
The city with its surprises, Queens with its good food and people I love.

The city lights fade away until it's only cars and trees.
Then it's just the trees.
The dark stillness of the night echoes even through the noise of the vehicle.
This night looks ominous, haunting.

It is not welcoming,
Unlike night in the city.

Nature envelops the whole scenery.
The moon, in its crescent shape, slowly rises and falls as the hours go by.
Stars eventually emerge from the sky (always a sight to see when you're from the city).
I concentrate on them really hard
As if they would disappear if I dare look away.

I miss the tall buildings and the streetlights.
I crave the lights that dot the city skyline and the warmth that comes from the city that never sleeps.
This part of the state is sleeping now,
Yet the forests seem suspiciously restless in the dark.
Only the stars overlooking the trees know what goes on in there.

It is hard to sleep when my mind is racing.
Bouncing back and forth, from New York City to Rochester.

I slowly ease up to the tranquility of the night,
To the hundreds of miles of hills and flatlands,
With no skyscrapers for hours.
My city girl mind relaxes.
I embrace the serene terrain.

We pass by Pennsylvania, the Pocono Mountains that I might have mistook for clouds.
We go up to Binghamton, drive by Syracuse.
The only lights are from billboards advertising storage spaces and obscure law firms.

Finally, I see the name of my school,
On medical centers and street signs, and am at peace.
I'm in known territory again.

I call my dad back in NYC when I get off the bus.
My call wakes him up from sleep.
I tell him I made it back safe.

It's hard leaving the city you grew up in,
no matter how many times you have to make the journey away.
But eventually, when you arrive at your destination,
A place where you've already started building a life,
You feel better.

Journey Back (Tracy)

I've returned to New York in every way possible, I think.
Regurgitated through the mouths of the Holland and Lincoln
Gliding gracefully over the Verrazzano
Sunburned on the ferry back from Sandy Hook
Down that Hudson River Line, like Billy Joel sang about
On a plane flying so low over Brooklyn and Queens that I can pick out Greenwood Cemetery, and my first apartment, and my next apartment
On my own two feet over the George Washington Bridge
(this is not an exhaustive list)

So here's what you need to know: New York doesn't care if you were gone, but it always welcomes you back.
I don't mean that there's no warmth to be found in the city. It's there, if you know where to look for it.
I mean that the city goes on without you while you're away, the way the earth spins on its axis every year, the way your own breath flows in and out: without you doing anything about it.
So when you come back, you're dropping into a scene already in motion. You have only to remember your place in the choreography.

Other cities speak in smiles and whispers
They show you proudly their neat and manicured lawns
They are polite and presentable, like a nice suit dress, like church clothes

New York dresses only for itself. It contains all the wonders of the world but needs to show you nothing, for it has nothing to prove: It is what it is, and you can choose to be in it or outside it.

When I come back to this place I love, I take a deep breath and let its chaotic symphony welcome me back in.
The blare of car horns, the heels on hard pavement, the indelible *bing-bong* of the subway doors
The motorbikes that buzz below my window, the heavy footfalls of my upstairs neighbor, and my clanging radiator singing me to sleep
And I feel the peace and contentment of knowing I'm home.

THAINÁ THEODORO

Thainá is a twenty-year-old student at Grinnell College majoring in political science and gender, women's, and sexuality studies.

MENTEE'S ANECDOTE:

While Nandini and I were discovering our shared passion for political science, we stumbled upon a writing project that intrigued us both in *Here & Now: Girls Write Now 2024 Anthology.*

NANDINI KALANI

Nandini (she/her) is a freshman in college with a fervent love for cinematography, traveling, piano melodies, and the occasional indulgence in a well-crafted passion fruit gelato.

PEER MENTEE'S ANECDOTE:

Thainá is an exceptional and imaginative individual. Our shared enthusiasm for civic engagement and social justice has strengthened our bond as college freshmen, guiding us through the whirlwind transition from high school to university life. Delving into political science, advocacy, and activism work together, we've found solace in navigating a male-dominated field as empowered women. It's a joy to connect with someone who shares so many common passions. Through our collaborations, I've cherished the opportunity to learn, grow, and laugh alongside Thainá, finding inspiration in her unwavering dedication and vibrant spirit.

MR. CUPID TAUGHT ME THERE IS MORE TO LIFE

THAINÁ THEODORO

Content Warning: Addiction

In 2023, I had an apprenticeship program at Mr. Cupido's drug rehabilitation NGO, Second Chance Outreach in Cape Town. Every day I learned about the lives of others and the true meaning of a second chance.

Every morning, my friends Julia, Isa, and I would meet halfway between our houses at 8 a.m. As broke students, we had a system where someone different called an Uber each day. When we arrived at Retreat, a township in Cape Town, the driver would warn us to be careful. However, Retreat quickly became a second home for us.

As soon as we got out of the car, Mr. Cupido would be there waiting for us with his friends who sold oranges on the street. He would always buy us some for breakfast. That's what made Mr. Cupido special—he made us feel like we belonged. Whether it was by giving us fruit, salads, or freshly baked goods, he always went out of his way to make us feel welcome.

The building where Mr. Cupido worked was both partially a church and his office, and it had an aura of hope. Being there reminded me that everyone is living for the first time.

Julia used an unbranded laptop, Isa had a 2000s ThinkPad, and I used a box computer; it was a learning experience. The three of us managed to make it lighter, typing over fifteen profiles and stories of addiction. We found ourselves sharing what we had learned from different people's experiences. We heard from couples, parents, and friends, and saw how much people are affected by characteristics they cannot change. This made me appreciate Mr. Cupido even more.

As I digitized all of his financial books, I saw that he paid himself the least. Mr. Cupido suffered from years of addiction and went to rehab but did not find a space to grow there. He was ignored, and it took him a lot of effort to get through it. His past pictures may prove shocking to anyone who sees the laughing and kind Mr. Cupido who always goes out of his way to help others. When talking about his measly salary, he would frequently say that his greatest blessing was rather helping people the way he would like to have been helped.

I am inspired by Mr. Cupido's selfless acts of heroism. He has dedicated his life to saving others in his community, and his empathetic nature has made a significant impact on dozens of people's lives. It takes a special kind of person to be able to dedicate their life to helping those in need. I have tried ever since to emulate Mr. Cupido's bravery and kindness in everything I do.

NYILAH THOMAS

Nyilah Thomas puts pen to paper to obsess about love, loss, religion, and her daily experiences in poetry, prose, and personal essays.

MENTEE'S ANECDOTE:

Asma Al-Masyabi is one of the greats. Reading Asma's pieces always invokes so many emotions, images, and ideas, leaving me stunned like a deer peering into headlights. Her work hits home, and her feedback is a delight. I love Saturdays at 3 p.m., because that's when I get to catch up with Asma about our lives and, even more recently, share a mutual love for spoken-word poetry and even a playlist for performances. I hope to one day see Asma perform, because her voice journeys you into the poem. Remember her name, folks; she's that good!

ASMA AL-MASYABI

Asma Al-Masyabi writes poetry, personal essays, and stories that stain her fingers dark with ink. She tries to find her reflection in these musings.

PEER MENTEE'S ANECDOTE:

Nyilah Thomas is the kind of writer whose work you can't read just once. I could write a long list of the things I obsess about in her writing—the bold voice, the perfect amount of humor, the way she separates her stanzas, but I don't have the word count for that. I love learning more about her through her beautiful poetry and prose in our weekly sessions, and all our time spent together geeking over our favorite poetry. Nyilah is the one who truly introduced me to spoken-word poetry, and my YouTube algorithm thanks her profusely.

I'M AFRAID YOU'LL END UP SEEING ME THE WAY I SEE MYSELF

NYILAH THOMAS

One by one, her words vanished until there were none le—

my mouth lives as a rusted gate, aged from words sheltered within for so long.
closed for so long you'd think it's a casket, earthworms and atomic bombs lay dormant, bones of all the "i wish i would's and could's" claw on its metal hinges.

such a buried, haunted thing.

begging to be let out, explored, consumed. i want to breathe you, but these pearly whites won't concede. their manifesto was scribed by martyrs and anarchists who burned bridges—burned hopes of ever finding something worthy of destruction.

Girly's with pretty pretty eyes and clean skin ooze hearty laughs,
and my cheeks outstretch themselves in
an attempt to remain open

long enough for something—
anything to escape.

hellfire scorches my lips, making them chapped.
burns my tongue and swells my gums.

"be quiet, girl."

see how there's no *Y* in this statement? i'm no girly.
just a mute thing.

my knees release their stiffness and propel me to run.
run away, girl. you don't belong
here.

there once was a time when words were holy ground, and Men would worship its feet like a false god, sacrificing themselves daily for something worth praising. Men would caress my skin, and grip firmly my jaw.

"Speak," He ordered.

my mouth released all its contents; every word, every syllable, and every idea flourished. everything i had was birthed into the atmosphere, the biggest explosion of the cosmos to occur in that century. i was an enigma of warrior's wounds, accelerant of earthquakes.

Helen had nothing on me, but Troy did.

He knew i was not worthy of being an idol. then,
Murphy created His First Law. You know the one.
Everything that can go wrong, will.

thus, my words became a bunched basket of empty cradles. my teeth snarled at the aspirations of syllables, my tongue rolled into every other word like bowling pins, and my gums swelled at the idea of ideas—swelled at the idea of ever being heard
again.

i became and remained just a poor little mute thing.

finding this out, the Men stoned me, cracking every one of my words open.
leaving them gaping,
defenseless.

massacring my words for the survival of their own, and soon

i forgot how to move,   how to breathe,   how to speak.
my voice became formless, and my throat remained a barren well of
soot and blood—praying to one day ooze as its Ancestors did.

NAVYA VASIREDDY

Navya (she/her) is a high school junior who is passionate about journalism, and if she's not at a café, she's likely baking or walking with her family.

MENTEE'S ANECDOTE:

My mentor of almost two years, Ambika, has become one of my biggest supporters. She has inspired me to explore new genres, including poetry and memoir writing, and her encouragement instilled the confidence I have today to share my voice with the world. With her help, I've discovered how I can effectively convey my emotions, experiences, inspirations, and voice through my work. Her support, however, extends beyond my writing. Ambika has stuck with me through my ups and downs, helping me recognize that growth follows every rough patch. I couldn't be more thankful for Ambika and her infinite support.

AMBIKA SUKUL

Ambika is a program manager at Citibank, a poetry enthusiast, and a foodie traveler.

MENTOR'S ANECDOTE:

Navya is a highly intelligent and personable young woman, and is especially praiseworthy for her dedication to tasks and exceptional writing skills. Navya is a talented writer, and it has been a pleasure working with her these past two years.

TRADITION

NAVYA VASIREDDY

"tradition" is a poem that captures the beauty of my family's annual holiday traditions and how my struggle with change has impacted my perception of the constants in life.

the doorbell rings, and the winter season begins—
my sister enters, followed by my younger cousins from connecticut, my older cousins from virginia and arkansas, and all my aunts and uncles.
suddenly, the house is chirping, energetic, and loud,
just like every other christmas break.

the break begins with a customary trip to target,
our cart overflowing with boxes of milano cookies, takis, and powdered sugar donuts.
my cousins run around target, the nine of us crowding every aisle we enter—
our first holiday tradition.

the grinch plays on the television,
as we sit on the floor of our family room,
gluing gumdrops onto the gingerbread house with a mountain of icing—
our second holiday tradition.

we drive to lake hiawatha,
home to a quaint downtown and my childhood ice-cream parlor.
laughter lights up the street,
ice cream dripping down our cones—
our third holiday tradition.

the echoes of our chatter can be heard into the night,
as my cousins and i make our way around morristown greene.
the trees are lit with strings of lights,
and the lampposts are decorated with luminous snowflakes.
we walk through the cold, beautiful downtown—
our fourth holiday tradition.

we circle around the christmas tree,
gifts piling under the tree for my cousins and our parents.
my cousins sport our comfortable holiday attire:
plaid pajama pants and a plain t-shirt.
the adults record our reactions,
faces glowing with joy at their presents—
our fifth holiday tradition.

however,
this year is different.
my younger cousins are now at the age
where their voices sound deeper,
and they have grown independent.
they now kneel in family photos;
and use familiar slang, cracking jokes that i'd hear my classmates make.

my older cousins have also changed.
once the remaining two seniors graduate,
i will be the only one left in high school.
conversation topics vary from college to internships to extracurriculars,
and i am suddenly on the sidelines of every discussion;
time fleets quicker than any of us would like.

the thing is,
i changed too.
i grew more confident,
more vocal about my needs.
i expressed my feelings of exclusion,
and my cousins responded with support.

i began to realize:
perhaps change is nice—
new experiences, new memories, new traditions.

as we grow older, we will learn more about each other and ourselves,
forging an even stronger connection.
though the constants are treasured,
the unpredictable circumstances open doors to fresh ideas
. . . and i'm excited to see what's next.

MALIA-FAY VAZQUEZ

Malia-Fay Vazquez is a Chelsea-based writer who is obsessed with magical realism, literary fiction, and her dog, Jojo. She is interested in the human condition in literature.

MENTEE'S ANECDOTE:

Steph and I met only about a month ago, but we quickly bonded and talked about anything and everything related to books and our lives! Her style and genres of writing are really powerful, especially since she explores forms and genres I haven't explored yet! Steph has supported me in writing applications and let me know about any interesting writing opportunities she thinks I might enjoy. She is such a sweet and caring person!

STEPH AUTERI

Steph Auteri is a New Jersey writer for *The Atlantic*, *VICE*, and other publications. Auteri is also the author of *A Dirty Word* and the founder of Guerrilla Sex Ed.

MENTOR'S ANECDOTE:

Malia and I were paired up midyear, which made me nervous, but we immediately bonded over our mutual love for needlework and jigsaw puzzles and the fact that we're both clearly book nerds. She has ideas for everything from a school magazine to a community enrichment project and a truly extraordinary-sounding novel. By the end of our first call, I was amazed by Malia's ambition. Since then, I've been lucky enough to see some of her work, quirky little gems of speculative fiction that cross genres and blur the lines of reality, and they are so my jam!

THE LETTERS OF THE MAGIC FRIDGE

MALIA-FAY VAZQUEZ

January 14, 2024—425 East Delancey Street, Apartment 4D, the back of the vintage fridge near a jar of pickles.

Dear Casey,

I wish I could explain the feeling I get eating kimchi straight out of the jar at 2 a.m. I only slightly regret it when bursts of energy knock into me, spices reach my throat, and the fiery coals ignite in my lungs. It's strange when I'm sitting on my kitchen floor, legs crossed in front of the dryer, watching clothes spin and tumble. I scoop up more fermented cabbage, bringing it up to my tingling lips, and the pressing point in my chest seems to ease a little.

Getting up in the morning is hard. You know that more than anyone, but today took more than it gave. I can't seem to wipe the sleep from my eyes, yet they won't close for more than a minute. I'm sorry I don't like talking about the accident; I know how helpless you feel when you can't do anything for me.

Up until this point, I've been slowly inching toward the comfortable sheets of darkness the kitchen seems to promise. I close my eyes, and the lights continuously flicker in a humming rhythm, the breeze kissing my skin. It's the gentle thrum of the dryer at my back and the cool floor underneath my toes that keep me on the ground.

I imagine how different it would be if you were here with me, cross-legged on the floor, feeling the delicious burn in your lungs as the fluorescent lights flicker above us, and you whisper stories to me of when you were younger.

Tell me more; tell me all of it. You're all I think about, and I could just die sitting next to you as we lean over this jar of fiery heaven and secrets.

Love,
Kai

P.S. I left some pancit in the fridge. (I'm not sure if you guys have microwaves in the nineties—or if the container will even reach you with this note—but it might take longer for it to heat on yours. I know you have the late shift again, but it's super-quick to make, I promise.)

Dear Kai,

The thoughts of you seem to swirl in the ink of my pen. It's nearing midnight, and the stillness of the night wraps around me like a comforting shroud, the humming energy of your words breathing into the void. Your description of kimchi-induced euphoria is, by all accounts, a masterpiece. I can almost taste the tangy spice on my own tongue, imagining the way it quickens your heartbeat. Your nights are filled with such peculiar rituals—finding solace in the simple act of eating by a dryer. It's endearing, and so quintessentially you.

Finding those pockets of peace is so hard sometimes, where time seems to slow, and the weight of the world lightens just enough to let me breathe. As I write, the Cranberries are playing in the background (I think you would love them), and I really want to make you sinigang (Filipino sour soup). I'm not sure why, but I want to make a meal for you, like an impulse. Not leave a container for you in the fridge, like we always do, but prepare a meal for you. You'd lean on the doorway, smiling as you watch me at the stove, and I'd smile, wearing a pink apron you'd get me for Valentine's Day. We'd talk about everything. We would exchange the day's tales—mine penned on paper, yours spun from vinyl—and the record store's own melody, a symphony of stories and songs. "Linger" would be playing in the background as I see the way your face lights up when you try my sinigang. Our smiles would mingle in the airy scent of tamarind and tomatoes, much like how I can sense your smile as you read this letter. It's moments like these, enveloped in music and memories, that I feel closest to you.

Keep savoring the good, no matter how fleeting, and cherish the laughter, even if it's tinged with sorrow. These fragments of delight are yours, and no voice—no matter how stern—can take them from you. As for the pancit, rest assured, we do have microwaves here in the nineties (I'm a little concerned you thought we didn't). And though I might not be able to enjoy your cooking *with* you, in 1.5 minutes, I'll have a piece of your world.

Always here,
Casey

P.S. Left you two army-sized containers of sinigang for you to try. (Describing it as an impulse might have been putting it mildly.) Also, I think you'd love the album *Everybody Else Is Doing It, So Why Can't We?*

SOPHIA VENABLES

Sophia Venables is a proud 2023–2024 Collaboratory "Elder Mentee," creating poetry and comedy. When she's not writing, Sophia works for a global nonprofit law firm.

MENTEE'S ANECDOTE:

Jennifer is not only a brilliant mentor, but also a phenomenal human being. Her ability to "meet me where I'm at" in both my personal and creative lives has been such a joy. In terms of creative growth, she brings a wealth of knowledge to our pair sessions, regardless of the topic or genre. We have spent hours writing jokes, finding just the right poetic words, and discussing story structure. In terms of personal growth, with Jennifer's support, I have found the courage to pursue my longtime creative goals and the resilience to see them through. Thank you, Jennifer!

JENNIFER L. BROWN

Jennifer L. Brown is an author of middle-grade and young-adult novels. When not writing, she enjoys walking her dog or perusing a bookstore.

MENTOR'S ANECDOTE:

I have loved working with Sophia this year. She brings boundless enthusiasm into our sessions, whether she's exploring a new medium or delving further into an old favorite. She has such a facility for language; it's been a pleasure to watch her turn that skill toward crafting a killer metaphor in a poem or punchline in a joke. I'm awed by her bravery in trying new things and her ability to check in with her feelings as she decides which goals to pursue. I am excited for her future projects and feel privileged to accompany her on her writing journey.

PRESENT

SOPHIA VENABLES

If you've lost someone, may the specifics of this poem be relatable.

You cannot reschedule
grief
like a lunch date—

this morning,
brimming with
expectations

(and you're
already
running late)

please pencil in
at your earliest [in]*convenience*
this unwelcome

guest—the fog that
swirls,
gnawing your veins

making fossils from
your larynx and
quicksand from your

rib cage,
stalagmites sprung
from your shoulders and

valleys drilled into
your collarbone.
Only then,

with the earth now
sunk
into each

poisoned pore,
will mourning smile
and ask,

if you would like
to do this
again, sometime soon.

NYLAH WATKINS

Nylah Watkins is an award-winning writer and a senior attending Douglas Anderson School of the Arts for creative writing.

MENTEE'S ANECDOTE:

Ashley has supported me in a way I didn't know I needed. We have created a strong relationship, built on passion and trust, and she has been a vital part of my development as a writer this year. It has been so fun to see her and speak with her. We talk about school, writing, hobbies, anything that's on our minds. Every time we meet, I am just excited to hear what she thinks about my work, to share my writing with someone who I value so deeply.

ASHLEY ALLMAN

Ashley Allman is a Seattle-based writer and communications professional. She is the author of the novel *Pachamama* and has published fiction, nonfiction, and academic work in *Superstition Review* and the *Desire to Escape* anthology, among others.

MENTOR'S ANECDOTE:

Nylah is an incredibly hardworking, insightful, and creative student. The opportunity to work with her and to be trusted with her writing has been a gift. I admire the clarity of vision she has for her future—it's impressive for someone as young as she is—and the dedication she has for bringing that vision into reality. Nylah is a promising young poet with a strong voice, a keen sense of social injustice, and a talent for writing lyrical narrative. Wherever her creative journey leads, I'm fortunate to have been present at one of the mileposts along the way.

SOME GIRLS

NYLAH WATKINS

After Joy Harjo's "She Had Some Horses," "Some Girls" is a piece about women, their beauty, and their worth.

Some girls are birds of morning
Some girls are sirens of night
Some girls are made of stars
Some girls are basins of tears

I am not these girls

Some girls are fat
Some girls are thin
Some girls don't own a scale
Some girls have never lived without one

I am not these girls

Some girls are pretty
Some girls are plain
Some girls glow like a red moon
Some girls dull like a forgotten pond

I am not these girls

Some girls stuff their bras
Some girls suffocate their legs
Some girls cage their stomachs
Some girls starve their guts

I am not these girls

Some girls have hair that breezes like wind
Some girls have eyes like the sky
Some girls have hair that curls like waves
Some girls have eyes like the sun
Some girls have hair that defies gravity
Some girls have eyes like death

I am not these girls

Some girls are little girls, wrapping their heads with towels, squealing
 at their inches
Some girls scream as relaxer burns fester
Some girls sizzle curls till they're straight as bone
Some girls watch their hair wither and fall out

I am these girls

Some girls have "dirt skin" so
Some girls scrub until skin bleeds raw
Some girls rub chemical cream until melanin disappears
Some girls hide from the sun

I am these girls

Some girls hear, "you don't have enough for a man to grab on to"
Some girls hear, "how can you have no ass—you're Black"
Some girls hear, "your body is a distraction"
Some girls hear, "you will never be pretty enough to love"

I am, I am
I am these girls

I am a girl who sucks in her stomach
I am a girl who is skin and bones
I am a girl who stuffs her pants because
I am a girl who hates her hips

I am a girl who longs for Beyoncé hair, but
I am a girl who will never have it
I am a girl who is made of tears
I am a girl with eyes like death
I am a girl who will never be beautiful enough to love

I am these girls
I am, I am

SIERRA J. WILLIAMS

Sierra is a freshman at the University of Pennsylvania. Originally from Staten Island, she now resides in Atlanta. She loves the arts and writing poetry.

MENTEE'S ANECDOTE:

Creating and growing with my mentor, Caitlin, for a second year has been an extension of our enlightening and creatively driven experience. Caitlin continues to help me so much, from editing and revising my poetry to motivating me and helping me see everything with more clarity and precision. Without her, I would not have accomplished everything I have. She is a great mentor, inspiration, and encourager. With this song, she helped me synthesize my ideas and inspired me to dive deeper into using colors to tell one narrative that offers a glimpse into different external-internal moments of the same story.

CAITLIN CHASE

Caitlin Chase is a mother, mentor, creative, and strategy consultant for cultural organizations and emerging brands. She lives and works in Washington, D.C.

MENTOR'S ANECDOTE:

This marks the second year of creative collaboration between Sierra and I, and it continues to be a joy to explore different forms of expression—from poetry to personal narrative—and to examine the possibilities of language together. Sierra is incredibly curious, insightful, and motivated, and it is a privilege to think, learn, and create alongside her!

EASY TO YOU: A SHOEGAZE SONG

SIERRA J. WILLIAMS

In this song, I was inspired to explore the genre of shoegaze music and songwriting. I sought to imbue this song with stages of isolation and romantic grief, using settings, colors, solitude, and abyss-like imagery.

Lying around
Not doing anything
Waking up to stare at the ceiling
Sleeping to feel no pain

Copy paper dreams
My mind just draws a blank
Black and white thoughts (of you) run violent
Colored static to fill the silence

I'm standing near
The edge between the world and the moon
I just hope you won't forget me
'Cause I know that everything comes
Easy to you

Near the edge of the blue
I just hope you won't forget me
'Cause I know that everything comes
Easy to you

Feeling around in the darkness
Forgetting my own name

Reaching out to resurface
But the weight (of you) remains

Rising up to see a light in view
I remember when the sun shone boldly
Pull away from the shackles that hold me
Opening my eyes to the truth
(without you)

I'm standing near
The edge between the world and the moon
I just hope you won't forget me
'Cause I know that everything comes
Easy to you

Near the edge of the blue
I just hope you won't forget me
'Cause I know that everything comes
Easy to you

TATYANNA WILLS

Tatyanna Wills is a freshman in college studying psychology. She has a habit of writing, but not about herself—except for that one time.

MENTEE'S ANECDOTE:

Meeting Elizabeth has definitely improved my writing and my ability to speak out as a person. Not only has she provided a safe space for me to talk about my experiences, but we have also been able to connect on multiple subjects. Elizabeth has helped me grow not only as a writer, but as a person.

ELIZABETH KOSTER

Elizabeth Koster is a writer, teacher, and cat mom in New York City.

MENTOR'S ANECDOTE:

I've enjoyed our conversations about writing, as well as our in-depth discussions about human nature and human rights. Tatyanna's work is powerful and moving. It has been inspiring to speak with her about her process and to see her transform pain into beauty.

1985

TATYANNA WILLS

Content Warning: Cursing, Homophobia, Sexual Content

This piece showcases a former guitarist for a popular band reminiscing on her experience as a young lesbian in the 1980s.

I've tried to "fix myself" numerous times in my life. Homosexuality wasn't exactly seen as a normal thing back then; sure, there were the Stonewall riots and the AIDS crisis bringing a new sense of humanity to these people for anyone who had eyes and a tiny bit of compassion in their hearts for others. I had a gay uncle who I shared many fond memories with, and I remember visiting his house after school. But fitting in was not usually my experience, especially in our neighborhood.

They were always the other, the deviants. Destined to be outcast by good, hardworking, civilized Americans like ourselves for the rest of our lives. One of *them* couldn't possibly be Miriam, couldn't possibly be me. The last time I tried to fix myself I was eighteen and fresh out of a relationship. Actually being able to love a woman was out of the question. When I'd first been propositioned by a fan of our band, I'd said "fuck it" and ignored whatever my gut was warning me about.

It probably didn't matter anyway. I was gonna be fine. If I could just ignore the nagging feeling in the back of my head, perhaps I could even have some fun with this guy. Though I doubted it. I wasn't attracted to him; I don't think anyone could've been. He wasn't the type of guy you got with for his looks. He was attractive because he looked like he was enjoying himself. He was older, about thirty-five, with this badly cut shaggy hair, stubble, and smoke on his breath. We went to his van, which was decked out in hippie décor. You would've never guessed he'd listened to a single second of Maria y Las Estrellas, yet here I was sitting on some kind of strange tapestry on the floor because I was too weirded out by the dirt on the couch to sit on it.

"So are we gonna get this started or are you just gonna sit there looking stupid?" he asked.

"Huh?" I blurted out in reply, caught off guard by the sound of his voice, sure he had spoken to me as we walked to his van, but perhaps I hadn't really been paying attention. My mind often ended up wandering to other things—to different, better scenarios.

Deep down, I knew I didn't want to do this. I didn't want to be here. I wanted to be at home, watching a shitty teen movie with Maria, lying in her arms, thinking about how the moment would last forever, that at any moment if I turned to look to my side I would see her there with me, holding my hand, instead of me holding some man's.

I craved that ignorance more than anything, but I had already gotten here and so I figured I might as well finish what I'd started.

"I, uh, um." My hope of making a sly remark or even a cheesy attempt at flirtatious banter exited my lips as a stutter, to my own chagrin.

I think it was at this point that the man noticed my reluctance; he sat next to me and placed a hand on my shoulder in some sort of comforting gesture. "You know you don't have to do this if you don't want to. I won't hold it against you. Look, I understand you're young and hot and I'm twice your age and also hot." I chuckle at that last statement, which he doesn't appreciate; I see his face contort into a frown that he quickly brushes off. "Listen, what I'm getting at is that I know you probably want an experience or something, but this shouldn't be something you force yourself into. I don't want you leaving this van with any regrets, now, do you hear me, doll?"

I looked down at my hands. Maybe he was right; I didn't have to do this, even if I so desperately needed to be fixed. Maybe I could wait a little while, could live in bliss for a few years before I was forced to become some man's wife, or even worse—a mistress.

Maybe being straight could wait awhile. I fiddled with my thumbs, the silence permeating in the room for what felt like an eternity before the man quickly got up to his feet with a huff. "All right, then." He groaned, stretching. "How about I get us some beer, okay? Lighten the mood a little bit." I stared at him blankly as he walked out of his van to go buy some beer from the local gas station down the street, leaving me alone with my thoughts.

CAMRON WRIGHT

Camron Wright (she/hers/her) is a 2023 graduate of Howard University who is an emerging writer and playwright.

MENTEE'S ANECDOTE:

Olivia and I are very alike. They don't drink coffee, but like tea or the occasional hot chocolate, and we both love going to museums, dialogue, and visualizing every single detail for our stories. Being Olivia's mentee for the second year has been amazing. We encourage each other to write through our doubts. I am so lucky to be her mentee.

OLIVIA GOOD

Olivia Good is a Brooklyn-based writer, producer, and editor of podcasts, museum audio content, and audio description.

MENTOR'S ANECDOTE:

Camron and I have been a mentee-mentor pair since last year, but we finally met in person a few weeks ago. Walking into the coffee shop in Brooklyn where we met up, it was a thrill to see her face and give her a hug. When I first started getting to know Camron, she was a busy senior at Howard University. As of January, she is now a busy New York City resident, interning in the press department at American Ballet Theatre and working as a writer's assistant on a Columbia University School of the Arts theater production, *In the Bronx Brown Girls Can See Stars Too*, written by Amalia Oliva Rojas. Camron continues to impress me with her maturity, creativity, work ethic, and kindness!

LET'S BE FIVE

CAMRON WRIGHT

"Let's Be Five" is a story about reflecting on the first semester of college and having to make the decision to be your own person.

"Playtime is over. Lay down," I say.

She jumps on the bed, trying to reach the popcorn ceiling. How did this jellybean of a child gain more energy? Maybe if I say it with more authority she will listen. I add bass to my voice.

"Layla Lewis, go to sleep! Don't make me count to ten!"

She jumps higher and faster. I look around at my old ballet-pink bedroom walls, now speckled with golden crown stickers that make the room hers. I try to remember all the times I played here alone. I want to remember the last time I was happy enough to smile so widely, to laugh as hard as Layla does. Those moments don't last forever. I should let her have this, but I need a break.

"One."

"Two!" she says.

"No, that's not how . . ." I start to say.

I don't know how I expect the rest of the world to listen to me if my younger sister is not fazed by my authority.

"Layla, I want to go to sleep. Please lay down."

"One hundred more minutes!" she says. "Jump with me, Kyra! Pleeeeeeease! Pleeeeeeease!"

I lay my head against the white headboard and exhale so deeply that Layla giggles.

"You sound like an elephant. PPPPHHHFFFF!"

Layla squeals, her feet inching toward my legs as she jumps. Not only is she ignoring me, but now she is mocking my existence.

My first spring break from college has turned me into a free babysitting service. My parents need to come home from their so-called date night and deal with their child. The sooner they return, the more time I'll have to watch Netflix in peace. I lay on the pink princess comforter and close my eyes to pretend I am sleeping. Maybe she will take the hint.

"Kyra!" she says.

I feel the springs jolt as those kindergarten feet come closer. Then they suddenly stop. I guess I won. I open my eyes to a stubby little finger about to touch my nose. Layla jumps to her feet and screams as if she is trying to wake the dead, finding a new rhythm at the edge of the bed as she continues her antics. I have one option left, though I regret thinking about it already.

"Let's play a game," I say.

"GAME!"

She gains excitement while her feet are off the ground. Her pink silk bonnet flies up and her tiny body, draped in a Cinderella-blue nightgown, hits the twin mattress. Why didn't I think of this twenty minutes ago?

"Candy Land!"

"No, we are playing Dreamland!" I say.

For the first time in my life, a kindergartener rolls their eyes at me. I know it won't be the last time this week.

"Close your eyes. Tight enough so the bad dreams won't sneak in," I say.

Surprisingly, she listens. Layla crosses her legs and places her hands in her lap. She takes being a princess a little too seriously.

"Here's how you play. I say one sentence and then you say two sentences after me, okay? But your eyes have to be closed the whole time."

Layla's bonnet shakes up and down in agreement.

I close my eyes, putting myself in Layla's world:

Once there was a dragon who lived in the tallest castle in the world.

He had orange scales, blue teeth, and breathed green fire every time he talked.

He was a friendly dragon that wanted to protect the princess, but he was bad at his job.

The dragon would not let the princess do anything she wanted to do.

She wanted to eat cake and the dragon said no. She wanted to jump on the bed and the dragon said no again.

She wanted to change her major and the dragon said no.

But the princess did not care.

She wanted to have fun because princesses do whatever they want to do.

So the princess ran from the dragon.

I look at Layla as she skips my turn. It doesn't matter, because her eyes are still closed. I low-key want to see where she is going with this story. As she continues, her voice becomes quieter.

One night when the dragon was sleeping, the princess threw a birthday party. With balloons and a bouncy house and presents. She invited all the other princesses. Then the dragon woke up while they were singing and started to breathe fire. But the princess told him no and then . . .

"What happened next?" I say.

I open my eyes to see Layla's body slumped over at my side. I should poke her just to make sure she is sleeping, but I don't want to risk it. I angle my feet toward the beige carpet, getting ready to stand, although I want to be in Layla's world for a few seconds longer. I stand anyway, taking the blanket from the foot of the bed to cover her. She always says that she gets cold at night. I turn out the lights and exit the princess's room.

OLIVIA WRONSKI

Olivia Wronski is a writer and artist in their second year of college with passions for dance, music, and video games.

MENTEE'S ANECDOTE:

Working with Louise has been such a memorable and fun experience. I truly felt like we clicked, and it has led to such an enriching writing adventure. Much of our work is a collaborative effort, which stems from a wonderful blend of our common interests in food, culture, and our differences as people. I give all the credit to Louise for being an incredible guide and mentor in discovering new ways of expression through writing with an equally vast amount of prompts to further guide our riveting writing adventures.

LOUISE LING EDWARDS

Louise Ling Edwards is a writer and educator who lives in Columbus, Ohio, and enjoys long walks, listening to podcasts, and cooking delicious food.

MENTOR'S ANECDOTE:

Working with Olivia is an exciting and rewarding way for us to grow together as writers. Whether we're laughing together or working quietly, it's fun to bounce ideas off each other and be in a space where we can share creative energy. I've enjoyed learning about Olivia's interests in performance poetry through leading community studios together and exploring new artistic forms with each other—PechaKucha, zines, graphic design, and terza rimas (a rhyming poetic form showcased in our work in the anthology). I'm so glad I've gotten the chance to collaborate with such an insightful artist by working alongside Olivia!

CYCLE OF SEASONS

OLIVIA WRONSKI

A collection of poems that showcases our collaborative efforts as a pair. The collection delves into themes of growth, nature, and self-reflection.

I.

Winter truly begins when the flurries of snow
Waltz down, down, down
Collecting at my sock-warmed toes.

Summer truly begins when the cicadas sound,
And the sweltering heat ripples in the air
And the summer night, fireflies leave me spellbound.

Autumn truly begins when warm-colored leaves fall everywhere,
Waltzing like their snowy sisters
And the wind picks up from a gentle breeze one day out of nowhere.

Spring leaves behind soft breezy whispers
Of summer beach days spent lounging,
Oh to think soon we will once again be with biting winters.

Winter to summer to autumn to spring, the cycle of seasons is so grounding,
With breezy winds and spring sun, I look toward winter's cold fun.
From winter's cold fun, I look toward autumn's surroundings.

Each season feels like rebirth, like a new era of me has begun.
Yet, as each season passes, pieces of the old me stick out of my body like threads undone.

II.

To be a woolen doll, spun from sheep-soft threads,
What colors tell the story of the lives I've lived
And the days I've passed?

What pieces of me are picked out by sewing needles,
Tucked back in by crochet hooks,
Cut off with the sharp silver blades of scissors?

How complex are the stitches of my torso,
Whipstitched to protect my edges,
Ladder-stitched for a completed finish?

Or am I just made from the negligent hands of a child,
Who could not tell the professional stitches of a master
From the clumps of yarn they shove together in small hands?

III.

When light shines against my hands they glow red
and sometimes I wish I could feel soft warmth
like a vegetable garden tended:

functional and growing in swaths
of green that scream I am cared for
and the green peppered with kernels of color: corn

filled with sun, orange face of pumpkins. Earlier, July tomatoes
    outpoured
matching the heat that outlines my hands. The beams
radiate through my skin. How can I know in my core

that I am still growing, when I no longer grow taller and fruit does
    not gleam
from my body? Please sew me a map. Sew me
a path. Sew me into the ground where I came from by a stream

where I can grow again. Drink me in, bee.
Bite my leaves, ant. Sometimes, maybe, I don't need to know
that I am growing. I just need to know my body can foresee

another season. That seeds can be blown
and land where they may be grown or not grown.

IV.

And can you hear the cicadas buzzing?
Those strange periodical bugs that only emerge
every 13 or 17 years. Their percussing

muscles sucking their torsos in and out. Merge
music and body. Suck in your chest
so your ribs buckle one by one. Deform, reform, resurge

300–400 times a second. I'm at my best
in a chorus where no one can hear me, but I know I'm singing
and we're creating sound and summer. But most of the time I'm nesting

underground in an outlandish goblin mode. I fling
clothes that pile in mounds and then spend days tunneling
through them. I could live in this soft cocoon of earth spinning

into cloth spinning into all the shapes of my old bodies. I could smuggle
myself back into childhood. I could live most of my days as a nymph.
I could spend 15 years there. I could snuggle

most of my life. But once in a while, when it's warm and dry, I'll un-stiff
myself from the burrow. We'll paint the sky with our bodies, as if they were hieroglyphs.

V.

papers of poetry stapled together like patchwork,
gardens patched from seeds and soil
catching flower petals like I can catch the words

in my ear. They spiral around my cochlea, coiling
through my bloodstream in quick steps.
outside, fireflies blink to the rhythm, lights like sizzling oil

reminding me of drops of sesame-colored gold specks.
Cook me a meal filled with all the seasons
cycling through time makes me reflect.

I think of changing tastes and shifting reasons
I am an unraveling spool of thread and it is my season of spring.
I live and relive, coming alive again, blazoned

to tie it all off with a bow, I take the end of my string
make two loops and twist them together on an upswing.

JULIA WYSOKINSKA

Julia Wysokinska is a first-year college student who enjoys testing out new coffee shops with friends, reading creative nonfiction, and wandering through Central Park.

MENTEE'S ANECDOTE:

This is my third year with Jamie as my mentor, and I am forever indebted to her for being so supportive at each step of my development as both a writer and a person. Our conversations never fail to inspire and motivate me, and I feel unbelievably lucky to have been paired with such a kind, generous, and perceptive mentor. Jamie has helped me explore many different genres, and I'm immensely grateful to be her mentee and to call her a friend.

JAMIE DUCHARME

Jamie Ducharme is a health correspondent at *Time* and the author of *Big Vape: The Incendiary Rise of Juul.*

MENTOR'S ANECDOTE:

So much has changed in the three years I have known Julia. I met her (through a screen, during the all-virtual pandemic years) as she was beginning her junior year of high school. Since then, she has grown as a writer and a person, settling into her first year of college with grace and poise. One thing that has not changed in the years I have known Julia? She is unfailingly kind and good-humored, with a superhuman work ethic and a willingness to face any challenge head-on. I am confident I have learned more from her than she has from me.

FLOOD OF INFORMATION

JULIA WYSOKINSKA

A live studio interview goes off the rails.

The rain had forced pretzel vendors on the street to pack up and push their carts into storage. They would not be back to business until the next day, when the forecast predicted sunny skies to become the norm once again. As Josephine scurried into the forty-five-story building eleven streets south of Central Park, holding her coat over her head rather than draped over her back and arms, she dreamed of being in a dry environment with less probability of slipping in just a moment. She proceeded to smile at a doorman who let her into the building and waved at the elevator operator who helped her get to the correct floor.

Once their journey up was over, the elevator operator gestured toward the opening doors and Josephine stepped out onto the navy-blue carpet. A blond broadcast technician nearly knocked her off her feet as she raced to the control room, though Josephine had managed to swerve out of her way and escaped with just a brush against her shoulder.

"Are you the data analyst?" inquired a voice from across the hall.

Before she could confirm her identity, the lead anchor had made his way over to Josephine and stuck out his hand, expecting a handshake. As Josephine reciprocated his gesture, his lips curled into a smile and revealed his artificially white teeth.

"Nice to meet you," he said, revealing that their first two interviews on his show had not left a strong impression on him.

They walked down the hall leading to the recording studio, but not before stopping for a beat to let a pair of camera operators through the doorway, lugging a large camera on wheels with an unclear, pixelated monitor.

A redheaded man of average height sauntered in front of the desk just as the anchor was in the middle of furiously reciting tongue twisters from memory. His leisurely pace and furrowed brow glaringly contradicted each other, and all Josephine could do was imagine what his news would be.

She did not have to wait long to find out, as the man cleared his throat and managed to say, "Sorry, folks, it seems like we'll have to stick to airing commercials for a little while longer. Looks like the storm's interfering with our tech, but we'll get it back up and running in no time."

The anchor scoffed and complained while waving his hands in the air, though Josephine had already blocked his voice out. She had hoped they would have more time.

She feared dashing out of the interview now would arouse suspicions, so she remained perfectly still and composed in the swivel chair provided to her. All she could think about was getting back to her apartment in Lower Manhattan, newly made more spacious following her acrimonious breakup with her partner of ten months.

As soon as the last hastily packed bag of belongings was hauled out of her apartment, she got in a taxi and drove all the way to the most expansive grocery store in nearby New Jersey. With cartons and cartons and cartons of supplies in tow, she called a rideshare service and made her way back to TriBeCa. She then proceeded to make the same trek three more times.

"I'm going to run to the restroom while we wait for the cameras," she offered, as most people on set scrambled to get the cameras rolling.

"Go ahead, Jo. It seems like we're going to get a late start on today's broadcast, but we'll just bump the meteorologist to make up for lost airtime," yelled a producer as she blinked rapidly, seemingly to get an eyelash out of her eye. "Hurry back, though."

Josephine pushed her chair in neatly and made a beeline for the window in the hall, bolting right past the restrooms. She watched as the downpour grew outside. She tucked the front strands of her hair behind her ears, closed her eyes, and took a deep breath. Then she peered down at the sidewalk and discovered a flock of pigeons lying motionlessly on the ground. It was like they had dropped right out of the sky instead of seeking shelter from the storm.

The rain continued to collect down below. The city's drainage grates were overworked and overpowered, and water rose at an accelerating rate, with no sign of stopping soon in sight. Soon, doormen would have to bunch fabric up near their doors and prepare for floods with every opening. The storming clouds were so dark they seemed purple. Her eyes darted back down just a few seconds later with the blindingly bright lightning that lingered in the atmosphere.

While returning to participate in the interview, Josephine picked up the incoming phone call from her secretary, who informed her about her boss's insistence that she return to their office building at once. Josephine understood the menacing, ransom-note-esque letters that poured into their headquarters were not threats of an impending chemical attack, but rather warnings.

HUDA YASEEN

Huda (she/her) is a high school junior based in Michigan. She enjoys creative journaling, reading, and binging K-dramas, all while snuggling with her cat.

MENTEE'S ANECDOTE:

Karen has gone above and beyond what a mentor does, supporting me since our first meeting and always having my goals in mind. During our virtual sessions, we would not only focus on our writing skills, but also have lighthearted discussions about our life aspirations. But it did not end there. She was willing to answer any random writing questions I had at any time of the day and help me edit last-minute drafts. It was a truly memorable time for me, as I found myself supported, giggling, and smiling from ear to ear.

KAREN MAZZA

Karen (she/her) is still finding herself after retiring in 2022. In her free time, she reads books, works in her garden, and mentors.

MENTOR'S ANECDOTE:

Huda has been an amazing mentee. She is bright, enthusiastic, and generous. I am amazed at her zest for writing and life in general. She encouraged me to work with her on the anthology and was as supportive as could be. Despite her being incredibly busy, when we meet we always joyfully run over our planned time.

HEIRLOOMS: A STORY OF THE CONNECTIONS WE HOLD TO THE OBJECTS WE CHERISH

HUDA YASEEN

For this pair piece, we each wrote about a family heirloom. From an authentic kilim rug to an opal ring, these treasured objects are valued for the stories they tell, the cultural traditions they uphold, and the intergenerational bonds they form.

"THE KILIM RUG" BY HUDA YASEEN

I stared at the sight before me, perplexed. My eyes watered in an effort to make me blink, but I couldn't. Its vibrant hues of purple and red enraptured me. For one last time, I indulged in its grandeur. It was an Iraqi kilim rug, a traditional flat-woven tapestry handcrafted by authentic artisans. And though it was beautiful, it was time to store the rug beneath the newer artificial and manufactured carpets, where it would remain until the next guest arrived.

It was a rule in my grandmother's home that the kilim rug was not for daily use, but rather for seating guests to dinner at special events. The rug's exclusive appearance in the house emphasized its special quality to me even more. The woven rug illuminated the room with its imperfect beauty. Despite its rough edges and numerous scratches, the handcrafted rug exuded warmth and character that no manufactured carpet could equal. I traced my fingers over the intricate patterns and motifs, feeling the depressions and lines of the tight yarn woven with meticulous craftsmanship. With each flow of the weave, I was reminded of the labor and history that went into each thread. Its imperfections spoke of the local tribal women who handcrafted it in the 1900s, and the fading natural tint was an ode to the personality sewn within its wool yarn. The patterns felt almost symphonic, composing a story of an era long before me. Though woven, the centered star beamed, signifying everlasting happiness and good prosperity. The geometric eyes circled each corner of the star, staring directly at whatever evil may befall this house. Last, the pixelated triangular patterns that adorned the rug's border mimicked the waves of the Euphrates, symbolizing the vitality of running water in life.

As much as I wanted to keep it out so I could admire its beauty every day, I knew that it must be preserved. With a sigh, I rolled up the beautiful rug. Though it wasn't seen daily, its significance lived on, reminding me of the history of my family and its tribal women, who told a poem through their handcraft and whose strong threads were able to be passed down through generations.

"THE OPAL RING" BY KAREN MAZZA

For as long as I could remember, my aunt wore her opal ring on special occasions. It was a simple ring with a rectangular-shaped stone in a plain gold setting. It had been a gift from her parents, who intended to present her birthstone in the style of a ring. However, the birthstone was chosen mistakenly based on her astrological sign rather than her birth month. She was born in September—it should have been a sapphire.

We often joked that wearing an opal that wasn't your birthstone brings bad luck. She had some of that—estranged from her father, divorced, with two young children, and diagnosed with lung cancer and emphysema later in life. Despite all that, she was, to me, the coolest aunt.

She would wear the ring when we went to the ballet and weddings and on holidays. Eventually, she began saying, "Since you are the October baby, this will be yours someday." I treasured those words, not because the ring had great monetary value, but because it was hers.

We had begun spending Christmas at her daughter's home, and in 2019, those words became a reality. As we were hugging goodbye, she handed me a ring box. "It's yours now. I wanted you to have it while I was still here." As I opened the box, the opal ring revealed itself, away from the hands of its owner. At that moment, I immediately felt a connection to the ring. Perhaps it was the fact that this was my correct birthstone, or maybe it was the unwavering promise that moved me. But, either way, I knew I had the responsibility to cherish her ring. After all, it was my embodiment of her, despite it not being her true birthstone. She passed away this past July. But every time I wear that opal, I'm brought back to the wonderful memories she created, not only with me, but also with my husband and children. She will always be the coolest aunt.

MANAR YASEEN

Manar is a current college freshman in Michigan who has a passion for exploring historical romance novels and trying out new recipes whenever she can.

MENTEE'S ANECDOTE:

Working with Allison, I've realized she hasn't been just a mentor throughout this whole writing process, but also a friend. She supported me in my endeavors to enter the world of writing and resonated with me on many topics I wanted to write about. This journey wouldn't have been as enjoyable had it not been for Allison's support.

ALLISON KELLEY

Allison Kelley is a Brooklyn-based comedy writer, essayist, and coauthor of the feminist joke book *Jokes to Offend Men*.

MENTOR'S ANECDOTE:

Working with Manar and getting to know her through her writing has been a joy. She is overflowing with story ideas and has a rich imagination. The hardest part has just been deciding which one to start first, which is a great problem to have! I can't wait to see what Manar dreams up next!

THE ODD ONE OUT

MANAR YASEEN

The beauty of cultures lies within the intricate differences they hold. But when comparing them, one can't help but notice how humans interact, even if it's not in the best light.

Basrah, Iraq. 2015, Eleven years old

I sat in my usual spot on my bibi's* Arabian cushion floor set, occasionally smiling and gesturing to the plate of date cookies. Bibi's overzealously decorated living room beamed with the laughter and chatter of the town's Ahwari† women. Delicate teaspoons clung against golden-rimmed Arabian Finjan‡ cups, and the sun's ever-so-radiant beams illuminated each of the women's carefully chosen bangles and khaleeji necklaces. The women's children's liveliness rang across Bibi's courtyard, their childhood delight befitting the warm summer air.

"Did you hear?" one auntie said as she leaned forward toward the huddled women and pursed her lips, waiting for their responses. Auntie Rania, one of Mama's distant cousins seemingly obsessed with the status of each individual in the town, instantly commented, "Is it about the Sheik's daughter?"

Tsk tsk tsk. Bibi's room boomed with the dissatisfaction of disapproving tongues. My ears perked as I instinctively took small sips of chia to overhear their hushed whispers.

"Poor woman, her father's soul departed right after she remarried," Auntie Farah mused with a sigh.

A stunned silence engulfed Bibi's living room as all heads whipped in her direction, the once casual, lighthearted atmosphere evaporating

* Bibi: Iraqi dialect endearment term for Grandma.
† Ahwari: Semitic people that reside in the marshes of Iraq.
‡ Finjan: Arabic word for coffee.

into an uncomfortable awkwardness. Clearly irritated, Auntie Salma's nose flared, and she placed her hands on her hips. "Poor woman? She's anything but that! How could a Sheik's daughter, of all people, not even attend her father's funeral and frolic with her new husband so freely?"

A few murmurs of agreement could be heard as the women averted their gaze. Some nodded in agreement, while others shifted uncomfortably in their seats. But it was too pronounced not to notice the sparkle in each one of the women's eyes. *Ah, yes,* they finally had something new to work their tongues about.

Bibi's room was lively again, but this time with the wagging of these women's tongues. Each morsel of the truth, or what could be considered as such, was dissected into nothing more than meaningless gossip.

Why wouldn't she contribute to her father's funeral funds? Why didn't she attend it? Did her father treat her unwell, or was she just insolent? And my, oh, my, who could be her new husband?

The judgments were swift yet fierce. There was no helping it now. This information was far more scandalous than the typical family squabbles Ahwari women enjoyed conversing about. Perhaps Auntie Farah laid a trap, but I wouldn't take the bait of naïvety, so I just sat and watched the scene unfold.

America, 2021, Seventeen years old

The afternoon sun hung low across the sky, casting its last rays over the pristinely mowed grass of my neighbor's yard. The wind sent tantalizing wafts of sizzling meat and spices in the air. My younger siblings' and the neighboring children's laughter echoed across the vast land while adults in floppy hats and expensive sunglasses lounged on canopy chairs.

I rolled out a picnic cloth under the shade of an elderberry tree, patiently waiting for my hamburger to finish cooking on the grill. But waiting was never my strong suit, so I resolved to listen in on the adults' chatter. "Thank goodness Christie isn't here," Paige fanned while scanning the neighbors for any of Christie's relatives. "I know! Who would've expected her sudden pregnancy announcement?" Anya declared in a hushed tone. Her husband followed right behind her, nodding in agreement.

"We've decided that our kids won't be hanging out with her son at her house anymore. We don't want to normalize anything to the kids." Nick furrowed his brows as he glanced at his rowdy children. Mama and Baba shot each other puzzled looks. It was a subtle exchange, but I knew their confusion. *Hadn't she always been single?* Yet, despite their confusion, they didn't utter a word. The revelation would play out on its own, something I also learned a while ago. Surely enough, it did. "It's so unfortunate her son won't have a father," Tanya remarked, with a hint of ironic worry wrinkling her face. The neighbors all murmured in agreement as I stared expectantly at my parents' still composition, my stomach rumbling unease.

From there, a casual vitriol engulfed the adults' conversation, and I shared a look at my parents. It was clear that they hadn't expected Iraq's social dynamics to play out so similarly in America. But it was simply something they would eventually accept. It's human nature to establish hierarchy, regardless of culture. And it's human to sit and listen and not be the odd one out.

HEESEO YOON

Heeseo (she/her) is a high school junior who has a profound love for writing, drawing, and mint chocolate-chip ice cream.

MENTEE'S ANECDOTE:

Yaddy and I have had an extremely positive relationship. From Yaddy, I was able to learn ways to build confidence not only in writing, but also in real life. As a veteran writer, she assisted me through one of the most tumultuous times in my high school career by continuously introducing writing opportunities and helping me. Working with Yaddy has been the most valuable experience in finding my identity as a writer and as a young woman.

YADDY VALERIO

Yaddy is a passionate writer and the creator of the *Cafecito Time con Yaddy* podcast. She has been published in the *Manhattan Times* and by the Dominican Writers Association.

MENTOR'S ANECDOTE:

When Heeseo and I had our first session, I knew our relationship would go well. Heeseo's passion for writing and journalism inspired me to keep writing my stories. Heeseo also has been dedicated to her studies; she has started to look at some colleges and asked me questions regarding the process. Heeseo is motivated to continue pursuing writing, and she has applied to numerous writing contests and is starting to apply for summer internships.

DENIAL

HEESEO YOON

We all run from our roads.

Once, I walked across a road—
A road that I had crossed as a child,
A road that I knew well.
But that day, the road was oddly quiet.
It was quite peculiar, thinking back.

There was not a single person
Not even a brush of wind
Not even the chatter of birds
That used to fill my ears with joy.
It was almost as if time had stopped.

Then I saw a tiny dot far away.
As I approached the dot,
I realized it was

A girl.

A little girl, about eight years old
Wearing a simple white dress.

Her purple eyes were fixed on me—
No,
Eyes can't be purple.
It was probably the light.
Anyway,
There was a fierceness in her eyes

That I wouldn't expect from a child,
Especially from

A girl.

"What are you doing here?" I asked.
Just walking.
"You shouldn't be out so late."
It's morning.
"No, it's the evening."
What makes you think it's the evening?
"It's dark, and nobody's out and about.
You, especially a girl, should not be out at this time."
And what makes you think I'm a girl?
"You're wearing a dress . . . stop this nonsense.
What is going on?
Things aren't supposed to be like this."

At those words, her fiery eyes suddenly lost their fire.
This place has changed.
You know that.

Her eyes were filled with sadness.
It was as if she was . . .
pitying me.

"No, nothing changed," I said angrily.
"Today is just a strange day.
The road will be normal by tomorrow."

The girl shook her head.

Things have changed.
The past is the past.
Nobody crosses this road anymore.
Not a single person
Not even a brush of wind

Not even the birds that used to sing to your ears.
No one.

At this point, I knew the girl was deranged.
I quelled my anger
And patted her small head.

"You'll know better when you get older,"
With a teasing poke to her forehead
I continued on my way
Across the road.
I walked

Walked

And walked.

When the girl had turned back
Into a mere dot in the distance,
I started running.
Running

Running

And running.

My hair slapped against my face.
The winds greeted me.
I heard a distant bird calling.

See? She was wrong.
Everything was still in place.
She was just a little girl blabbering absurdity
As little girls usually do.
It can't mean anything,
Could it?

CAROLYN ZHENG

Carolyn Zheng is a high school junior with a penchant for procrastination and reading who also occasionally happens to write.

MENTEE'S ANECDOTE:

It has been a hectic junior year for me, but I'm so glad that Davia has been here for me throughout all of it. She's always so supportive of my endeavors, even with me constantly changing my mind. Our monthly meetings have been a safe space for me to create without worrying about the stress-inducers of my school and personal life. With all of my writing, Davia encourages me to continue, helping me to break free from negative thought patterns. Davia's writing also motivates me to attain that level of craft. I can't wait to continue writing with her!

DAVIA SCHENDEL

Davia Schendel is a writer, musician, and filmmaker. She also writes a newsletter, *Zeitgeist Deterrent*, and composes scores for film.

MENTOR'S ANECDOTE:

It has been my second year working with Carolyn, and I am constantly awed by how she incorporates so many passions into her life. Along with her writing, she also plays in a musical ensemble, participates in athletics, and works part-time—all on top of her studies. She inspires me every time we meet. Her curiosity and enthusiasm for pursuing multiple creative outlets, whether it's music, fiction, or poetry, fuels my own initiative and makes me look forward to our meetings. It's a great honor and pleasure to know her, and to have seen her artistry unfold over this past year.

FROM 3 TO 6

CAROLYN ZHENG

Content Warning: Implied Violence

A call is made at three in the morning.

She told me to come pick her up
At three in the morning
With my mom's gray Cadillac
That stank of faint traces of cigarettes
So I drove and drove, down past that last lane
Away from the lives and lights of the city
Into the complete darkness of dreary streets
Where people silently scream
And no one comes running
'Cause they're already running from life

When headlamp light shines on her
She's leaning with one leg bent
On a broken concrete wall inside chain-link fence
Has a Hollister white jacket on her back
And torn-up jeans with fishnet stockings on her legs
With knee-high boots that *click-clack*
As she takes a step
She walks over to the Cadillac
Yanks the shotgun door open
Then takes a seat inside
On top of the plastic cups and wrappers
And quickly shuts the door
To block the drone of the outside night

Red handprints litter her bare skin
Dried-up blood is stuck under her black nails
She keeps staring out the window
At dull scenery passing by
At the dead sky
At the flashing film inside her mind

Her gaze is somewhere far away
But her eyes
Are still the same, determined, cold steel gray
And we stay silent all the way
Back to the comatose, gross buildings we always see
Until she whispers
To something, somewhere out in the world
But it never passes her lips

MICHELLE ZHENG

Michelle (she/her) is a high school senior who enjoys reading, cooking, learning about dentistry, and trying out new food places in the city.

MENTEE'S ANECDOTE:

Mary has been an amazing mentor! From the beginning, she has not only given thoughtful edits but has also made sure I understood each edit. She has also given me tremendous help during my college application process. I truly mean it when I say I don't think I have met anyone as kind and hard-working as Mary. At the start of our sessions, she always makes sure to have a brief discussion about the beginning of the week, which I always appreciate. She shares the most interesting and fun facts about her life. I can't wait to learn more from her!

MARY DARBY

Mary Darby is a vice president and senior writer for Burness, a public interest communications firm that works exclusively with nonprofits to advance social change.

MENTOR'S ANECDOTE:

One thing I love about working with Michelle is how she weaves her Cantonese heritage into her writing—and she does it with so much love, grace, and humor. I have learned about Cantonese foods, traditions, and the role that they have played in Michelle's life. However, I am terrible at pronouncing the Cantonese words that she uses! I am also touched by how her parents' oral health problems resulting from lack of dental care in China have inspired Michelle to become a public health dentist, something she is passionate about. I feel privileged to have been her mentor this year.

THE SACRED DNA OF SUPERMARKETS

MICHELLE ZHENG

From the outside, you'll see only a brick building with a sign indicating its presence as a supermarket. But a step inside the market and this personal essay will transport you to a new world.

To the untrained eye, a supermarket is *only* a supermarket: a busy yet serene retail store that sells groceries. Yet, as an experienced and loyal customer of ethnic supermarkets in New York City, I can attest to supermarkets being more than a place to shop: they are a place of belonging.

All Chinese Americans growing up in South Brooklyn know the big three Asian supermarkets: Good Fortune Supermarket, Fei Long Market, and iFresh.

As I approach my favorite, Fei Long Market, the open doors welcome me to a new world.

Endless aisles of food stand before my eyes; yet it's the produce section that grabs my attention. Dozens of aunties and uncles tug at the plastic bags, struggling to get the ends to open. Children push heavy carts with their caved-in shoulders, already tired of the trip. Meanwhile, other young children run wild after one another.

As I observe the scenery, my nose is hit by the contrasting smell of the seafood section to my right and the warm, sweet smell of cake from the left. I make my way toward the produce section, where I hear a multitude of voices: *Oh, where is the noodles aisle? Wa, yī hé cǎoméi cái yīkuài qián!* (English translation: Wow, only one dollar for a box of strawberries!) English mixes with dialects like Mandarin, and standard Cantonese mixes with subdialects such as Toisanese, reminding me of how something as simple as food links people from different parts of the world.

It's the beauty in such small yet impactful things that makes supermarkets so appealing to me.

Truth be told, I hated going to the supermarkets when I was younger, even though I love them now. I wasn't a fan of the seafood section, which always had a distinctly fishy smell, or the wet floors. I wasn't a fan of the busy crowds at these supermarkets. I wasn't a fan of the long hours I would spend, waiting for my family to buy the groceries. Yet I bonded with my family in those markets, and for that, I do *not* regret going to this day.

From my mom and grandma, I learned how to grocery-shop. To many people, grocery shopping is an innate skill that everyone just knows. I didn't know how to *properly* grocery-shop, but I learned from the best: my family. Perhaps that's why I would only be put in charge of choosing snacks and restricted to observing on those trips. Still, I learned how to pick the best *bok choy* (English translation: Chinese cabbage) from my mom. *Choose the one with bright green leaves and a firm stem.* I learned how to pick fresh fruits from the fruit king himself, my dad. *Choose the firm yet plumpest fruits* was the general tip.

I know to most people a supermarket is *only* a supermarket, but to many families like mine, an ethnic supermarket has the DNA that connects people from all over the world. Inside these ethnic supermarkets, you will find different products of different ethnic origins sitting next to one another. You might find Vietnamese sriracha sauce beside Japanese Kewpie mayo in the sauces aisle. Below, you might spot bottles of Chinese Lao Gan Ma.

For millions of people, these supermarkets are also places of belonging. They are like time capsules that they can use to travel back to their childhood and remember their favorite foods. Even though I'm no longer eleven years old, I go back to these stores with the hope that I can reclaim a small hidden part of myself, knowing that I'm always welcome.

Regardless of how well connected you are to your culture, you can always go to these markets to experiment with food, explore different cultures, and of course shop. Whether you feel strongly or loosely connected to your culture, you can always depend on ethnic supermarkets for connections to different places or, perhaps, a reminder of your childhood. Even people who want to explore different cultures can step inside an ethnic supermarket for a glimpse. If they take the time to walk through the aisles, they might even understand what's important to each culture.

That's why I will never tire of supermarket trips; you'll find me in New York City, exploring different ethnic supermarkets: from Chinese grocery stores to Eastern European food shops. Hopefully, you, too, will see a supermarket as more than a supermarket—as a place for connection, exploration, and even adventure.

CHELSEA ZHU

Chelsea is a writer exploring short-form poetry and microfiction; she cherishes Fridays, snow days, and Raspberry Creme Kit Kats.

MENTEE'S ANECDOTE:

Whether we're reading scripts, talking about Owala bottles, or sharing our impulses to write, Katie brings me so much laughter and joy. Every conversation with Katie shows me how similar our experiences and feelings are as we navigate the shared excitement and challenges of settling into a new job or experiencing sophomore year. I am so grateful for our life updates and writing exercises, motivating me to generate new questions and ideas. Katie's helped me trust my creative process. She's shown me the power of having a mentor, friend, and supporter. She's taught me to believe in myself and in others.

KATIE SONG

Katie Song is a New York–based writer, producer, and avid watcher of nineties rom-coms and TV shows. She currently works for *TV Insider*.

MENTOR'S ANECDOTE:

As someone who has their hand in many pots, Chelsea immediately struck me with her multifaceted skills and interests. From her poetry, to her sportsmanship, to her activism in her community, Chelsea's bravery in her voice and writing has inspired me and my own—let alone how easily we lose track of time giggling and lamenting about our trials and day-to-day adventures. Chelsea is gracious, hilarious, and so open-minded when it comes to our future as young writers. This is truly the beginning of a beautiful friendship.

UNIVERSES, DRIFTING: A TEMPORAL HAIKU COLLECTION

CHELSEA ZHU

We capture little moments of friendship, revelation, beauty, and stillness while exploring the brief and transformative form of haiku.

staircase—
constant movement
of new faces

footsteps rippling
into sound—
the rhythm of raindrops

a new wash on
my lips, perhaps berry or brown
let's try again

snapshots of last september
conversations lost
in the lunch courtyard

soft crunch of
autumn leaves
drifting cherry blossoms

during a sunshower
white keys
from my neighbor's piano

shoreside—
younger me holding
mason jar

sleek in black and gray
I stretch like we all used to
breathing in the day

I hit the green button
to hear friends, many miles away,
we squeal on the street

in a charter bus
I watch two geese
cross the road

by the river creek
two names fading
on a paper boat

every month I trim
my nails—cut
down memory

lemon berry buttercream
sixteen, twenty-one, twenty-four candles
a flame for one

marking my progress
with pen on paper
my feet on the floor

new mascara bottle—
I watch an eyelash fall
in the bathroom mirror

I click on a light
picturing the faces
I'll see at the end

WRITING PROMPTS FROM THE GIRLS WRITE NOW COLLABORATORY

Despite the limitless possibilities of storytelling, not everyone feels free to tell their own. Girls Write Now has opened up the world of storytelling to those who have been ignored or silenced—and to all of us who need to hear these stories to better understand the world around us.

For a quarter-century, Girls Write Now has stood as a beacon, shining light on the inherent resilience in storytelling and advocating for the transformative power of diverse voices in underrepresented communities. We do this through our unique, holistic model combining mentoring, community, and learning. Championing not just writing, but the whole writer, our curriculum is rooted in social-emotional learning, which builds the core competencies needed to be resilient, balanced, and fulfilled human beings expressing creativity and leadership. Now this model is expressed through what we call The Collaboratory, a hub that allows mentors and mentees across more than thirty-two U.S. states to meet, create, and inspire one another on their writing adventures through all stages of life.

Within the Collaboratory, mentors and mentees meet one-to-one in Mentoring Sessions, in small seminar-style Studios, and in synchronous and asynchronous project-based courses called Learning Journeys with carefully designed objectives. We offer a variety of resources, from mentorship, to author salons, to self-paced, human-centered learning journeys. Throughout all of these gatherings, writers are exploring a wide range of topics, genres, and media, from fiction, poetry, memoir, and scriptwriting to college, career, leadership, and activism.

The revelation of the journey is how every story is told, and that journey starts with a prompt. Through the following exercises generated in our Collaboratory over the past year, we invite you to join us. We hope that the pages of the *Girls Write Now 2024 Anthology* fuel your passion to write—*Here & Now.* The call to write is even more than an invitation—it is our innate right to self-expression.

Intro by Emily Méndez, Girls Write Now editor-in-residence, with prompts from Learning Journeys and Studios overseen by Community Managers Margery Hannah and Jessica Jagtiani

PROMPTS

INTERCONNECTEDNESS

Bringing words to life can be an isolating journey. At Girls Write Now, we work passionately to encourage, support, and celebrate our talented community of writers. Use the prompts below to interact with the communities you value or to guide you to the community you want to discover.

CONNECTING WITH THE ENVIRONMENT

Tell us about your favorite texture from the natural world. Imagine touching it. What memories does this specific sensation bring up for you?

—**MENTOR ELLEN AIRHART**, facilitator for Environmental Journalism

MEMOIR: STORIES THAT SHAPE US

We each have a different way of describing our relationship with our environment and what is around us. How would you describe being caught in the rain or witnessing a rainbow?

—**MENTOR MELODY SERRA**, facilitator for Memoir: Stories That Shape Us

FIND YOUR THIRD PLACE

Third places are the public areas we go to beyond home and school/work; they can be physical or virtual spaces. Girls Write Now is a valued third place for our community of writers and leaders. What is a third place that is meaningful to you and why?

—**GIRLS WRITE NOW STAFFERS EMILY RIGBY AND KATHRYN DESTIN**, facilitators for Intersectional Voices in Editorial Committee: Accessibility of Stories

REWRITING THE NARRATIVE: REDEFINING PHILANTHROPY AND GIVING BACK FOR THE NEXT GENERATION

We spend time in our Committee Studio decolonizing Philanthropy, eliminating all we've presumed about it in favor of what resonates with our desire to build legacies for the next generation, aka NextGen. Tell us, as a story, how you learned to give? What does "giving back" look like to you?

—**GIRLS WRITE NOW STAFFERS CHELLE CARTER-WILSON AND KELSEY LEPAGE**, facilitators for NextGen Philanthropy: The Story Changes

WRITING YOUR WAY TOWARD YOUR BIGGEST IDEA(S)

Take five to ten minutes to "speak"—through the art of writing—life into your wildest entrepreneurial dreams. Write all of your thoughts down, forgetting any perceived limitations. What business idea might you pursue? Who will your idea help, and how is it different from other solutions that may already exist? Identify one step you can take toward developing this dream into reality.

—**MENTOR ASHLEY SOWERS**, facilitator for Passion, Purpose, Profit: From Idea to Enterprise

BUILD A HOME FROM POETRY

Read the poems "Perhaps the World Ends Here" by Joy Harjo and "Duplex" by Jericho Brown. Then build a home with words and consider writing in Brown's "duplex" form. What are the components of "home"? What are some ways that you build a sense of home? Is "home" in your body? Is it an ancestral place? Is it a place where you are or that you can only imagine?

—**MENTOR ALUM ANN VAN BUREN**, facilitator for Open Your Heart Here: Generative Poetry Writing (annvanburen.com)

ILLUMINATING YOUR SETTING

Imagine you have a magic wand that can whisk you away to anywhere—real or pretend. Describe or sketch your arrival in this place, using imagery and sensory details.

—**MENTOR KRISTINA CUNNINGHAM BIEGLER**, facilitator for Graphic Novels and Visual Storytelling

A WRITER'S ELEMENTAL MAGIC

The children's TV show *Avatar: The Last Airbender* features characters that wield fire, air, water, and/or earth as a bending form. These elements match the elements of astrology as well! Considering the act of writing as your very own form of magic, describe which element(s) you'd associate with it and why.

—**MENTOR MELANIE HORTON**, facilitator for The Astrology of the Writer Within (melaniehorton.com)

WRITE OUTSIDE THE BOX

Write an essay about a specific memory in a nontraditional format, such as a recipe for a fancy dessert, a birthday party shopping list, or a letter to someone you admire.

—**MENTEE SHELLEY YANG**, facilitator for Rediscovering Writing Through Nonfiction

THE ELEPHANT IN THE ROOM

Write a one-page scene between two characters where neither of them is addressing an uncomfortable truth. How might you use action and dialogue to demonstrate discomfort and indirect communication?

—**GIRLS WRITE NOW STAFFER JULIA ANDRESAKIS**, facilitator for Before The Marker Snaps: The Feature-Length Screenplay

THE ART OF INTERVIEWING

To write about yourself (and others) without paralyzing fear is to have confidence in your ability to tease out the illustrative details, anecdotes, and symbols that represent a life. Read a profile of an individual whom you're either familiar with or not and list out what you believe may have been the interview questions the writer posed to their interlocutor. Then ask a friend or family member if you may interview them, and come up with your own series of questions for the task. (Optional: Write the profile, too!)

—**MENTOR ALUM HEATHER O'DONOVAN**, facilitator for Cringe! How to Write About Yourself Without Paralyzing Fear

PAST, PRESENT, AND FUTURE SELVES

Many people believe that all versions of yourself walk with you every day. From your little self to your higher self, you have access to the emotions, language, and stories these versions hold. Use these prompts to reacquaint yourself with a voice you miss.

WRITE YOUR OWN HISTORY

Think about a concept, a person, or a thing that means a lot to you. This can be extremely specific or more general. Then write a poem about your own personal history, or a made-up history, with what you chose to think about.

—**MENTEE ASMA AL-MASYABI**, facilitator for Poetry in Motion

OPEN WRITING & CREATING

Select a picture that you've taken, ideally from two-plus years ago. What do you remember most clearly about this day, and what do you wish you remembered? What does the picture mean to you, and why have you kept it?

—**GIRLS WRITE NOW STAFFER LISBETT RODRIGUEZ**, facilitator for Open Writing and Creating

DIVINE YOUR DESTINY

Seeing is believing! Commit a wish to paper by writing a dream horoscope based on the upcoming moon cycles: a new moon is for setting intentions and the full moon for celebrating your accomplishments.

—**MENTOR KIKI T.**, facilitator for Beating Writer's Block with Astrology

THE POWER OF FASHION

Picture the first thing you wore that made you feel truly powerful. Describe how it made you feel. What did it give you the courage to do?

—**MENTOR FARAN KRENTCIL**, facilitator for Fashion Writing 101

COMING OF AGE

Young adulthood is a tumultuous time and coming of age is rough work. Let's try to build a character out of insecurities:

- What are a few traits this character dislikes about themself?
- What are a few traits this character dislikes about other people?
- What does this character envy in others?
- What are things this character likes to complain about?

—**MENTOR AMY ZHANG**, facilitator for A Novel Approach for Young Adult Fiction

INVITING THE MUSES: WRITING POETRY IN COMMUNITY

Write an epistolary (letter) poem to yourself or to someone you love. Write the poem so that it provides comfort to you or the reader in future times of need.

—**GIRLS WRITE NOW STAFFER AZIA ARMSTEAD**, facilitator for Inviting the Muses: Writing Poetry in Community

INTROSPECTION

Introspection stems from the Latin word *introspicere,* meaning to look inside. Dive deep by exploring your innermost thoughts, memories, and emotions with the following prompts.

JOURNALING: AN EXPLORATION OF THE UNCONSCIOUS

Journaling is a mental, emotional, and spiritual exercise that helps you build strong "emotional muscles" to deal with life's difficulties and uncertainties. Think about a time when you felt undeniably authentic and true to yourself. Journal about it. When was it? Where was it? What made you feel like this? How exactly did it feel, and how can you cultivate that feeling in your daily life?

–**GIRLS WRITE NOW STAFFER JESSICA JAGTIANI**, facilitator for Journaling: An Exploration of the Unconscious

FINDING ART IN THE BODY

How is your heart today? Before responding, spend a quiet moment checking in, perhaps by placing a hand on your chest or closing your eyes to inquire from within. When you're ready to respond, try to do so using two different storytelling methods—one that's comfortable and one that's unfamiliar or new. For example:

- Journaling + intuitive movement within your body
- Poetry + doodling a portrait of your heart's emotion

–**MENTOR RICHELLE SZYPULSKI**, RYT 200, facilitator for Cultivate Creative Compassion with Yoga

GETTING PERSONAL

Write an incomplete list of things you should know by now—don't try to list everything. Just go with what comes to mind when you think, *I should know by now* . . . Use this as inspiration for a longer piece that focuses on patterns you notice or a few list items.

—**MENTOR PRISCILLA THOMAS**, facilitator for Nonfiction: Telling Truths

KICK-START YOUR BLOG

Pick a topic that you are interested in exploring and write down three potential blog posts based on these three questions:

- What is a unique perspective that you bring to the topic?
- What excites you about this topic?
- What is misunderstood about this topic?

—**GIRLS WRITE NOW STAFFER VAHNI KURRA**, facilitator for Writing for the Web: Blogging

MULTIMEDIA JOURNALISM AND SOCIAL JUSTICE STORYTELLING

Write about a time you were asked a really good question about yourself/your opinion (e.g., what are you most proud of, what do you dream of, a personable "how are you?"). What did it feel like to have someone clearly show an interest in you/your interests?

—**GIRLS WRITE NOW STAFFER KATHRYN DESTIN**, facilitator for Multimedia Journalism and Social Justice Storytelling

WRITING A PURPOSEFUL MEMOIR

Memoirs have a specific focus. Think about what your focus would be for your memoir by writing a purpose statement. An example of a purpose statement: "My purpose is to tell the story of the house I grew up in and left because I want to educate the public about the effects of gentrification on families in New York." Then decide what the most important thing that you want your audience to know is and focus on telling that story in your memoir.

—**MENTEE FIONA HERNANDEZ AND MENTOR LEONORA LAPETER ANTON**, facilitators for Memoir: Tracing Your Memories

VISUALIZING LANGUAGE

Part of creativity is allowing yourself to be an observer. Embrace the vividness and expression around you through various artistic forms, such as color, collage, dance, photography, and more.

PAINT WITH YOUR WORDS

Colors have a special way of showing up in our lives, and sometimes we connect with specific colors more than we do others. As there is power with color energy, there is also power in expressing gratitude. Write a love letter or thank-you note to your favorite color or have your favorite color write a love letter or thank-you note to you.

—**MENTOR DANIELLE M. CHERY**, facilitator for Where Colors Do the Talking, author of *Peers, Cheers, and Volunteers*

BRINGING ART TO LIFE

Find an image or a piece of artwork that speaks to you. It could be a painting of a person, a photograph of a landscape, or an image of a specific object—whatever you find is fine. Now write a story that brings that image to life. Use your imagination to give it a backstory, a conflict, a memory, or even a soul. See how far your creativity can go!

—**MENTEE CHIAMAKA OKAFOR**, facilitator for Fiction: Adventures of Storytelling

EXPLORING THE SELF THROUGH VISUAL ART

Using your preferred art materials, create a collage that focuses on an emotion currently washing over you. After you have visually depicted that feeling, create a written piece as a response that reflects what you have learned through your visual exploration of the emotion.

—**GIRLS WRITE NOW STAFFER SALLY FAMILIA**, facilitator for Romanticize Your Life Through Collage

A TANGO OF TALENTS: WRITING AND DANCE

Watch a video of a dance performance of your choice. Then write a poem based on the emotions the dance evoked for you.

—**MENTEE OLIVIA WRONSKI AND MENTOR LOUISE LING EDWARDS**, facilitators for Poetry: Exploring Emotion Through Performance Poetry

EXPLORING THE ART OF THE CRAFT

Once again, the words do not find you. The blank page mocks you. The pencil is sharper than ever. *I am alone in this*—you convince yourself. Not on our watch! Use the following prompts to inspire new ways of engaging with the art of the craft.

WRITE A PIECE . . . WRITE IT AGAIN!

Write anything for ten minutes. After, see what you like or don't like. Rewrite the entire piece, incorporating your own previous feedback. No peeking at your first piece!

—**MENTEE SHAYLA ASTUDILLO**, facilitator for Editing: Practicing Writing

A CREATIVE RENAISSANCE FOR SELF-EXPRESSION

Write a short story set in the future, in which the main character finds a letter in an unopened book, plunging them deep into the rich personal life of another—love, loss, guilt, power, all of it. Use ChatGPT to help you develop a *fresh* storyline using a two-step prompt such as this one: 1. "What are three clichés about protagonists in novels?" And then, 2. "What are some ways these clichés can be turned on their heads?" Use ChatGPT's response to help you stay away from common plot/character tropes and add complexity to your story. Consider AI a tool in a writer's toolbox and a way to inspire your creative process. Note: You can use the same two-step prompt for any genre or character in your book (e.g., "what are some clichés about villains in murder mysteries," etc.).

—**MENTOR ASHNA SHAH**, facilitator for Writing & AI: Trading Fear for a Creative Renaissance

UNLOCKING CHARACTER

What's something your character would do in private that they wouldn't let anyone see them do in public? Write that scene. See where it leads—you might learn something new about your character!

—**MENTOR MEREDITH WESTGATE**, facilitator for Elements of Fiction, author of *The Shimmering State*

UNLOCKING THE STORIES AROUND US

Free-write for fifteen minutes about whatever comes to mind when it comes to the words: "ice shower, everyone else's mess, and the nature of nothing." Maybe the three elements relate, maybe they don't. What are you thinking? Where are you? Show us.

—**MENTEE NICOLE ITKIN AND MENTOR HOLLI HARMS**, author of *For Abby* and "Cereal and Fire," facilitators for Sparking Ideas Through Prompt Writing

THE ART OF THE AUTHOR BLURB AND WHY IT MATTERS

The Art of the Author Blurb: You've finished writing your book—now what? Start thinking about promotion, beginning with the author blurb. This blurb typically lives on the front or back cover and is a great form of promotion for your book. Here's the best way to secure a testimonial from an author:

- Brainstorm mentors and writers you admire.
- Draft a letter that entices your dream author to read your book (or excerpts from your book). The hope is that this author gives you a blurb.
- Why is a blurb important? It engages the reader to pick up and buy your book.

—**GIRLS WRITE NOW STAFFERS VAHNI KURRA AND MOLLY MACDERMOT**, facilitators for Print Anthology: The Making of a Book

MEET THE GIRLS WRITE NOW ANTHOLOGY CURRICULUM WRITERS

Azia Armstead is a community coordinator at Girls Write Now. Azia is a poet from Richmond, Virginia. She holds an MFA in poetry from New York University, where she received the Goldwater Fellowship. Her honors include: finalist for the 2019 Furious Flower Poetry Prize judged by A. Van Jordan, honorable mention for the Arts Club of Washington's Scholarship Award for Poetry, and finalist for the 2023 Nine Syllables Press Chapbook Contest. Her work has appeared in *Boston Review, The Quarry, Rattle,* and *Obsidian*. She currently lives in Brooklyn.

Annaya Baynes (she/they) is a fellow at Girls Write Now. They're passionate about liberation for all people and creatures that go bump in the night. As an undergraduate at Spelman College, she worked on Spelman's social justice podcast, *The Blue Record*, and the reproductive justice-oriented podcast *Black Feminist Rants*. They served as a co-chair of Girls Write Now's 2024 Anthology Editorial Committee.

Sally Familia is a community coordinator at Girls Write Now. Sally is a queer Dominican artist who explores identity, the natural world, and interpersonal relationships through poetry, collage, and Reiki. Sally received the Academy of American Poets Prize for the poem "The Trouble with Reminiscing" and was nominated for a Pushcart Prize for the poem "Esperanza, Republica Dominicana." Their work appears in the anthologies *New York's Best Emerging Poets, Genre: Urban Arts, BX Writers,* and they have two upcoming publications in the forthcoming anthology *¡Pájaros, lesbianas y Queers . . . A volar! An LGBTQ+ Anthology of Dominican Transnational Writers*. Sally is currently working on their first collection of poems.

Margery Hannah is the community manager for curriculum at Girls Write Now. She is a Harlem-based multigenre writer and mother of three daughters. A ghostwriter for many years, she is the founder and publisher of the online magazine *The Literary Purveyor* (theliterarypur veyor.com).

Jessica Jagtiani is the community manager for engagement and experience at Girls Write Now. She is an interdisciplinary artist, educator, and researcher of Indian German heritage residing in New York City. Jessica holds a doctor of education in art and art education from Teachers College, Columbia University. Her research centers on the formative dimensions of intuition, bridging indigenous wisdom with contemporary scientific perspectives to foster a balance of the intuitive and the rational mind within Western educational paradigms. Jessica's artwork has been exhibited nationally and internationally, and her scholarly contributions extend to various publications, including chapter three of the book *Developing Informed Intuition for Decision-Making.*

Vahni Kurra (she/hers) is a senior community & marketing coordinator at Girls Write Now. She is a multigenre writer from Brooklyn, New York, with roots in the American Midwest and Southern India. Her writing can be found in *Peach Mag, Oyster River Pages, and SweetLit,* and on her blog, *Shloka Slush*. She served as a co-chair of Girls Write Now's 2024 Anthology Editorial Committee.

Emily Méndez is an editor-in-residence at Girls Write Now and a native New Yorker raised in Queens. She is also a Girls Write Now mentee alum who is passionate about creating accessible, human-centered learning journeys for all, particularly for children with disabilities, and is pursuing occupational therapy. In her free time, Emily finds joy in watching telenovelas and reality TV, crafting personal essays and letters, and spending quality time with friends and family.

ABOUT GIRLS WRITE NOW

We are a powerhouse of voices that have been ignored or silenced for too long. We are a pipeline of talent into schools and industries in need of new perspectives. As a community, we follow our hearts and—through bold, authentic storytelling—inspire people to open theirs. We are Girls Write Now.

For more than twenty-five years, Girls Write Now has been breaking down barriers of gender, race, age, and poverty to mentor the next generation of writers and leaders who are impacting businesses, shaping culture, and creating change.

In thirty-two states and growing nationally, Girls Write Now matches female and gender-expansive young adults from systemically underserved communities—more than 90 percent of color, 90 percent high-need, 75 percent immigrant or first-generation, and 25 percent LGBTQIA+—with professional writers and digital media makers as their personal mentors. Mentees' multigenre, multimedia work is published in outlets including *Teen Vogue* and *The New York Times*; is performed at Lincoln Center and the United Nations; and wins hundreds of writing awards. Mentees are also featured in Girls Write Now's podcasts, films, and print, including *On the Art of the Craft: A Guidebook to Collaborative Storytelling*, a community-produced collection published by HarperCollins in 2024.

Girls Write Now sends 100 percent of its seniors on to college, and continues to support them in school, career, and beyond through professional development, strategic networking, and lifelong community bonds. In addition to being the first writing and mentoring organization for girls, Girls Write Now continually ranks among the top nonprofits nationwide for leadership and capacity-building in the field, and for driving social-emotional growth for young people. Girls Write Now has been distinguished three times by the White House as one of the nation's top youth programs, twice by the Nonprofit Excellence Awards as one of New York's top ten nonprofits, by NBCUniversal's 21st Century Solutions for Social Innovation, by Youth INC for Youth Innovation, and as a DVF People's Voice Nominee. Reaching more than 500,000 youth, Girls Write Now is a founding partner of the decade-strong STARS Citywide Girls Initiative.

TEAM

Julia Andresakis, *Marketing & Web Design Coordinator; Mentee Alum*

Azia Armstead, *Community Coordinator*

Annaya Baynes, *Fellow; Mentee Alum*

Marian Caballo, *Learning Design Intern; Mentee Alum*

Chelle Carter-Wilson, *Creative Director of Marketing & Communications*

Renisha Conner, *Editorial & Production Intern; Mentee Alum*

Kathryn Destin, *Special Projects Coordinator; Mentee Alum*

Morayo Faleyimu, *Senior Editor-in-Residence; Mentor Alum*

Sally Familia, *Community Coordinator*

Spencer George, *Senior Marketing & Development Coordinator*

Margery Hannah, *Community Manager*

Irene Hao, *Learning Design Intern; Mentee Alum*

Dolores Haze, *Editorial and Production Intern; Mentee Alum*

Ellen Rae Huang, *Director of Development*

Jessica Jagtiani, *Community Manager*

Mi So Jeong, *Operations Manager*

Vahni Kurra, *Senior Community & Marketing Coordinator*

Kelsey LePage, *Development Manager*

Molly MacDermot, *Director of Special Initiatives*

Kenna McCafferty, *Fellow*

Emily Méndez, *Editor-in-Residence; Mentee Alum*

Elmer Meza, *Salesforce & Systems Manager*

Maya Nussbaum, *Founder & Executive Director*

Daniella Olibrice, *Director of People & Culture*

Emily Oppenheimer, *Senior Grants Manager*

Ayana Perkins, *Fellow*

Emily Rigby, *Community Manager*

Lisbett Rodriguez, *Programs & Systems Senior Coordinator; Mentee Alum*

Jeanine Marie Russaw, *Community Advisor*

Erica Silberman, *Director of Engagement & Partnerships; Mentor Alum*

Monique Sterling, *Graphic Designer*

Zuzanna Wasiluk, *Learning Design Intern; Mentee Alum*

BOARD OF DIRECTORS

Judith Curr, *Board Chair*
Gati Curtis, *Vice Chair*
Bruce Morrow, *Secretary*
Mustafa Topiwalla, *Treasurer*
Cate Ambrose, *Finance Chair*
Lynda Pak, *Tech Committee Chair*
Stephanie Gordon
Lavaille Lavette
Maya Nussbaum, *Executive Director*
Ellen Archer, *Board Chair Emerita*

TEACHING ARTISTS, GUEST ARTISTS, SPEAKERS & HONOREES

Azia Armstead
Olivia Arnold
Nicole Avant
María Barrios Vélez
Grace Bastidas
Alex Budak
Sam Cammarata
Maile Carpenter
Noni Carter
Christina Cazanave-McCarthy
Jessica Clancy
Christiamilda Correa
Ayesha Curry
Stephen Czaja
Anaïs DerSimonian
Kathryn Destin
Jen Elmashni
Sally Familia
Ylonda Gault
Ross Gay
Nicole Glover
Colleen Hamilton
Bob Hammer
Merle Hoffman
Kylie Holloway
Arianna Huffington
Congressman Steve Israel
Jessica Jagtiani
Elise Jayakar
Ollie Jayakar
Valerie June Hockett
Maja Kristin
R. F. Kuang
Melania Luisa Marte
Madeline McIntosh
Michael Mejias
B. Michael
Emi Nietfield
Erin O'Connor
Lama Rod Owens
Zibby Owens
Morgan Parker
Kristie Raines
James Rhee
Traven Rice

Sheena Daree Romero
Jasmine Rosario
Andrea Salas
Mara Santilli
Savannah Sellers
Liz Sgroi
Hilary Smith
Molly Stern
Jill Stoddard
Nehanda Thom
Krishan Trotman
Katie Wargo
Danielle Whyte
Jon Yaged

GIRLS WRITE NOW AMBASSADORS

FOUNDERS $250K+

Maja Kristin
Jane Lauder

TRAILBLAZERS $100K+

Ann & Bob Hammer

LEADERS $50K+

Ellen Archer & Jeffrey Gracer
Amy & James Ramsey
Kate Stroup & Matthew Berger

INNOVATORS $25K+

Raymond & Gloria Naftali Foundation
Zibby & Kyle Owens

CHAMPIONS $10K+

Judith Curr & Ken Kennedy
James M. & Margaret V. Stine Foundation
Mustafa Topiwalla
Brent and Ann Wilson Family Foundation

SUPPORTERS $5K+

Anonymous
Berger Family Foundation
Gati Curtis
Forsyth Harmon

Maya Nussbaum & Todd Pulerwitz
Lynda Pak
Nicolas Rohatyn
Alina Roytberg
Susan & Sophie Sawyers

VICE CHAIRS $2.5K+

Cate Ambrose
Rachel Bloom
Stephanie Gordon
Catherine Greenman & Richard D'Albert
Agnes Gund
Lavaille Lavette
Bruce Morrow
Kelly Murphy
Robin Thede
Jon Yaged
Marie & John Zimmermann Fund

PATRONS $1K+

Marci Alboher and Jay Goldberg
Nisha Aoyama
Maria Aspan
Jennifer Burkinshaw
Jill Cohen
Rachel Cohen
Cohn Giving Fund
Anne B. Fritz & Libbie Thacker
Anna Gomez
Lynne Greene
Janice Horowitz
Susan and Robert Koroshetz
Anna Kubicka
Robert Levin
Jacob Lewis
Brendan Lowe
Eric Ma
Molly Meloy & Jeff Fitts
Linda C. Rose
Elaine Stuart-Shah & Nirav Shah
Lisa & Frank Wohl

GIRLS WRITE NOW PARTNERS

GAMECHANGERS $100K+

Estée Lauder Companies
News Corp
Pinterest
RBC Foundation
The Upswing Fund

LEADERS $75K+

BBDO
BIC Corporate Foundation
HarperCollins Publishers

VISIONARIES $50K+

Comcast NBCUniversal
Genesis Inspiration Foundation
Macmillan
Penguin Random House

INNOVATORS $25K+

GFP Real Estate
Mattel: The Barbie Dream Gap Project

CHAMPIONS $10K+

Adobe
Amazon Literary Partnership
Dotdash Meredith
WealthEngine, an Altrata company

CREATORS $5K+

Anonymous
Bloomberg
Kickstarter
Kyndryl
Nike
Yen Press

SUPPORTERS $2.5K+

Alloy Entertainment
The Feminist Press
Mischief
Target Circle Guest-Directed Giving Program

ANTHOLOGY SPONSORS

Penguin Random House

amazon literary partnership

We are grateful to the countless institutions and individuals who have supported our work through their generous contributions. Visit our website at girlswritenow.org to view the extended list.

Girls Write Now would like to thank Dutton, including Christine Ball, Maya Ziv, and Grace Layer, for their help producing this year's anthology, and Amazon Literary Partnership, which provided the charitable contribution that made this book possible.